DANCING THE SKIES

[signature]

August 2019

DANCING THE SKIES

David Roome

The Book Guild Ltd

First published in Great Britain in 2019 by
The Book Guild Ltd
9 Priory Business Park
Wistow Road, Kibworth
Leicestershire, LE8 0RX
Freephone: 0800 999 2982
www.bookguild.co.uk
Email: info@bookguild.co.uk
Twitter: @bookguild

Typeset in Adobe Garamond Pro

Printed and bound by CPI Group (UK) Ltd, Croydon, CR0 4YY

ISBN 978 1912881 901

British Library Cataloguing in Publication Data.
A catalogue record for this book is available from the British Library.

This book is dedicated to all those friends of mine who also flew in the Royal Air Force and who were killed on duty: there were far too many of them.

CONTENTS

Acknowledgements   ix

Abbreviations   x

High Flight   xiii

1.   Sunward I've Climbed   1

2.   Early Days   5

3.   Sign on the Dotted Line   10

4.   Learning the Basics   23

5.   Land of my Mother   36

6.   Summer in Devon   47

MAJOR   51

7.   Aggressive Defence   62

8.   Tyger, Tyger, Burning Bright   71

9.   Getting Around   102

10. Midway   110

11. One Year to Go   120

12. Patter, Patter, Patter 129

13. Back to Yr Fali 131

14. The Mighty Phantom 144

15. The Trappers 161

16. Taceval and Staff College 182

17. A Very Special Place 187

18. Command 192

19. Return to Bentley 205

20. Personnel and Training Command 217

21. Commander British Forces Northern Iraq 222

22. Plans and Budgets 225

23. Swansong 232

24. Delta Jets 235

25. FRADU 254

Annex 261

ACKNOWLEDGEMENTS

This book would never have seen the light of day without the incomparable assistance of Bob Cossey who, as a very accomplished author, provided me with helpful advice at every stage. I must also thank my wife Sandy for her patience while I locked myself away in front of a screen, and also to her and to my children Steve and Ellen for their positive criticisms and for proof-reading. The Hawk photo on the jacket is of me attacking HMS Westminster, a Type 23 frigate, while working in the English Channel and was taken by a Royal Navy Fleet photographer. The air-to-air photographs of the Gnat in Chapter 24 are courtesy of Ian Seager, while those of the Vampire and BA747 formation in Chapter 22 are thanks to Jack Pritchard. Finally, the photo of Sandy and me together in 2009 is courtesy of David Penprase and is from his book on the people of Porthleven in Cornwall entitled Harbour 2 Harbour and published by d&j publishing, Flagstaff House, Porthleven, TR13 9DZ.

ABBREVIATIONS

AAR	Air-to-Air Refuelling
AEW	Airborne Early Warning
AMTC	Aeromedical Training Centre
AOC	Air Officer Commanding (of a Group)
AOCinC	Air Officer Commanding in Chief (of a Command)
APC	Armament Practice Camp
ATC	Air Training Corps or Air Traffic Control
ATS	Auxiliary Territorial Service
BBMF	Battle of Britain Memorial Flight
CAA	Civil Aviation Authority
CARU	Control and Reporting Unit
CCF	Combined Cadet Force
CFS	Central Flying School
CFSO	Command Flight Safety Officer
CIRE	Command Instrument Rating Examiner
DME	Distance Measuring Equipment
EFTS	Elementary Flying Training School
ETA	Estimated Time of arrival
ETPS	Empire Test Pilots' School (Boscombe Down)
FAC	Forward Air Controller
FEAF	Far East Air Force
FL	Flight Level (altitude above the Transition Altitude)

FTS	Flying Training School
GH	General Handling
HP Cock	High Pressure Fuel Cock (feeding fuel directly into the engine)
IF	Instrument Flying
ILS	Instrument Landing System
IMC	Instrument Meteorological Conditions
IRE	Instrument Rating Examiner
IRT	Instrument Rating Test
JP	Jet Provost, also Junior Pilot on a sqn
KT	Knot (speed in nautical miles per hour)
LP Cock	Low Pressure Fuel Cock (feeding fuel from the tanks to the high pressure side of the fuel system)
MRG	Master Reference Gyro (on the Lightning)
NCO	Non-Commissioned Officer
OC	Officer Commanding
OCU	Operational Conversion Unit
OO	Orderly Officer
OTU	Operational Training Unit
PE	Physical Education
PMC	The President of The Mess Committee (of an Officers' Mess)
QFI	Qualified Flying Instructor
QGH	Controlled descent though cloud procedure
QRA	Quick Reaction Alert

RAAF	Royal Australian Air Force
RCAF	Royal Canadian Air Force
RLG	Relief Landing Ground
RNZAF	Royal New Zealand Air Force
SASO	Senior Air Staff Officer
SCT	Staff Continuation Training
SDO	Station Duty Officer
SHQ	Station Headquarters
TWU	Tactical Weapons Unit
UAS	University Air Squadron
UHF	Ultra High Frequency (radio)
USAF	United States Air Force
VHF	Very High Frequency (radio)
WW1/II	World War 1/II

RAF RANK ABBREVIATIONS

APO	Acting Pilot Officer
Plt Off	Pilot Officer
Fg Off	Flying Officer
Flt Lt	Flight Lieutenant
Sqn Ldr	Squadron Leader
Wg Cdr	Wing Commander
Gp Capt	Group Captain
Air Cdre	Air Commodore
AVM	Air Vice Marshal
Air Mshl	Air Marshal
ACM	Air Chief Marshal

HIGH FLIGHT

Oh! I have slipped the surly bonds of earth
And danced the skies on laughter-silvered wings
Sunward I've climbed and joined the tumbling mirth
Of sun-split clouds – and done a hundred things
You have not dreamed of; wheeled and soared and swung
High in the sun-lit silence. Hovering there
I've chased the shouting wind along, and flung
My eager craft through footless hall of air;
Up, up the long, delirious, burning blue
I've topped the wind-swept heights with easy grace,
Where never lark, nor even eagle flew;
And while, with silent, lifting mind I've trod
The high untrespassed sanctity of space,
Put out my hand, and touched the face of God.

John Gillespie Magee
Fg Off RCAF
1922-41

BORN IN SHANGHAI, CHINA to an American father and a British mother, John Magee began his education at the American School in Nanking in 1929 but in 1931 he moved with his mother to the UK and attended Rugby School from 1935 to 1939. He developed his poetry whilst at the school and in 1938 he won the school's poetry prize. In 1939 Magee visited the United States but the outbreak of World War II meant that he was unable to return to Rugby for his final school year. He earned a scholarship to Yale University in July 1940 but did not enrol, choosing instead to enlist in the Royal Canadian Air Force in October of that year.

Magee's posthumous fame rests mainly on this sonnet, which he started just a few months before his death in December 1941 in a mid-air collision over Lincolnshire. In his seventh flight in a Spitfire he had climbed to 33,000ft and as he climbed he was struck by words he had read in another poem – 'To touch the face of God'. He completed his verse soon after landing and it is now a most famous poem.

1

SUNWARD I'VE CLIMBED

ON THE EVENING OF Monday 30 November 1936 those on the upper floors of 192 Muswell Hill Road, now the Muswell Hill branch of the Royal British Legion in northwest London but then a maternity home, could look southeast across London and watch as the Crystal Palace burned to the ground. The great glass and metal relic of the 1851 Great Exhibition had originally been erected in Hyde Park, held the largest amount of glass of any building and got its name when the playwright Douglas Jerrold wrote in *Punch* a year before that it was 'a palace of very crystal' – the name caught on. After the exhibition was over the building was re-erected, somewhat enlarged, on Penge Common next to Sydenham Hill. Over the next ninety or so years it was used for a variety of purposes including in 1911 the Festival of Empire to mark the coronation of King George V. During World War I it became *HMS Victory VI*, a naval training establishment, and later it was also the first home of the Imperial War Museum. At 500ft above sea level Sydenham stands 150ft higher than Muswell Hill and as London lies in a bowl there is nothing to obscure the view from one side of the city to the other: the fire fascinated thousands around London that night in 1936. Ten years later to the day in 1946 I started my life in that Muswell Hill maternity home, where my mother, Nell, had been admitted as labour started. She and my father, Arnold, had come from their house in Kingsbury eight miles away to his parents' home in Crouch End to await the birth. They lived in Kingsbury for only another ten months and then moved to Knoll Drive in Southgate, from where my father caught the Tube each day to his job with the stockbrokers

Cazenove, within sight of the Bank of England. Those were still the days when they all wore the same 'uniform' of a dark suit, a Homburg hat and carried a tightly rolled umbrella – always tightly rolled but hardly ever to be used. The firm gave the 'boys' the task of re-rolling any brollies which had been unfurled and they competed with each other to achieve the slimmest result possible. Dad also wore a stiff, detachable collar above his shirt and each week the square cardboard box of used collars was exchanged for another from the firm in Harrow which would launder and return these items to starched beauty. Grandfather Roome worked for the same firm in the same role and retired in the year I was born: there were family expectations that I would follow the same path.

My mother's side of the family was very different, coming from Portmadoc (now Porthmadog) in North Wales. My maternal grandfather, always known to me by the Welsh '*Taid*' (pronounced Tide) was a well-known estate agent and auctioneer in and around the Lleyn Peninsula and down as far as Machynlleth in mid-Wales; he also ran a shop in Portmadoc selling ironmongery, soft furnishings and furniture. Very well known around the town for his usual dress of 'plus-fours', Taid never owned a car and was content to walk to and from the houses he was asked to value; he was still walking five miles or so every day until a fall at the age of ninety-three in 1981 resulted in a broken hip and this put paid to his exercise. During WWI he was already too old for military service but volunteered to aid the war effort and spent some time with a pickaxe handle guarding the road and rail bridges over the Menai Strait separating Ynys Môn, the Isle of Anglesey, from the mainland. He and his wife, Annie, had six children, the youngest of which was Nellie, born in 1920. On leaving school she joined the Midland Bank in Wrexham until 1940, when she joined the Auxiliary Territorial Service (ATS) and soon found herself helping to man an anti-aircraft gun defending London. Anti-Aircraft Command was formed on 1 April 1939 and operated from Glenthorn, a building in the grounds of RAF Bentley Priory on the hill above Stanmore in northwest London, the home of Fighter Command and a place at which I was to serve many years later. General Pile, the Commander, invited a female engineer called Miss Caroline Haslett to inspect a gun battery in the Surrey Hills and give her opinion on the capacity of women to do this work. She spent several Sundays there and assured the general that women could do the job, so from then on women manned everything except the guns themselves. They drove and serviced the trucks, acted as sentries and despatch riders and operated other equipment such as rangefinders; by doing so they released men to carry out the heavy work in the gun pits.*

Nell enjoyed the camaraderie of the Army and progressed, via the award of a commission, from managing a gun in 1940 to managing the ATS Band in 1945. In charge of a group of woman musicians in occupied Europe, she took the band through France and Belgium where, just after the end of the war, she met Captain Arnold Roome, who had experienced a more varied war. After leaving school he followed his father into Cazenove in the City of London, but soon after his twenty-second birthday war once more came to the UK and he joined the Royal Army Service Corps. Training preceded going to France in late 1939 with the British Expeditionary Force, only to join the frantic rush back toward the Channel after the Blitzkrieg of May 1940. Commanding a small group of trucks, he then had the task of destroying them by pouring sand through the oil filler cap and running the engines until they seized. He then found himself on the beach at Dunkirk, where he spent six days before getting away on *HMS Sabre*, one of the last Royal Navy ships to leave, and this brought him back to the UK early on 3 June. Now with almost no transport, the Army commandeered the fleet of coaches operated by the Southdown Bus Company and Dad was ordered to collect one and drive it back to his depot. He had never driven any vehicle of such a size before but nevertheless set off down a narrow road, to be faced within two miles by another vehicle trying to go in the opposite direction. As the other driver would not give way, Dad reversed for almost a mile before the road was wide enough for the other truck to pass, after which Dad found that the coach was now jammed firmly in reverse gear and so he had no option but to continue reversing for almost three miles until he came to a garage in a village where the problem could be fixed!

In 1941 Lt Roome was sent to North Africa and a year later helped to supply fuel and ammunition to the tanks and guns at the Battle of El Alamein. Unlike the German Army which used the eponymous 'Jerry Can', the British Army was slow to realise the value of using well-made,

---

* Excerpt from *Roof Over Britain – The Official Story of the AA Defences 1939-42*

reusable fuel cans, and transported fuel in thin-skinned four-gallon fuel cans, the bottom tier of which usually collapsed under the weight of those above as trucks bumped across the desert. It was common for fuel to gush out each side of the cab as trucks came to a stop, close to both the hot engine and exhaust – hardly the best way to 'get the fuel to the front'! After North Africa, Dad's war continued through Sicily and Italy until not far from Venice where a German mortar round landed fifty yards in front of him and forty-nine yards behind another officer in conversation with Dad. The other man was killed but Dad's only wound was a piece of shrapnel which went through his right foot just behind the toes. His subsequent evacuation down Italy was partly by Dakota, the first time he had flown and 'not the nicest way to start' was his later comment, and then by hospital ship back to Britain. U-boats were still active and Dad later said that throughout the passage home every man who could do so spent every night on deck scanning the sea for tell-tale signs – luckily nothing occurred and they reached Blighty safely.

After recovering from his wound Dad went back into Europe and it was in Antwerp at the end of 1945 that he met Lt Nell Parry. They married in that city on 18 February 1946 and those with good arithmetic will be able to work out that forty weeks on from that date is the end of November: there is little doubt I was conceived in Belgium!

2

EARLY DAYS

MANY OTHER BOYS OF my generation were going to be engine drivers when they grew up, but I was particularly lucky as I actually had an uncle who was one. Dei Thomas was married to my mother's eldest sister, Siân, and lived further along the Lleyn Peninsula in Pwllheli. On holiday I would often be allowed to join him as he worked the railway along the south coast of the Lleyn and down toward Aberdovey. I would treat the cotton waste given to me on the footplate with great reverence as long as it retained the smell of steam, coal and light oil, and will never forget the special occasion when he allowed me, at about fifteen, to drive the Cambrian Coast Express, an eight-coach mainline express, as it started its journey back to Paddington from Pwllheli.

However, in 1956 a film was released which would change my life. *Reach for the Sky* starred Kenneth More and was the story of Douglas Bader who, as a young Royal Air Force pilot, seemed to have the world at his feet playing rugby for the RAF with the potential to play for England. Posted to join 23 Squadron at RAF Kenley, he became one of the three pilots who formed the RAF Aerobatic Team for 1923, along with his friend Geoffrey Stephenson and led by Sqn Ldr Harry Day. In December 1931, after a lunch at Woodley Airfield near Reading, he was goaded into showing off and attempted a slow roll at very low level when, to use his own phrase, he 'didn't apply enough top rudder' and one wingtip of his Bristol Bulldog touched the ground: the crash virtually removed his legs. Someone with fewer guts (or 'bloody mindedness') would in all likelihood have not survived but Bader went on to master prosthetic legs and

Paternal Grandparents with my father, me and sister Helen. 1951

returned to RAF flying during World War II. I saw the film of the book[*] in 1958 and decided that I now wanted to be fighter pilot. I could see it mapped out. 'They' would give me a Spitfire and a polka dot scarf (not absolutely necessary) and with luck I would get to keep my legs. Over seventy years after Bader's accident I was to be given a fascinating account of the event by a man who watched it happen as he cycled back to school after lunch at home, but I'll leave the details of that for later.

Although my parents accepted my change of plan, it did not go down very well with my paternal grandfather. Apart from the Great War, which he had spent in the Army, Grandpa had spent his entire working life at Cazenove. He and my grandmother lived in Crouch End in North London and remained, as far as I could see, locked in the Edwardian era. The very popular TV comedy series *Dad's Army* had Arthur Lowe playing Captain Mainwaring, a pompous bank manager who loved the status given to him as the unit's commanding officer. My grandfather was Captain Mainwaring's spitting image, right down to the glasses and the moustache. In my grandparents' house in Wolseley Road the front room, or parlour, was kept for special occasions and it was in that room on one such visit that my grandfather asked me what I was going to do when I grew up.

When I said I planned to be a fighter pilot he told my father, 'Take the boy away and don't bring him back until he has come to his senses!'

---

* Brickhill, *Paul. Reach for the Sky: The Story of Douglas Bader* DSO, DFC. London: Odhams Press Ltd., 1954. ISBN 1-55750-222-6.

I don't remember how long it was before we returned, though needless to say the subject was not raised again! By the time I saw *Reach for the Sky* we were living in Surrey not two miles from RAF Kenley where much of it was filmed for, after spending my first nine years in Southgate in North London, the family had moved to Coulsdon where, after passing my Eleven Plus exam, I gained a place at Reigate Grammar School. Here I existed reasonably happily and in 1960, on joining the third form, I was introduced to the Combined Cadet Force (CCF), which all boys were required to experience. Time in the Army section was the initial requirement, but after passing the appropriate time and tests a transfer to the RAF section was possible. This I completed and exchanged khaki for light blue to find something that interested me greatly: I responded with enthusiasm and progressed well within the RAF section. I well remember my first air experience flight, in a Chipmunk at RAF White Waltham in 1962. Sitting in the back cockpit I watched as the pilot took off and flew out to a free area before asking me if I wanted to try flying the aircraft. I most certainly did but being left-handed it was automatic for me to hold the control column in my left hand. Subsequent instructions

Star Camp RAF South Cerney 1964

My parents 1981

from the front to increase the power necessitated a change of hand and the astute pilot in the front seat obviously spotted this, asking me to confirm that I was indeed flying left-handed. 'Well, lad, you had better get used to flying with your right hand if you're going to be a pilot.' The master at school who ran this section, Dick Griffiths, encouraged me to go on gliding courses which were also held at RAF Kenley and to join the section rifle shooting team: the section subsequently won the Royal Air Force Small Arms Association Assegai Trophy for 1964. Without any doubt, however, the icing on the cake was my selection to attend a CCF Star Camp in the summer of 1964. This was two weeks at RAF South Cerney near Cirencester, the Initial Training School for those seeking to become aircrew officers (and at least five of those in the photo on page 7 became RAF officers); it was a chance for the cadets to see what might be, and for the staff at South Cerney also to evaluate the potential of the cadet. Most importantly the camp included ten hours' assessed flying in the Chipmunk, the RAF's elementary trainer, and I flew my ten hours under the tutelage of Flt Lt Graham Smart, who subsequently wrote up his assessment of my flying ability. I also had my one and only trip in an Avro Anson from the Fighter Command Communications Squadron, based at Bovingdon outside Watford.

To achieve the standard required for a Direct Entry Commission I had to gain at least five GCE (General Certificate of Education) 'O' Levels, including English and maths which should not have proved a problem except that while at school I failed to apply myself to subjects which did not hold my interest. Indeed, the phrase '… could do better if he tried' or similar crops up frequently in my school reports. I failed to gain the requisite 'O' Levels by one, and four were insufficient to progress into the sixth form. In due course I had a one-sided interview with the headmaster, Mr Holland who, having told me that Reigate Grammar School and I were parting company, asked me what I would do. My response of 'I intend to be an officer in the Royal Air Force' elicited the patronising 'I may be wrong about some things, Roome', implying that such an event was a very rare occasion, 'but you will never be an RAF officer.' On that less than auspicious note was my schooling terminated, but Dick Griffiths had been talking to the RAF Schools Liaison Officer for the area, who suggested that I might be granted an educational waiver, usually reserved for those who had gained extra qualifications since leaving school. I applied immediately. I had already completed the RAF's 'pre-selection' tests at the Officer and Aircrew Selection Centre at RAF Biggin Hill and in early November 1964 I was told that my application had been approved, subject to successful completion of the second part of the application procedure. I later received a letter from the Schools Liaison Officer in Southampton who said that he knew 'of no other case where an applicant of your age (seventeen) has gained such an educational waiver'. Although I can never be sure, I wonder if my CCF Star Camp report played any part – perhaps I have an 'O' Level in Chipmunk flying!

3

SIGN ON THE DOTTED LINE

WHILE I AWAITED NEWS from the Royal Air Force about joining dates, I had taken a job in a local garage, KLM Motors of Coulsdon. There I was a dogsbody in the stores but realised after a short while that the system was in something of a mess and I volunteered to tidy it up and streamline it. The storekeeper, one 'Dinty' Moore (it was the generation when so many people had a nickname based on their surname – 'Chalky' White, 'Smudge' Smith, 'Dinger' Bell, 'Nobby' Clark and so on) gave me free rein and I enjoyed the challenge of listing, cataloguing and racking the various items. I had passed my driving test early in 1964 and the garage also often gave me the task of driving the spares Minivan, usually across London to Henley's, the main Jaguar agent in Colindale, and manoeuvring the van through the busy London traffic was excellent driving experience. Another regular task was to move the various cars on and off the forecourt at the beginning and end of each day (they were locked in the main garage workshops overnight). This I enjoyed, as there was always a wide range of motoring hardware, including various models of Jaguar. Most of these were saloons, but occasionally there was an 'E' Type to move, and as I slid behind the wheel I would imagine owning one of these beautiful vehicles. The stores counter was also the servicing desk where owners would drop off their cars for servicing. One lucky day an 'E' Type owner – an airline pilot – came in to leave his car for a few days but asked if someone would come down to Gatwick and bring the car back as time was short. I jumped at the chance and revelled in the fifteen-mile drive back up the A23. Even better, I then had to drive down again to Gatwick a few days later to deliver the car back to its owner.

Enjoyable though the driving was I was delighted to receive notice that I should report to RAF Biggin Hill for completion of the formal selection process. I duly presented myself for the two or three days of interviews, medicals and tests, the first of which was to produce a urine specimen, and we were each given a glass phial and told to queue 'over there' once we had done the necessary. I overheard another candidate saying, 'I went as I came through the door and my bladder's empty.' 'Don't worry,' said the next in line, 'have some of mine.' I wonder whether that resulted in two failures or two passes! One moment of worry for me came during the eyesight tests, when I found difficulty in reading the lower lines of the letter board. The technician expressed considerable surprise at my failure and asked me to confirm what I could read: I tried again but still could not progress below about the mid-point. Then he looked himself. 'Oh dear, I am SO sorry, I haven't switched the backlight on.' I could then read to the foot of the display! Eventually I had completed the process and walked out across the road from the main gate to await a bus back to Bromley station. While at the stop, a sergeant appeared and shouted to me, 'Are you Roome?' I acknowledged this to be so and he came across to tell me that I had only put down pilot as my number one choice. 'You have to fill all three choices,' he said and when I asked what most put down he replied that pilot, navigator and AEO (air electronics officer) were the norm. I agreed, he filled in the missing lines on the form and went back across the road, thus completing my application to become an officer in Her Majesty's Royal Air Force. I had also stated that I could join with little notice. Things moved quite quickly and in late November a letter arrived telling me to report to RAF South Cerney, where I had been for the CCF Star Camp, on 11 January 1965. This time, however, I would be an officer cadet on 208 Course of No.1 Initial Training School. My parents now told me that I had been left some money by a great-aunt, to be given to me on reaching twenty-one or when I started my career, and that I was now richer by some £400. I spent £350 of it on my first car, a green Austin Mini, and in early January I loaded my worldly possessions into it and set off westwards for Gloucestershire.

Along with about twenty-five others who made up 208 Course I was to start air force life living in a barrack block and in the first few days signed on (as an airman, like all officer cadets), and drew all manner of kit, uniform, PE kit, bedding and linen, books, cleaning materials and so on and so forth. Some of it seemed to be very out of date and all our uniform shirts had detached collars with studs front and back, but that was the way it was then. On the second day I was attested, stating that '*I, David Christopher Roome, swear by Almighty God that I will be faithful and bear true allegiance to Her Majesty Queen Elizabeth The Second, Her Heirs and Successors, and that I will as in duty bound, honestly and faithfully defend Her Majesty, Her Heirs and Successors in person, Crown and Dignity against all enemies, and will observe and obey all orders of Her Majesty, Her Heirs and Successors, and of the Air Officers and other officers set over me. So help me God.*' I signed and my flight commander Flt Lt Stuart Greenslade witnessed as the Attesting Officer. On the same form was my contracting to sign on as an airman for five years from that date. I was 'in'.

Life as an officer cadet at South Cerney was 'full on'. In the barrack block for the first month each of us had our own bed space, which had to be ready for inspection at any time other than when we slept. Each and every morning we made our bedding into a bedpack in which the two sheets were folded ensuring that the stripes sewn into the linen were square and central, then the three blankets were positioned to sandwich the sheets (stripes also central) and the whole wrapped in the last blanket. To pass muster the resultant rectangle had to be a thing of beauty. A ruler placed down the stripes would show them all to be perfectly in line and the whole bedpack was placed at the head of the bed above the other items on display for inspection, polished to a high gloss where possible, including the ubiquitous button stick, a brass slide which went behind other brass items while they were cleaned. Needless to say, the button stick itself had to display the same shine. The wood floors were polished in a like manner – woe betide any cadet who didn't take their boots off before entering the room – and even the ablutions had to give the appearance that no one had ever used them and that they were all brand new, even though they were of wartime vintage. We had one enterprising cadet who decided that the work required to achieve the acceptance of either the drill sergeant or inspecting officer (praise was an impossible dream and a cursory nod would be all that we could hope for) was all too much. Leaving his bedpack made up he slept underneath his bed in a sleeping bag. Of course, he was eventually found out, his bedpack was reduced to its component parts and he was awarded no end of 'restrictions' to teach him a lesson. These restrictions meant that life was even more hectic. Apart from having to parade twice in the evening, at 1800 and 2200 in full uniform, belt blanco'd, and boots and brasses shining, we were given extra tasks to complete in the early evening; it might be sweeping the hangar floor or polishing some door handles, but I also remember being told to paint the concrete blocks along the front of the hangar 'black/white/black/white'. As they were 'white/black/white/black', I started to paint but once no longer under scrutiny it made eminent sense to lift each block and transfer its position. Of course, the flight commander returned after a leisurely stroll around the hangar to find me carrying one of the blocks! That misdemeanour got me some more 'strickers'! It wasn't always the permanent staff who would make our life hell either, as on the odd occasion members of more senior courses would run riot through the block and leave us with more cleaning to do before the morning deadline.

The days were taken up with a variety of events. Inevitably drill and PE were very high on the list as the staff tried to shape, mould and near beat us into prospective officers. There was much emphasis on fitness and South Cerney airfield often played a part in this. It is a grass airfield with a roughly circular perimeter track around it, and we would get to know the two miles of that peri track very well indeed. Sometimes we would simply be tasked to run around it, but then there were the times we did so each carrying a medicine ball, or three of us carrying a gym bench between us. During the run, the physical training instructor would stop us now and then to complete some extra exertions before setting off once again. The cadets on the course before ours had found themselves one foggy Gloucestershire morning running around it in freezing fog, with the grass white with frost. Deciding that they couldn't be seen and a shortcut would save both time and effort, they took a direct route across the grass in the middle of the airfield. All was well until the fog lifted and the footprints left in the grass told the tale: the penalties for so doing ensured that this was never repeated.

During that first month the only time off was on Saturday afternoon as coursework continued up to noon on the Saturday. Sunday morning was church parade and we all turned out in sports jackets and slacks, each wearing a hat as required by the South Cerney dress rules. Church of England and Roman Catholic services were held in the appropriate church buildings on the camp, but I had been brought up in the Congregational Church and like the Baptists, Methodists and other 'odds and sods' we were taken into Cirencester by bus to attend services there. Saturday evenings were also free, although we had to be back in the block by 11pm, or 2300 hours as we now termed it. Occasionally a late pass to midnight was granted, though as the pubs closed around eleven it was not generally something we took advantage of. At the end of January came a day of particular note. On 30 January we were all given the day off to permit us to watch the funeral of Sir Winston Churchill on television, which I well remember doing in the South Cerney NAAFI.

At the end of the first month there was a written test in which I failed to achieve the pass mark for maths, with the result that I was immediately re-coursed to join 209 Course, starting in February 1965 and could look forward to another month in the barrack block. It was a nasty shock, but I passed the exam next time and said goodbye to bedpacks and the barrack block as we moved down to the comparative delights of No.2 officers' mess. This was a hutted set of 'temporary' buildings which from September 1939 to October 1946 had been the home of HQ 23 Group, controlling the RAF's advanced pilot training. It was situated in front of and below the main (No.1) officers' mess, a grand three-storey building typical of the 1930s Expansion Scheme and one of the largest officers' messes built during that period. Cadets lived in No.2 mess for the two-month duration of the leadership phase of the course before moving into No.1 mess for the final month. Life was a bit easier during this intermediate phase of the course and we had individual rooms and a 'proper' mess instead of the NAAFI cafeteria. The public rooms of the mess – the anteroom, bar, dining room and kitchens – were in a separate block and entry was by means of several wooden steps up into an entrance hall and then through either of two sets of batwing doors, each with six opaque glazed panels. Once through the doors a corridor ran down left to the anteroom and bar. Ahead were the kitchens (out of bounds to cadets) and to the right was the dining room. The reason for all this detail is that it provides the background to a fascinating tale which occurred the night before our course was to depart for our leadership camp in the Brecon

Beacons. Early in the morning an airman was detailed to come down to No.2 mess and prepare packed lunches for the cadets. He arrived around three in the morning and started work in the kitchens but was interrupted by the sound of someone in the hall and he came out to investigate, as he should have been the only person in the mess. As he described it later, he looked down the corridor toward the anteroom and saw a man walking up towards him wearing darker than the usual blue uniform trousers, fur-lined flying boots and similar lined jacket, and muttering in 'an American' accent about 'those damned lights'. The airman demanded to know what the officer was doing in the mess but he walked straight past him and then went out through the batwing doors of the exit, without the doors moving! This event was duly recorded by the orderly sergeant in the main guardroom at the opposite end of the camp after the airman arrived at a sprint and gabbled his story out. We cadets only heard the story after returning from our leadership camp, having gone without our packed lunches! Several of us then tried to find out the background to 'the ghost of No.2 mess', and the story was that in about 1943 a bomber returning from a raid had diverted to South Cerney. While trying to land it had crashed into the Belman hangar, a corrugated iron hangar. The crew had been killed and it was thought that the pilot had mistaken the obstruction lights (which during the war were blue in place of the usual red) on the roof of what later became the mess, for the perimeter of the airfield. As he flared for the landing the aircraft hit the hangar which lay beyond the mess. The pilot concerned had been a Canadian. The final fact that appeared to corroborate the tale was that the RCAF uniform was of a darker blue than that of the RAF, appearing to bear out the cook's account. Unfortunately, I could find no record of such a crash during the war but if that ghost is still prowling around South Cerney he must have difficulty, as the building was knocked down soon after all officer training left at the end of 1967.

The leadership phase, while continuing the drill, physical training and lectures on such aviation subjects as aerodynamics and airmanship, also brought in those exercises we had seen a taster of during the Biggin Hill selection – the 'three oil drums, two pitch poles and a length of rope to get four people across a chasm' type of exercise. However, in April we were also shown what would happen if we were ever flying an aircraft at height and the oxygen system failed. South Cerney had a hypobaric chamber and we were all given the experience of hypoxia, a lack of oxygen. Six of us at a time climbed into the chamber and sat in comfortable leather seating along the sides, each with an oxygen regulator and mask attached to a flying helmet. With a doctor in the chamber with us, the pressure inside was reduced to half that at ground level, equating to an altitude of 18,000ft. The three of us on one side were then told to switch off our oxygen and each of us was given a simple task: one had to write his name and address over and over again, another had to count up to a hundred and back and so on. The other three cadets were then treated to a display of increasing inanity as the lack of oxygen became apparent. Writing became a scrawl with the pen continuing off the paper onto the knee, while the cadet counting became to all intents and purposes a drunkard, incapable of simple addition. Although it was all very amusing there was a very serious learning point. Each of us was told to remember the symptoms we felt as the hypoxia took hold, for one day we might have to face the problem for real and the memory of this event might be a lifesaver. For me, the tingling in my fingertips and feet, and the loss of concentration would be my triggers. We would all experience deliberate hypoxia again at other stages of our training, but this was our first real insight into what could go wrong when flying at altitude.

Such practical events were few and far between and most teaching was by lectures, some more enjoyable than others. One of the most enjoyable airmanship lectures will always stick in my mind, however. It would also have been around April when the instructor whose task it was to impart this morning's piece of knowledge, Flt Lt Chris Salwey, announced that we would hold the session outside on the grass in front of the hangar offices. It was still very chilly but to question such a decision was, of course, unthinkable. We duly sat outside and the lecture continued until the faint sound of piston engines approaching at speed swelled into a roar and between the hangars at about 30ft above the ground a Mosquito swept out across the airfield and began a most impressive beat-up. Chris Salwey had obviously been aware that this would be happening and we all stood in awe of this beautiful aircraft as it raced back and forth across the field with big, graceful wingovers at the end of each pass. Eventually, after a full five minutes of exhilarating joy, the Mosquito departed back to its base, RAF Little Rissington, some fifteen miles to the northeast. It was being flown by the Commandant of the Central Flying School (CFS), Air Commodore H A C 'Birdy' Bird Wilson, who had had a very successful wartime career as a fighter pilot and was now about to go out to Hong Kong as the Air Officer Commanding. He had displayed the 'Mossie' each summer during his time as Commandant and perhaps it was his final trip at 'Little Rissie'; in any event we most certainly enjoyed it!

There is a sad ending to the story of that Mosquito, TA639. For the 1965 summer display season the aircraft was flown by Flt Lt Chick Kirkham, a great gentleman who I later had the pleasure of serving alongside at RAF Valley. After Chick Kirkham's last display of the 1965 season on 3 October that year, the aircraft was placed in No.4 hangar for the winter. However, the extra work required to keep this historic aircraft serviceable was not to the liking of some of the engineering senior NCOs, who went to OC Engineering Wing to complain about the time spent on Mosquito support. They wanted the aircraft grounded but this was refused. However, they were allowed to move the aircraft from No.4 hangar to No.5 hangar, which had one very important difference: it was the only hangar at Little Rissington that was heated, with several hot air blowers on the roof girders, each with wide canvas pipes reaching down to duct hot air to the working level a few feet above the hangar floor. The Mosquito was deliberately placed by one of the ducts and over the winter the hot air played on the glue joints used in the aircraft's construction. The constant heating caused the glue to fail, resulting in the complete loss of structural integrity and the aircraft was permanently grounded. Such sabotage by engineers would now attract serious disciplinary measures, especially on such an iconic and irreplaceable aircraft, but the perpetrators were never punished.

Back at South Cerney we officer cadets of 209 Course went off in April to carry out our leadership camp in the Brecon Beacons. At the end of this camp I was summoned by my flight commander and informed that I had failed to achieve the grade and would be re-coursed once again. This was a bitter blow, for I had no warning that things were not 'up to spec' and it was with a heavy heart that I faced the prospect of another eight weeks in No.2 mess and the entire leadership phase again. However, there was a silver lining to this particular cloud, for South Cerney was to host the 1965 World Gliding Championships and our accommodation was required. Off we went for five much more relaxed weeks at RAF Shawbury outside Shrewsbury before returning in mid-June to repeat the leadership camp, for which I was designated the Flight Leader. This time my flight commander declared my leadership abilities to be fine, saying, 'You're no Winston Churchill, but I can't see why you failed the first time.'

So now I could begin to see the end of the course, and as a member of 211 Course I moved into No.1 mess, the 'proper' officers' mess. We were given final fittings for our uniforms and officers' peaked 'service duties' or SD Cap, although the white band around it signified that we were not yet officers. We would only remove the band on the day of our graduation and commissioning. Dress rules in the mess were clear-cut; after 1900 on weekdays the only uniform to be seen was worn by officers on duty, usually only the orderly officer (OO) and the station duty officer (SDO). Everyone else wore a suit, though on Wednesdays (which was sports day across the Service) and at weekends a sports jacket was acceptable. Much work was also spent practising for our graduation parade, which finally took place on 21 July 1965. I was selected to be the parade commander for the event and the reviewing officer was Gp Capt Wallace, the station commander at RAF Shawbury where the course had spent most of May and June during the gliding championships. I was now appointed to a direct entry permanent commission (A) on the supplementary list which meant that subject to satisfactory completion of pilot training I was guaranteed a commission to the age of thirty-eight. I was now Acting Pilot Officer (APO) Roome with a very thin stripe on my No.1 uniform, so thin it was just about invisible from fifteen feet. Nevertheless, it was a real stripe and I was very proud of it, so proud that I wore it back to Reigate Grammar School and walked into the headmaster's office. 'What are you doing now, Kilbey?' was all Mr Holland said, so I turned on my heel and left!

Even now I was not to leave South Cerney, for 211 Course was to be the first to carry out thirty-five sorties of Chipmunk flying as a form of primary flying training before starting on the Jet Provost. During August we got used to being officers, though the line between officer cadet and APO was a fine one. One day I was walking back to the officers' mess with another friend on the same course, Rod Newman, when a stentorian voice bellowed 'Gentlemen! I am saluting you!' On looking around we saw Warrant Officer Peake, the South Cerney Training Wing Warrant Officer and a man we all feared. Although he was a good one hundred yards away, his right arm was rigid against the peak of his hat and I knew that, as the officer closer to Mr Peake, it fell to me to return the salute. This I did, but obviously not well enough because the response was 'NOT LIKE THAT! NOW STAND STILL!' We froze and waited as Mr Peake marched (he never walked) over to us. 'Now, gentlemen', intimating that we were anything but, 'how do you salute?' Our response came together as we snapped out 'Up the longest way, down the shortest way, Mr Peake!' while our right arms displayed the proper salute. After several more attempts to prove we knew how to salute, Mr Peake allowed us to go on our way. 'Blimey,' said Rod, 'and we thought we were officers!'

During our final month as officer cadets we had also been introduced to the dining-in night to inculcate this Service tradition into the cadets. Such dinners were originally for mess members 'dining in the mess together' and had originally been every weekday night, but by the mid-1960s it had dropped to a monthly function. Dress for the evening was mess kit, consisting of a blue monkey jacket with gold rank braid, a white waistcoat over a stiff-fronted shirt with a detachable wing collar and high-waisted blue barathea trousers. On occasions when there were female guests the function became a ladies' guest night and white ties were worn. Later the mess dress rules changed and a 'golf ball' or 'Marcella' white shirt and a blue waistcoat replaced the 'penguin suit' for dining-in nights, though the full fig, for special occasions, was retained as an option for many years. These different forms of mess kit bring to mind an amusing anecdote which occurred several years later. When the Royal Air Force Regiment was invited to mount the guard at Buckingham Palace, the officer in charge of the guard was reminded to dress in mess kit each evening 'in case you're invited to dine with the Royal Family'. The officer concerned therefore spent each evening in his quarters in the palace wearing mess kit until the last evening, when a summons came and he found himself dining with The Queen and HRH The Duke of Edinburgh. During the meal the conversation turned to uniforms and the Duke pointed out that, while the Army had many different uniforms, even the RAF had some variations. Would the guard commander please inform Her Majesty of the differences? 'Well, Ma'am, we do indeed have two forms of mess dress – there is this one and then, for really special occasions…' and here he faltered. The Duke would not let it go. 'Yes,' he said, 'even you have two forms of mess dress, the one which you are wearing and then, for really special occasions, such as a private dinner with The Queen, you would wear your stiff-fronted shirt!'

As South Cerney officer cadets we would have no mess dress until we completed the course successfully and were commissioned, so for our first dining-in we wore our battledress with a white shirt and bow tie. Our introduction to this formal dinner started in the anteroom with pre-dinner drinks, usually sherry served by stewards. Everyone was on best behaviour and the squadron officers, our instructors, made polite conversation with us until the announcement from the mess manager, 'Gentlemen, dinner is served.' Now everyone put down their drinks and filed through the entrance hall to the dining room as a small band played 'The Roast Beef of Old England', as they still do as the call to dinner on such occasions. Everyone took their places standing behind their allotted chair until everyone was present when the President, usually the wing commander who was President of the Mess Committee (PMC), said a grace and we all sat down. The rules governing behaviour at these functions were to become very familiar as the years passed:

- On no account touch any of the silver (displayed on the tables and usually squadron or station trophies) before the Loyal Toast.
- Do not start eating before those on the top table have started.
- Divide your conversations equally between the people each side of you.
- Behave with dignity as befits such an occasion (again, *before* the Loyal Toast, afterwards was often a different matter!).

After the meal had been cleared away two decanters, one containing port and the other Madeira, would be placed in front of the PMC and another similar two in front of Mr Vice, usually the most junior officer present and seated at the foot of one of the tables, though at large dinners further decanters would be brought into use. The mess manager informed the PMC that all was ready and the PMC then removed the stoppers and passed the decanters to his left for each member to fill his liqueur glass while a steward shadowed the decanters with a jug of water for those who did not wish to take either port or Madeira. The decanters were always received in the right hand and passed on the same way (some maintained that the decanters must never touch the table as they passed round). When everyone had filled their glasses and the decanters had ended up back where they started, the PMC would bang his gavel, stand and command Mr Vice with the statement 'Mr Vice, The Queen!' Mr Vice would, in turn, stand and declare 'Gentlemen (or Ladies and Gentlemen), The Queen.' Everyone then stood while the musicians, who had played throughout the meal, played the National Anthem, after which everyone took their glass, raised it and declared 'The Queen' (NEVER adding the Naval 'God Bless Her') before sipping the drink and then sitting down. If there were officers present from overseas countries, the toast would then be repeated but with the words applicable to the country, 'The President of The United States of America' for example, and the musicians then played the appropriate anthem. Sometimes there were too many overseas officers present and then the toast would be 'The heads of state of countries here represented' – and the musicians didn't have to play!

After dinner, the toasts and speeches, everyone returned to the anteroom, and back in July 1965 I was treated to an evening the like of which would soon pass into RAF history. Mess games after the dining-in may still continue but they are a pale shadow of what went on that evening. One of the less dangerous was mess rugby, where the large leather chairs and sofas of the anteroom were placed alternately back to back and front to front, creating very large 'fences' or hurdles. The two teams took their places at each end, facing each other and the PMC or station commander started the game by throwing a ball into the centre of the 'fences'. Whichever team got their members and the ball to the opposing end first would be declared the winners and it was a case of anything goes! Another game was High Cockalorum, in which one team formed a line against a wall with one member having his back to the wall and the others scrummed down in a single line, usually of about eight officers. One at a time the opposing team ran and jumped as far as they could to land on the back of the line. As more landed at about the same point, those below had to carry the increasing weight on their back, exacerbated by the impact of the next to arrive. If the line could withstand all the opposing team arriving without collapsing, they were declared the winners! It was not long before this game was banned throughout the Service after several severe injuries, including broken spines. Thankfully no one suffered anything major that evening and we enjoyed much drinking, including several schooner races of pints of beer, and staggered off to bed much later, having seen our first Service dining-in night.

Between late July and the end of August I flew eighteen happy hours in Chipmunks at South Cerney under the tuition of Master Pilot Graham Forrester, and on 17 August 1965 I flew my first solo in a powered aircraft, flying Chipmunk WP896. I had finally 'slipped the surly bonds of earth' in a powered aircraft at my own hand and at last the future looked bright. It was now on to fly jets.

4

LEARNING THE BASICS

RAF SYERSTON OPENED FOR business on 1 December 1940 and was initially home to two Polish bomber squadrons of Wellingtons but in summer 1941 they left, to be replaced by a newly formed Canadian squadron, 408 (Goose) Squadron RCAF, flying the Hampden. Only six months later, on the day following the Japanese attack on Pearl Harbour, the Hampdens moved to Syerston's satellite airfield at Balderton just four miles to the northeast, and Syerston closed to allow the construction of hard runways in preparation for the four-engined bombers then coming into service. Five months later the airfield re-opened with two runways of 4,300ft and the main northeast-southwest runway being a shade under 6,000ft. The speed with which this was completed – and we should remember the same building programme was going on all over the east of England – is a reminder of just what can be done when the need arises, and it permitted squadrons equipped with the Lancaster to move in from May 1942, among which was 106 Squadron commanded by Wg Cdr Guy Gibson, soon to earn immortality leading 617 Squadron on the Dams Raid in May a year later. Also based there was 61 Squadron, and in November 1943 one of their Lancasters, piloted by Flt Lt William Reid, set off on a raid to Dusseldorf. As the aircraft crossed the Dutch coast it was set upon by a Messerschmitt Bf110 night fighter whose guns caused great damage, shattering the Lancaster windscreen and wounding Reid in the head, shoulders and hands. The controls were damaged, the aircraft was now difficult to fly and the compasses were put out of action. Not saying anything about his own injuries, Reid pressed on toward Dusseldorf but

23

the aircraft was soon attacked again, this time by a Focke-Wulf 190; the gunfire killed the navigator and fatally wounded the wireless operator. The Lancaster's guns were put out of action, the oxygen system disabled and on top of all this Reid himself sustained further injuries to his right arm. Having memorised the required course, Reid still pressed on to his target, which he reached fifty minutes later. He had continued on in such a normal manner that his bomb aimer, cut off from the cockpit by the comms failure, had no idea that his captain was injured and the bombs were released right over the centre of his target, a ball-bearing factory. Reid now set course for home, steering by reference to the Pole Star and sustained by oxygen from a portable bottle and administered by his flight engineer. At times semi-conscious, freezing cold because of the broken windscreen and half blinded by the blood from a head wound which kept streaming into his eyes, Reid managed to bring his defenceless aircraft safely back, landing at Shipdham in Norfolk. For this immensely brave action, Flt Lt Bill Reid was awarded the Victoria Cross.

Fifteen years later Syerston, now under the control of Flying Training Command, took delivery of its first Jet Provosts and two years later the station had the distinction of being the world's first to train student pilots on jet aircraft throughout. Syerston's airfield layout remains to this day, the three runways encircled by the perimeter track, with the teardrop dispersals and the one remaining hangar behind the air traffic tower. The airfield is bounded to the east by the Fosse Way and to the west by the River Trent, and the officers' mess, where I arrived in the first week of September 1965, was across the Fosse Way from the impressive straight drive leading to the main gate and station headquarters. The large expansion of the RAF was very well executed and the classic buildings of that period still impress today, though many at Syerston have been demolished. At the time of writing the station houses the RAF Central Gliding School and so the airfield remains active. It was not a large officers' mess, with the east and west wings being two-storey accommodation joined by a single-storey spine with the usual public rooms, anteroom, dining room, ladies' room, bar and billiard room, and had the kitchens to the rear. To cater for surplus aircrew, two rows of Secco huts had been built to the rear of the mess and this was where we students would live for the next eleven months.

170 Course started on 7 September 1965 with eleven students. After the inevitable endless form filling of the arrival procedure came the much more interesting trip to stores to be fitted for and to draw flying kit. For the first time I was issued with a 'bone dome', the hard outer shell that covered the cloth inner 'G' helmet with its earpieces for the radio (radiotelephony, or 'RT'), and to which was attached an oxygen mask with its integral microphone. Our flying kit included a thick blue aircrew shirt, under which in cold weather we could wear our string vests, made of real string! I never actually wore one of these, which looked as if it had been made by a trainee fisherwoman before she graduated onto proper fishing nets and was a string net in the shape of a tube, with heavy duty canvas shoulder strips to hold it in place! To complement these in the winter we had aircrew long johns, flannelette underwear secured by two rubber buttons which finished around mid-calf. Was this really what the well-dressed fighter pilot was wearing? Completing the ensemble was a grey flying suit which came with an integral belt and with buttoned pockets, and the 1952 pattern flying boot, heavy duty, rubber-soled leather boots with a wide top section into which some of the older pilots still tucked their flying suits and which could be cut off to make the boot appear to be an ordinary pair of shoes in the event of having to evade in enemy territory after baling out, something we hoped we would never have to do!

The very next morning we got straight down to business in ground school and for two weeks we spent all day learning the Jet Provost systems and checklists, and had lectures on navigation, meteorology, aerodynamics and so on. We also started to learn air traffic procedures, RT procedures and codes, and were introduced to the plethora of abbreviations common to the Services, like DME for Distance Measuring Equipment, more of which later, but there was also much use of 'Q' codes. These dated back to the time when much communication was carried out in Morse code and indeed, one of the course requirements was that we all had to be able to decode Morse sent at eight words per minute over a headset and at two words per minute on a signal light. Many of these Q codes have now disappeared though some, like QFE for airfield-level atmospheric pressure, or QNH for the pressure at sea level, are still in common use. I once went to the wedding of a signaller in the RAF, the trade that used Q codes for longer than any other, and at the reception listened as the best man read out the telegrams. One caused great hilarity among the (male) guests and comprised only a series of letters starting with 'Q'. I asked one of the signallers the decode, to which he said, 'It is a code for an aircraft to send to a submarine instructing it to signal its intended position and depth at midnight the coming night!'

To aid us in learning our Flight Reference Cards for the Jet Provost T.3 there was a cockpit trainer which to a degree mimicked the JP. Electrical power could be applied and some of the lights worked, enabling us to piece together what seemed at the time to be inordinately complex pages of checks and drills. Ground school would continue throughout the course but after the initial two weeks we spent a half-day at our desks and the other half at 2 Squadron in the hangar behind Air Traffic Control and the flight line of JPs. On 22 September I flew my first flight in Jet Provost T.3 XM409 under the tutelage of Flight Sergeant Smith. By the mid-1960s, SNCO flying instructors were already becoming a rarity and young SNCO instructors even more so. 'Smudge' Smith, the story went, had been commissioned as an APO and had completed his basic flying training before continuing to advanced flying training on the Vampire. Towards the end of this course on a solo trip he had decided to impress his girlfriend with a couple of low passes over her house. As Smudge himself said to us, 'If you're going to do some illegal low flying, only do one pass, because on any subsequent pass someone will be alert enough to take your number.' In his case it was the local policeman and Smudge was 'busted' back to sergeant pilot (and posted to a fighter squadron where he met several others who had met the same fate following flying indiscretions). That was something else that had died out by the mid-1960s, as flying offences now merited much sterner punishments, often dismissal from the Service.

About this time our course suddenly collected another fourteen students who were university graduates and because of the time spent on their university air squadrons had only had to spend four weeks at South Cerney. After an initial 'them and us' settling in period we soon all got on and would continue together on through the remainder of our training.

Although I flew my first two trips with Smudge, my primary instructor was Derek Bridge, who had also been NCO aircrew, but as a signaller on the Avro Shackleton before gaining a commission and transferring to pilot. At the end of his flying training, Derek was selected to go directly to the Central Flying School to become a qualified flying instructor (QFI): in air force parlance he was 'creamed off'. These first-tour QFIs usually progressed through to their aircraft of choice following their instructional tour and in Derek's case we would meet again as students on the same course when flying the Hawker Hunter at RAF Chivenor two years later, but now his job was to teach me how to fly, and, more importantly, how to land! With all students requiring plenty of practice in the circuit we made considerable use of Syerston's Relief Landing Ground (RLG) at RAF Wymeswold twenty miles southwest of Syerston and just outside Loughborough. This was a satellite of the main airfield and was manned by air traffic and fire personnel only when necessary. It was here on 11 October, after nine hours of instruction, that Derek told me to land from a circuit and taxi around behind the tower. As we taxied he replaced the pins in his ejection seat and unstrapped. Once stopped on the perimeter track he said words to the effect of 'I reckon you can probably do that on your own now, so do one circuit and land, then come back to here where I'll be waiting.' With that, he stepped out onto the intake step, strapped up the right-hand seat harness, disappeared down to the wing trailing edge and walked off to the tower without a backward glance! At last I was alone in a jet aircraft and despite my nerves, boy, did it feel good!

Once I had completed my first solo we went on to learn the various types of circuit other than the basic circuit. The flapless circuit was flown after a hydraulic failure when, with no flap available, the threshold speed was greater and it was harder to lose excess speed. The low-level circuit was flown when the cloudbase did not permit visual flight at the usual 1,000ft and the high-level circuit was flown when mist at low level made it impossible to see the runway unless the aircraft was climbed: we flew this at 2,000ft and selected idle power and full flap at the appropriate point in the finals turn. Then we started ranging further afield, doing 'sector recces (reconnaissance)'. In order to learn how to put out an emergency call I was shown and practised a 'Practice PAN'. There were three levels of emergency, starting with a slight raising of the pulse, perhaps for being 'temporarily uncertain of one's position' or, in truth, being lost! For this, the call on the emergency frequency was prefixed by the word 'Securité', said three times as are all emergency calls (why French was picked I never knew). If the emergency required urgent action to resolve, the call prefix became 'PAN' (not French, you will have noted) and if in dire straits, the highest level of emergency demanded a 'MAYDAY' (this, we learned, from the French (again) '*m'aidez*', or 'help me'). The practising of such calls could only be made using the 'Practice PAN' call. No one is ever meant to call 'Practice MAYDAY', though once when flying and monitoring – as all pilots are recommended to do – the international distress frequency of 243Mhz I did hear it: I then also heard the vitriolic response from the controller in the Distress Cell at RAF West Drayton!

It was on one of these circuit consolidation trips that I found myself (again with Derek Bridge) pounding the circuit at Wymeswold. Derek had another student and that morning he had sent him off solo with instructions to do some circuits at Syerston before flying down to Wymeswold for some more before landing. Derek would then get into that aircraft and carry out another sortie before recovering to Syerston. I got the reverse deal and Derek got me to land and let him out behind the tower once more. 'Do three more circuits and then go back to Syerston. I'll see you back in the squadron.' I duly took off, flew the three circuits and announced that I was 'departing the circuit for base' and before setting course (or thought I did). Now, as I have said, Wymeswold was a mere twenty miles southwest of Syerston and a direct line home would have the Fosse Way, a nice, almost straight, Roman road, on my right, while on my left would be the River Trent, which also ran directly past Syerston. How I managed to get lost is now beyond me, but get lost I certainly did. I was rushing around at what then seemed the phenomenal speed of 180kts and I hadn't got a clue where I was! Luckily an airfield appeared in front of me, though it didn't have a river to one side and a road to the other. It *did* have the word 'LANGAR' spelt out in paint on the runway (perhaps the RCAF, who operated from there at that time, also got lost now and again) and I realised that all should be OK if I turned onto north. Naturally Syerston appeared almost immediately and I was so relieved I felt as if I had flown across the Atlantic and found base! I didn't realise what a fool I had been until later that day when it sank in. Roughly fifteen years later I had become an examiner and was testing a student who also didn't pay enough attention to where he was going, this time in a Hawk at 420kts instead of the JP's 180, and turned onto the reciprocal of his required heading. When I pointed out his error he was convinced that he had 'screwed up' his 'trappers ride', but in the debrief I told him my story of getting lost within twenty miles of home base and showed that it happens to us all at some time: he was not to worry. That man was Mark Hanna who went on to fly the Phantom and later became a very accomplished display pilot and a good friend until his untimely death some years later.

Once students have passed the hurdle of first solo it is an advantage to vary their instructors and in November 1965 I flew a total of twelve sorties: three solo and the other nine with no less than five different QFIs, culminating just four days short of my nineteenth birthday by flying (and passing) the 'Spinning and Aerobatics Check' flight with my flight commander, Flt Lt Don Henderson. During the month I also was introduced to flight at high altitude. The T.3 Jet Provost could reach 35,000ft if one spent most of a morning climbing up there. We were required to do so, breathing oxygen through our economiser system (it would never be allowed today, when flight at these altitudes in an unpressurised aircraft requires 100% oxygen to be fed to the mask) and then we carried out a compressibility run to the maximum Mach number of 0.73M; in those days, only twenty years after the end of WWII, such events were judged simply a part of learning to fly a military jet. Less than eighteen months later I would be at almost twice that height and over twice that speed, 1.7M, learning to fly the Lightning.

It was also in November 1965 that one of our course members found that aircraft, even basic trainers, can bite. He had been sent off to practise, amongst other things, the approach to the stall. However, while he was doing so, the aircraft stalled fully and, he believed, entered a spin, something for which he had not yet been taught the recovery technique. As the ground approached and still not in control, he did the sensible thing and ejected. The Martin-Baker seat functioned as advertised and deposited him just outside Mansfield, from where he rang the squadron operations desk at Syerston. I was the duty student at the time and was somewhat surprised to hear this friend announce himself and ask to speak to his instructor. 'But,' I said, 'I thought you were meant to be flying.' 'Yes, that's why I need to speak to him,' came the response. Now, at the time the instructors were all having a meeting in the instructors' crewroom and had put a 'Do Not Disturb' notice on the door. They did not take kindly to me putting my head around the door and asking for one to come to the phone and it took more than one attempt to get their attention. When I announced that one of the students was on the phone the ridicule increased, but once I said that he was ringing because he had ejected, everything changed and I was almost mown down in the rush to the phone!

The course progressed through autumn, with general handling, navigation and instrument flying (GH, Nav and IF) with hurdles such as the BIFG (Basic Instrument Flying Grading) and later the AIFG (Advanced…), each of which allowed the solo pilot to penetrate cloud down to a lower height to recover to the airfield. The BIFG permitted a student to descend to 1,800ft and the AIFG to 1,200ft, by which time one had to be visual with the ground. In February 1966, after passing the Basic Handling Test, I was introduced to the 'hot ship', the Jet Provost T.4, on which most of the remainder of the course was to be flown. While the T.3 produced only 1,750lbs of thrust (unkindly called the 'constant noise, variable thrust machine'), the T.4 had 2,500lbs and (to us) went 'like greased weasel s**t'. Another facet of the course was how to navigate in the air and although visual recognition of a ground feature such as a river, power station or town was useful close to base, because aircraft now flew so much higher the primary means of navigating was to be by navigational aids, radio beacons which the pilot interpreted to confirm his position: this at least was the theory. In planning the flight, the required track was drawn on the map, but then this would be modified for the forecast wind during the climb to height and at the level to be flown. The next step was to draw various bearing lines from the departure airfield so that any drift from the planned track could be determined by getting a bearing from the airfield and the same drawn from the destination.

In the 1960s, the only rudimentary navigation aid available to the Jet Provost was the Distance Measuring Equipment (DME). The aircraft interrogated a ground beacon and the return gave the slant range from that beacon. On a map this could be shown as a range ring around the beacon. By selecting another beacon, another slant range could be plotted and where the two circles intersected was the approximate aircraft position. However, if the two ground stations chosen were each side of the planned track there were two points at which the range circles intersected, giving every chance of confusion in the cockpit. All our maps were covered in DME rings from those ground stations we might reasonably use, but to add to the problem, the selectors were two large Bakelite knobs, one with letters and the other with numbers. If, say, A5 was the selection for the DME at Marham in Norfolk and B7 that for Finningley near Doncaster, an aircraft over Peterborough could expect to see seventy miles on the Finningley beacon and thirty-two from Marham. However, the same readings would be seen if the aircraft was over The Wash, ten miles east of Skegness and fifty miles away from Peterborough! To compound the problem, when a new channel was selected it took what seemed to be an age for the DME to lock on and give a reading, watching the pointer sweep around the dial from 0 to 200 miles and back again and all the while covering the ground at three miles a minute! The map, with its drift angles and closing angles, groundspeed check points and so on, was now so cluttered that even with a completely clear sky so that the ground was visible from 18,000ft it was not easy to detect on the map what ground features lay below. Some, however, were easy and obvious – coastlines, railway lines and so on – and in the Syerston area the three big power stations on the River Trent were always an easily recognisable feature, even above cloud, for the heat from the cooling towers produced 'humps' of higher cloud above the cloud tops.

As well as learning to fly, our training as officers also continued. Each station maintained a twenty-four-hour roster of a station duty officer (SDO), generally of flight lieutenant rank, and a flying officer or pilot officer as the orderly officer (OO). Duty commenced with a briefing in the office of OC General Duties (GD) Flight at 0900 each day. In order to learn the ropes all students had to complete two spells of OO under training, shadowing the true OO of the day. Duties involved being present to salute the raising and lowering of the RAF Ensign, usually outside station headquarters (SHQ), inspecting the meals served in the airmen's mess and inspecting defaulters' parade early in the evening. I completed my spells under training and on 26 May 1966 I was on the list to be the orderly officer for 'real' and no longer 'under training'. I was sure that I was ready for anything that could be thrown at me. How wrong I was.

Syerston was not unusual in having a Station Formation Display Team and mid-morning the four JPs took off to practise their routine at medium level away from the circuit. A little later another JP took off and climbed up through cloud with an instructor and student, who were then presented, as they came out of cloud, with the four-ship team coming the other way! The singleton JP collided head on with the leader and both aircraft then hit the No.4 of the team who, flying in 'the box', was directly astern the leader. Amazingly, all aircrew survived, the leader, the instructor and the student all ejecting safely, while the No.4, who had seen the oncoming aircraft fractionally before impact, had thrown himself down across the empty right-hand seat as the wreckage smashed into his cockpit, flattening the windscreen and ripping off the cockpit canopy. The pilot, Bill Aspinall, then recovered the aircraft safely to Syerston. Meanwhile, the wreckage of the other two aircraft had thankfully caused no injury on hitting the ground and the three pilots floated down over parts of Nottinghamshire, one instructor landing on a pub roof where, despite it being before opening time, the landlord helped him down and then administered some alcohol 'to counter the shock'!

The station had, like all flying units, a formal plan to follow any aircraft accident and this worked well. However, the BBC had got to hear of it and the accident received coverage on the early evening news, omitting, as usual, any names of the aircrew involved. Relatives immediately jammed the telephone lines to Syerston and as the orderly officer I was detailed to sit by the phone and answer each call. This I did until another problem reared its head in the shape of a call from the orderly sergeant to say somewhat shamefacedly that he had just been thrown out of a barrack block containing Air Training Corps (ATC) cadets, and would I please come and sort them out! I went to the guardroom, from where I took the precaution of getting a couple of burly RAF policemen (known to one and all as 'snowdrops' because of the white cap covers they wore) and together with the sergeant we went along to the barrack block. I forget now what the cadets' anger was about, but the largest and most combative cadet was not about to be cowed by the sight of the orderly officer and announced that he and the others would now throw me out as well! A call to the two 'snowdrops', who had been waiting outside, quickly altered the balance of forces and soon two ATC cadets were sitting in the cells in the guardroom, minus their belts and shoelaces (a routine employed for those prisoners who might try to commit suicide and a great way to reduce aggression!).

Their tears evoked no sympathy in us and they were left there for the night to rue their antics. I thought that this must rate as the busiest spell of duty that could befall anyone but fate had one more card to play that evening. At about 2200 that night I got a call from the civil police to say that an airman from Syerston had been involved in a car accident and had, tragically, died in Nottingham Hospital. I was now informed that I was to act as this man's effects officer and had to go to his barrack block and remove his personal effects from there into store pending the appointment the next day of someone else to be the formal effects officer. No other period of station duty would be as hectic as that first one.

The area north of Newark was often travelled in the evenings, as there was a teachers' training college at Retford and the (mainly) female population were in great demand, not only by Syerston students but also by those from the Royal Air Force College at Cranwell, east of Newark. At the weekends there were often dances at Retford and many of us would go up for the evening. I well remember one very foggy night as I was leaving to drive back to Syerston I passed a young man dressed in the standard 'going out' clothes of sports jacket and slacks: he was trying to hitch a lift. It transpired that he was from Cranwell and had got to Retford with a friend. This 'friend' had found more success with a girl from that college and had announced that he was staying the night and the return lift was no longer available. I agreed to take the chap to Newark, but when we got there the fog was, if anything, worse and I took him all the way back to Cranwell. As we drove at a snail's pace in the (very thick) fog along the A17 I became aware of headlights coming up behind very quickly. The next minute a large truck overtook me going at what was a dangerous speed for the conditions, but no sooner was he past than his brake lights came on and he stopped in the middle of the road. The driver jumped out, came back to my window and invited me to get out of the car. I was sure that I had done nothing to antagonise him and didn't want to be attacked, but he was laughing and when I got out I could see why, for when I stood up my head was out of the fog and from his raised position in his cab the truck driver could see perfectly. Once he found out where we were headed he told me to 'stick behind' and I drove fast, completely blind, to Cranwell!

Another memory from evenings at Retford is amusing in retrospect. I had taken a girl out to a pub for the evening and on the way back to Retford

I stopped by a gate into a field, reversing in and anticipating a period of 'tonsil hockey' and other delights. Unfortunately, the track dropped away and turned, leaving a steep drop onto the field and my Mini very nearly went over it. Although it stopped before the edge, the rear wheels were just about in the air. I hoped the front-wheel drive would rescue us but the car had tilted sufficiently for them to lose grip and we must have looked like the coach did at the end of the film *The Italian Job*, half on and half off the surface. The girl was persuaded to (very slowly) get out and sit on the bonnet, which gave enough traction to allow me to drive out, but the muddy and cold girl then only wanted to go back to the college. Funny things, girls!

Formation flying, low- and high-level navigation, night flying and a full instrument rating followed and in July 1966, after two landaways, one to RAF St Mawgan in Cornwall and the other to RAF Acklington in Northumberland (later to become an opencast coal mine), I passed my Final Handling Test, meaning that I was now qualified to wear the RAF pilot's brevet, my wings. As we approached the end of the course we were also 'streamed'. Those who would go on to fly helicopters would go to RAF Tern Hill in Shropshire, future transport pilots would fly the Varsity at RAF Oakington outside Cambridge and those for the fast jet world, myself included, would head to Anglesey and RAF Valley to fly the Folland Gnat. However, the Gnat had suffered some problems in early service and so a proportion of the 'FJ' stream was to train on the venerable Vampire at RAF Swinderby, just the other side of Newark. At the time I was delighted to be told that I was to fly the Gnat, the very sexy, supersonic new trainer, but looking back, those on the Vampire learned a lot from this older aircraft: it would be almost thirty years before I would qualify on this de Havilland aircraft, both the T.11 that my friends flew at Swinderby and the FB.5 single-seater, and its later, more powerful stablemate, the Venom.

Our 'Wings' parade took place at Syerston on 20 July 1966, one day short of the anniversary of my commissioning parade at South Cerney. I was selected to be the No.1 Flight Commander for the parade and Air Vice Marshal R C Ayling, CB CBE, RAF, the Senior Air Staff Officer at RAF Flying Training Command, duly pinned the brevet onto my chest. My parents had come up to watch this event and after the parade there was the chance for us to show our proud relatives around the station. In a hangar was a Jet Provost which had been made safe for mums and dads to sit in. I got my father into the aircraft and found that he didn't want to get out! It later turned out that he had only joined the Army because his father had instructed him to do so. He confided to me that he would have much preferred the Royal Air Force and he would happily have spent the rest of the day shooting down enemy aircraft from that Jet Provost cockpit!

The graduation parade marked another step in the RAF careers of those of us who had been at South Cerney together, as our twelve months as acting pilot officers had passed and we were now 'gazetted' by an insert in *The London Gazette* showing us now to be full pilot officers. There was no rest for the wicked, however, and driving my 'new' Austin Mini Cooper, two years newer than my first Mini and with some slightly bigger horses under the bonnet, and once again full of all my belongings, it was off to RAF Valley and fast jet advanced training.

5

LAND OF MY MOTHER*

As I drove across England and into Wales in the summer of 1966, I joined the A5 road through Llangollen and Corwen before crossing the open moorland and dropping down to Betws-y-Coed. How well I would get to know this road over the next ten years. After Betws the A5 winds past the Swallow Falls and on to Capel Curig (one of the wettest places in the UK according to the Met Office) but then the land opens out and the grandeur of Snowdonia is displayed. As Llyn (Lake) Ogwen is passed, with the imposing bulk of Tryfan high on the left, the road turns sharply through about 60° and drops down the valley toward Bethesda and on to Bangor. Military pilots know this route well, for it provides one of the most exhilarating moments when flying at low level. Over most of the UK the minimum authorised height above the ground when low flying a fast jet is 250ft and a maximum speed of 480kts. For this A5 corner 420kts is plenty and the aircraft should be positioned over the road itself, on the southern side of Llyn Ogwen. Now the pilot is on the 'racing line' and as the end of the lake is approached the aircraft should be overbanked slightly beyond 90° (wings vertical). In this attitude all aircraft will descend, but if judged well, the aircraft now drops over the edge as the road crosses the end of the lake and is rolled upright down in the base of the valley, with the A5 now above and to your right. It is a great moment.

Such excitement was still a fair way off as 27 Course commenced Gnat training in the middle of August 1966. First, there was the inevitable

---

* The Welsh National Anthem is, of course, 'Land of My Fathers'.

joining procedure, filling out no end of forms to inform important areas at RAF Valley of our arrival, ranging from the station medical centre to the station bicycle store. Then came ground school, which was much more complex than that for the Jet Provost. The Gnat was a very complex aircraft – many would say unnecessarily so – and its longitudinal control system in particular was one of the most complicated I ever experienced. All who trained on the Gnat will remember it, mainly for the acronym STUPRECC, used to complete the emergency drill following a hydraulic failure in the air. The aircraft was usually flown in 'power', where the tailplane operated as a slab tail and the entire surface moved in response to control column deflection. The elevators could be unlocked from the slab (called follow-up), but in the event of a hydraulic failure the tailplane would eventually freeze as the hydraulic pressure dissipated. If this freeze occurred at the wrong angle, the elevators would not be powerful enough to maintain control and so it was essential that the hydraulics were exhausted with the tail at the optimum angle. The drill was:

S   Speed below 400kts/0.85M

T   Operate the Feel Trim to the ideal sector on the Feel Trim Position Indicator

U   Unlock elevators checking two clicks, white band, ELEV caption on

P   Select Tailplane Power to OFF (to ensure no hydraulic fluctuations would cause a sudden reversion to 'follow up')

R   Raise the guard on the Standby Trim switches on the console

E   Exhaust first the tailplane accumulator and then the same for the ailerons

C   Check operation of elevators, ailerons and standby trim switches

C   Change over trim switches to standby if required.

I have absolutely no doubt whatsoever that any Gnat pilot is able to recite that mnemonic in his sleep! As well as ground lectures, we were introduced to the cockpit emergency procedures trainer. This was a representation of the Gnat front cockpit, electrically powered to give a simulation of flight conditions, but behind the pilot's seat was a panel with switches to simulate failures for the front seat occupant to deal with. We students spent many hours, often late into the evening, in pairs and taking turns to be given failures in order to practise the correct emergency drills. For the first time we also had a full flight simulator which replicated the aircraft well and in which we could learn instrument flying, air traffic procedures and, most importantly, emergency drills. There was no motion in the sim as it was fixed to the floor but it was an excellent training aid. At Syerston there had been a Link Trainer for the Jet Provost (and a Meteor sim for specific instrument flying), but at Valley each student had to complete the appropriate simulator exercise before learning the equivalent air exercise. There were only eleven hours flown in the sim during a seventy-hour flying course, a lot less than is the case nowadays, and the primary use was training to cope with emergencies whilst 'in cloud'.

On 12 September 1966 I was introduced to the Gnat by my new instructor and, like everyone else, was amazed by the lightness of its controls, by its acceleration and by its amazing roll rate: this was a fighter in Training Command colours! The Gnat was originally built to have a roll rate of no less than 540° per second, one of the fastest ever, though this was halved by an electrical fuse (Fuse 13) when the undercarriage was retracted. The restricted rate was still extremely fast, more than enough for us students, and there was a Valley flying order which stated that if Fuse 13 failed in flight the aircraft was to be returned to base and landed. I had one such failure during the course when flying with a QFI, and we then both gleefully spent about fifteen minutes doing (very fast) aileron rolls as we took a very roundabout route back to Valley! My familiarisation ride on 12 September was followed by eight more dual rides but ten days later I flew the Gnat solo for the first time. On 10 October I first flew supersonic, for the Gnat was supersonic in a dive, and the course continued with general handling, instrument flying and some of the complexities of swept wing flight. This included maximum rate turning, when the aircraft is flown within the buffet caused by the wings reaching the angle of attack for maximum lift. A straight wing aircraft has an abrupt stall at which point the aircraft in essence stops turning, but a swept wing stall is less sharply defined and it is vital that pilots realise how to get the best rate of turn from their aircraft, a manoeuvre every fighter pilot can (and usually does) demonstrate with his hands! We were also introduced to flight at high level, for the Gnat could climb to 50,000ft. By international agreement all aircraft flying above what is called the transition altitude set their altimeters to a common pressure setting of 1013 millibars (mb) or hectopascals (hPa) and then altitude is reported in flight levels (FL), so 36,000ft is reported as FL360. In the Gnat we generally went to FL480, the notional limit for the oxygen system fitted to the aircraft, but every Gnat pilot I knew had continued the climb at some point to reach FL500.

Operating from Valley on the Anglesey coast, the Orpheus engine in the Gnat suffered from the salty atmosphere and periodically it was necessary to clean the engine of the salty deposits. These 'engine washes' took place early in the morning, sometimes as early as 0500, and required the aircraft to be started and taxied out from the flight line, across the short runway to the engine wash pan. There the pilot sat with the engine at idle while a soapy mixture was sprayed into the intakes, after which the engine was run at a slightly increased power setting to rinse and clean

Gnats over North Wales 1967

39

out the residue. It was, therefore, a given that students would be tasked to carry out these washes, often completing three or four before being allowed to return for breakfast. One of the joys of being on the course! At the course mid-point we had to pass a check ride called the progress check and then we began to see the advanced side of the Gnat, and to appreciate just what a joy it was to fly. Formation flying was followed by navigation, both at high and low level, and the excellent range of the aircraft on only 3,000lbs of fuel allowed us to range widely around the UK. In aviation, fuel weight (or more correctly, mass) is more important than volume, which varies with changes in different fuels' specific gravity. The Gnat was extremely frugal with its fuel and if climbed to 40,000ft after take-off could cover 850 miles. Several of the navigation exercises (NAVEX) included time at high level (where a jet aircraft obtains best range from its fuel) and time at 250ft above the ground (practising for a tactical approach to an attack or to delay detection). One of these exercises started by flying at 250ft over the sea from Anglesey to the Lancashire coast, then around the Lake District and southwest Scotland, before climbing up to 40,000ft and returning to Valley from east of the Isle of Man. It was on such an exercise I learned a lesson that I would remember for the remainder of my flying career and which would stand me in good stead when I became an instructor. It is not easy to judge height over the sea with only basic instruments (the Gnat had no radar altimeter) and I was almost certainly flying above 250ft as we passed Point Lynas on the Anglesey coast and headed toward Barrow-in-Furness. However, when my instructor criticised this and took control he descended to what seemed to be a dangerously low level. I was aware of two things: one, the view from the rear seat of the Gnat was not the best and two, my instructor had not done any operational flying but had been 'creamed off' from the Valley course to go to CFS to become a QFI. I knew that I was his first student after returning and that meant that his low-flying experience was 'not a lot'. As we raced across the sea I watched rime begin to form on the windscreen and was, frankly, terrified. When he then announced that we would go off to the south and look at a ship, and dropped the right wing, I pulled back on the control column, even though I knew that to override an instructor was a heinous crime. I had, however, stopped learning anything. That was the end of the sortie and my instructor flew the aircraft back to land at Valley. After a highly critical debrief (by him of me!) I requested an instructor change and had to explain to my flight commander my reasons for doing so. He was a very experienced pilot called 'Mac' McKenzie* who listened and announced that I would henceforth fly with him, so we set off again the next day to fly the same sortie. 'Mac' demonstrated 250ft above the sea, which was much higher than my instructor of yesterday had been flying and all went smoothly from there on. The important point I learned was that if you frighten your student he stops paying attention and doesn't learn. I never forgot that.

We all believe that cats have nine lives and perhaps the same is true for pilots because on 17 October 1966, when I had just twenty-two hours' experience in the aircraft, I used up the first of mine. I had been tasked to complete some general handling over mid-Wales before returning to fly some circuits at Valley. As my trip progressed I could see that there was a long line of cloud over Snowdonia and eventually there was a call for all solo aircraft to check in with their position and fuel remaining: the weather was closing in at Valley. Although I had plenty of fuel to make the diversion airfield of Shawbury, I was instructed to return to Valley, carrying out a Tacan dive procedure to fit in with others recovering. The Gnat had a sophisticated navigation display, exactly mirroring that fitted to the later marks of Lightning and to the Buccaneer, which was one of the things that made the aircraft such a good lead-in trainer. The Tactical Air Navigation (TACAN) display could be selected to read the distance and bearing to the selected beacon or to any offset point from that beacon. Operating from Valley, we used an initial recovery point, called 'Point Alpha', of the Menai Bridge, thirteen miles southeast of the airfield. Selecting 'TAC' on the navigation display then showed the bearing and distance directly to that offset point. Having received my instructions,

---

* 'Mac' McKenzie had learned to fly at the start of the war and after a spell on Hurricanes he progressed to fly the Hawker Typhoon. He joined a squadron which had the French 'ace' Pierre Clostermann on it and found himself often flying as Clostermann's wingman. Mac was not enamoured of Clostermann and told several tales which did not show the man in a good light. They both later converted onto the Tempest and then after the war, Mac went on to fly the jet fighters of the '50s and early '60s. He had many hours of flying experience and I respected him greatly. His life came to a tragic end a couple of years later when he was flying a cadet in a Chipmunk from Chivenor in North Devon and the aircraft spun into the ground. The inquiry judged that the most likely cause was that the cadet froze on the controls and Mac could not override him.

although I had not passed my instrument rating on the Gnat, I turned for Valley and asked air traffic to sequence me into the recovery system. I soon went into cloud but once ATC gave me clearance to fly the procedure I followed the display to a point about fifteen miles east of Point Alpha and then commenced my descent to 5,500ft, the safety altitude for flight in the vicinity of Snowdon. With a couple of miles to run I went to select the 'raw' Tacan to show me the direction to Valley and was horrified to find that it was already displayed. I had descended from a point roughly east of Valley itself and was now approaching the airfield overhead at about 6,000ft. I had to re-position and do it correctly, which would require me to go back east of the Menai Bridge, and I was now very aware of the restricted airspace around Valley. To the north, running east to west, was an airway into which we could only fly under positive control. To the southwest of Valley was a weapons range, another area it was sensible to stay away from, so I decided to stop my descent, put on power and retract the airbrakes, turn right and start the climb back up. I tried to do all of these things at the same time, but with my limited skill I simply overloaded myself and became completely disorientated. I was aware that the aircraft was not doing what I wanted but was not aware of what was actually going on until the aircraft broke out of cloud. I was in an almost vertical dive, approaching 400kts with full power selected and passing very rapidly down through 4,000ft, soon to impact in the middle of Trearddur Bay, northwest of Valley. Snapping the throttle to idle I pulled the stick onto the backstops and the aircraft duly responded, reaching level flight at just over 1,000ft. Although I had watched the sea approach in terrified fascination I had not blacked out and once level I found that the aircraft had registered a maximum 'g' count of 10g (the Gnat cleared maximum limit was 7g). Had the cloudbase been 1,000ft lower I would not have seen the surface in sufficient time to recover: it had been an extremely close shave. I recovered the aircraft to the airfield, landed and reported the overstress to the engineers. By the time I got back to the squadron my QFI was aware of the transgression and I was invited into his office to explain. 'Mac' McKenzie took one look at my white face and sent me back to the crewroom with orders to 'Get yourself a coffee and then come back'. As I walked into the crewroom another student on my course greeted me with a casual 'Good trip, then?' My response was to burst into tears! 'Oh,' he said, 'not so good?' When I had calmed down, and with my coffee, I returned to Mac's office, where he put his vast experience to good use, never admonished me but got me to talk through exactly what I had done and then said, 'Well, I doubt that you'll ever make that mistake again.'

To be in the Royal Air Force in the 1960s meant that almost inevitably one would lose friends and acquaintances in aircraft crashes, although the accident rate had reduced markedly since the previous decade. The very end of 1966 marked the first time that I experienced the death of someone I had known in flying, when on 30 December a Jet Provost from RAF Syerston crashed, killing both instructor and student: the instructor was Sqn Ldr David Noon, who had been my squadron commander during the Syerston course. There would be many more accidents to come.

As we approached the final weeks (we finished the course in January 1967) we students prepared to receive our postings with a great deal of trepidation. Although our posting to Valley from the basic flying schools had shown that we had all been classed as fit for swept wing aircraft, this term encompassed not only the Lightning and Hunter fighters, but also the Canberra and the V-Bombers, the Victor and Vulcan (the Valiant had been grounded in 1965). To a man we all wanted Hunters or Lightnings, but we were all required to fill out our preferences for posting: mine read simply 'Hunter, Hunter, Hunter' until Mac McKenzie had a quiet word. Having told me that he was recommending me for single-seat fighters 'as you would make a bloody awful captain of a crew at the moment', he told me quietly that 'if you want to fly fighters, you had better put down Lightning'. My preferences were duly changed to read 'Lightning, Hunter, Canberra', and in late January 1967 we learned that the allocation to our course of students was six to the Lightning, seven to the Canberra and six to the V-Force. This left one student, James Taylor, known to one and all as 'Wee Jim' because of his diminutive height. He was posted to the Hunter as it could take small pilots, though it didn't help him as after the Chivenor course he was posted to Bahrein and soon afterward flew at very low level past the range safety officer's post at Sharjah, ingested much of the radio aerial outside the hut and ejected. He left the Service soon afterward. Postings from earlier courses at Valley had often selected those toward the bottom of the course to go to the V-Force and there had been representation made to redress what the V-Force saw as an imbalance.

Accordingly, the six from our course to go to bombers were chosen by pin, an iniquitous method which had an adverse effect on several bright careers. One of those on our course, who had come second in the course placing, was Bob Eccles and he found himself sent to the Victor tanker fleet. He served his time there, rising quickly to become an aircraft captain and then volunteered for CFS to become an instructor. At the end of the Little Rissington course he returned to Valley as a Gnat instructor, during which time he was awarded an Air Force Cross for a brilliant forced landing of a Gnat in manual at Mona following an engine seizure. Bob later went to fly the Harrier and eventually completed a very successful tour on the Red Arrows.

I was, however, one of the lucky six destined to go to the Lightning and remember going across the airfield at Valley to the compound housing the Fighter Command Missile Practice Camp (MPC), where 92 Squadron were in residence on detachment from their base at RAF Leconfield in Yorkshire. When we went into the hangar I found myself immediately behind a Lightning looking into the lower (No.1) huge engine jet pipe of this absolutely massive beast. The top of the jet pipe was above my head and above that there was then another (the No.2 engine). Then atop all this was a fin which seemed to go on forever and a great slab-sided fuselage which stretched away into the distance. I was used to the Gnat, where one can look over the edge of the cockpit standing on the ground, whereas the Lightning's cockpit was almost twice as high and the pilot was seated higher than the top of the Gnat fin. It seemed to me to be too much for one person and I felt very nervous of trying to fly it. However, this was still a considerable time away for I still had to pass the Hunter Operational Conversion Unit (OCU) if I was to get my chance.

Delays were building in the RAF training system and I learnt that my course at 229 OCU RAF Chivenor would not start until May, almost four months later. Instead I was selected, along with Rod Newman, to go to RAF Cosford outside Wolverhampton and for two weeks stand each day in front of a Gnat placed inside the John Lewis store in Stoke-on-Trent as part of a recruiting exhibition. Rod and I duly drove up in our best uniforms to find that the Gnat was on the ground floor in the centre of the store and just opposite the cosmetics counter, where the prettiest girls were serving! Perhaps it would not be as bad as we feared. At the end of our first day we arrived back at Cosford and went into the officers' mess bar for a drink before changing for dinner. A squadron leader wearing the pilots' brevet came over and introduced himself as John Milner before asking how come two young pilots were at Cosford, a training school for aircraft apprentices. When we told him about the exhibition his response was to ask us if we would like to fly while we were there as he ran a small flying squadron of six Chipmunk trainers and two examples of the Vickers Varsity, a twin-piston multi-engined trainer used to train navigators and also pilots destined for the 'heavy' side of RAF flying. From that day on, only one of us went to Stoke-on-Trent each day while the other went flying! After a checkout with 'the Boss', our usual programme involved flying apprentices on air experience flights for about fifteen minutes each, fitting in three for every trip and doing a 'running turn-round', which meant taxiing in to the flight line, sliding back the canopy and waiting while the ground crew extricated one apprentice and replaced him with another. Once complete, the canopy would slide forward and with a tap on the shoulder we would be off again to introduce another young lad to the joys of flight. After the two weeks, Rod Newman went off to Bassingbourn to learn to fly the Canberra but I stayed on, to be joined in April by another four ex-Valley pilots. Mel Cornwell and I had been on the same course since Syerston, but the other three, Dick Northcote, Russ Pengelly and Andy Griffin, had finished the course behind ours and were also in the backlog 'hold'. Soon afterwards I learned that my Chivenor course was further postponed to June and I got the chance to try flying the Varsity, a very large aircraft it seemed at the time. The Varsity aircrew were a hoary old bunch of NCOs, two master pilots, two master navigators and two flight sergeant signallers, and very experienced they were too! I learned how to navigate using GEE, the navigation aid developed during the war, and am proud to say that one night, acting as the navigator, I navigated one of the Varsities from Cosford down to Gatwick where the pilots flew an ILS approach (we could fly practice diversions to Heathrow and Gatwick in those quieter days) and then navigated us back safely to Cosford. We also used the Varsity for kipper runs, when we would take one aircraft up to Machrahanish on the Mull of Kintyre and there load up with fish and shellfish to bring back to Cosford. Unfortunately, the sedate nature of the Varsity meant that our cargo had plenty of time to permeate the rear fuselage and the aircraft would stink of fish for days afterwards.

The pilot backlog in those days was just beginning to build up but in my case the delay between Valley and Chivenor was only three months, so in mid-May of 1967 my very pleasant interlude drew to a close and I set off southwest for Devon. I was going back into the training system, though no longer in Flying Training Command, as I was now in the famous Royal Air Force Fighter Command and for the first time in my life my next aircraft would be a single-seat fighter.

6

SUMMER IN DEVON

THE AIRFIELD SITUATED ON the north shore of the River Taw was originally given the name of the closest town, Barnstaple, but when the RAF decided to enlarge the site and build runways the name RAF Chivenor was chosen, derived from the thirteenth-century Saxon settlement of Chyvenor. Unlike the excellently designed and built infrastructure of the pre-WWII RAF expansion scheme of the 1930s, Chivenor was a hutted station and these huts, used by the personnel operating and supporting the long-range Whitleys and Wellingtons that searched for and attacked the U-Boats from 1941 to 1945, remained in use for many years, almost the only changes being the aircraft types. This failure to build modern accommodation resulted from the air ministry's reluctance to accept the airfield's permanence, although concrete hardstandings were built in 1952 to permit the operation of jets and a new control tower came a year later. 229 OCU arrived at Chivenor from RAF Leuchars in March 1951, equipped with de Havilland Vampire FB.5s and Meteor T.7s, and provided tactical training for pilots in the day-fighter role. Although the Vampires had given way to Hunters by the time Plt Off Roome rolled in through the gates, little else had changed. Behind the (hutted) officers' mess were the accommodation huts: those immediately behind the mess were the 'C' Lines and had ablutions within the same hut, and these housed officers on the permanent staff of the OCU. We students were most definitely 'below the salt' in the 'D' Lines, as our huts were separate from the ablution blocks. Each room had a coke stove for heating, a lino floor with one small mat, a bed, chest of drawers, a wardrobe and a chair. Thankfully our course was over the summer so I never had to light my coke stove, which was not very large and would go out during the night. The stories about them were legion; one in particular concerned an enterprising student who decided one winter's night that he would keep his stove going by loading up the coke through the small hatch high in the chimney (used for sweeping the chimney). As the chimney rose up through the room all the way to the roof he reckoned that the fire would stay warm all night, but instead the chimney blocked and the individual was lucky to be rescued from his room unconscious with carbon monoxide poisoning. Despite the privations of these huts, morale at Chivenor was high because we were all doing just what we had always wanted to do, fly fighters, and the Hawker Hunter was a great fighter to fly, with ten squadrons operational around the world from West Raynham in Norfolk, through the Middle East in Aden and Bahrein, to Singapore and Hong Kong.

28 pre-Lightning Course, running in parallel with 127 Day Fighter Ground Attack Course, started on 63 Squadron on 1 June with one week's ground school, and six days later I had my first Hunter ride in a two-seat T.7 before a further two dual trips, both of which were with Flt Lt 'Chunky' I'Anson. Chunky was a well-loved elder statesman at Chivenor. He had a boxer dog called Fred and each morning as we all walked over from the squadrons for the morning briefings he would arrive in his car, driving to park outside Flying Wing HQ beneath air traffic control. Fred always sat in the rear nearside passenger seat and as Chunky stopped to reverse into a parking slot, Fred's head would swivel to watch his progress, looking for all the world like a driving instructor. Another amazing thing with Fred was that he would always know when Chunky returned from a sortie. In the lovely summer weather, Chunky would walk out of the squadron to go to the line hut for his aircraft and Fred would follow only as far as the edge of the grass, where he would stop. Chunky would say, 'Stay, Fred,' and that is exactly what Fred would do, lying comfortably in the sun and ignoring the aircraft going past. Around an hour later Fred would jump up, rush to the edge of the grass and bark furiously at a Hunter taxiing back in after landing: it would always be Chunky. This very popular pilot and instructor was unfortunately killed in a small business jet in 1970 when, according to the CAA report, he fed in the incorrect rudder after a simulated engine failure just after take-off. I shall return to Chunky in a short while.

After three dual trips and a further one solo in the T.7, we then flew another seven hours in the single-seat F.6. There is something very special for a pilot when he first climbs into an aircraft that can only take one person; it's not the same as flying a two-seat aircraft solo and there will be many reading these words who can readily identify with this emotional moment. I shall always remember climbing up the ladder on the side of the Hunter and looking down along the fuselage to the fin before putting the left hand on the top of the windshield and the right on the cockpit canopy before stepping into the cockpit. The Hunter had a peculiarly unique smell and all Hunter pilots can remember it: I don't know exactly what it was, perhaps the mix of leather from the seat, old cordite from the guns, a particular oil; whatever it was I smelt it in all the other marks of the Hunter I flew – the F.6, T.7, T.7A, T.8, FGA.9, FR.10, GA.11, F.58, T.66 and T.75.

By the end of June I had completed eighteen hours in the Hunter and also completed the convex, IF (instrument flying) and FM (formation) phases. Formation was very different to that taught at Valley; here it was 'stick, search and report' as the No.2 of a fighting pair. We were practising to be wingmen and spent the majority of the time looking back behind the formation to confirm there was no threat approaching. Little quarter was given and it was not unknown for a staff pilot to return to Chivenor without his wingman, subsequently to administer a loud bollocking to the young man for 'losing' his leader. It was a hard school and although we 'enjoyed' the course, it was hardly the best way to teach inexperienced pilots to become fighter pilots. To a degree we would graduate despite the teaching but I loved it nevertheless. Then came the cine phase, where we practised tracking a target aircraft through the gunsight while its cine camera filmed our clumsy attempts at gaining a good firing solution. After landing, the film went off to be developed before a painful debrief in the cine room where a pilot attack instructor tore us apart for our pathetic flying. Then we moved on to the live air-to-air phase, firing the Hunter's 30mm Aden cannon at a flag towed behind a Meteor of 79 Squadron (a very brave bunch of pilots including one called Flight Sergeant Pete Boulter who, on one well-known occasion, came into our squadron in search of a foreign student who had actually put a round THROUGH the wing of Pete's Meteor, and delivered a firm punch to the chin!).

At the beginning of August, and newly promoted to flying officer, I started the night flying phase, which was one of the few areas of flight which seemed to terrify the big, bold, day fighter Hunter pilots. Indeed, when I later reached Singapore it reminded me of Chivenor as I witnessed the Hunter squadron achieving their statistical requirement to night fly. They would reach the Tengah overhead at 40,000ft at about 1855 (it gets dark in about five minutes in the tropics) and then carry out a maximum rate descent before landing at 1900 and claiming five minutes of night flying. I did my one dual night trip followed by two solo flights in the first two days of August 1967, and on 3 August set off for my fourth night trip on the Hunter, a twenty-five-minute climb to height west of Chivenor, returning for a QGH (a controlled descent through cloud procedure) and a few circuits. It did not go according to plan as can be seen from this excerpt from the RAF Fighter Command Flight Safety magazine for October 1967.

MAJOR

Flying Officer Roome was briefed for a night flying conversion exercise at 229 OCU RAF Chivenor. He took off in Hunter F.6 XF443 at 2026Z and the flight proceeded normally until he was outbound from Chivenor on a controlled descent. At about 14,000ft heading 110° in the descent the engine lost all oil pressure, the RPM fell quickly and the engine seized. As the RPM were falling Flying Officer Roome initially thought the engine had flamed out and tried a hot relight as he turned hard port towards Chivenor, informing them that he was going to 243.0Mc/s. This

he did on the standby radio set. He rolled out on a heading of 300° and when the standby radio warmed up he transmitted a MAYDAY call. This was acknowledged by Uxbridge ATCC who gave him a position and heading to steer for Chivenor. At about this time the controls reverted to manual so he selected power controls off, switched off all non-essential electrics and trimmed for manual flight. He cannot specifically remember closing the HP and LP cocks. He was handed over to Chivenor on 243.0Mc/s and homed to the overhead which he reached at a height of 6,000ft. Here he started a left-hand spiral descent and immediately went into cloud. Not his day was it? He broke cloud at 3,700ft about two miles east of Chivenor, north of the centre line of Runway 28: he turned hard port toward the airfield, selected undercarriage and flap down and tried to complete the S-turn back to starboard to line up with Runway 28. He decided that he would not achieve this so he levelled the aircraft wings and ejected successfully. Flying Officer Roome was uninjured and the aircraft crashed into a railway cutting one and a half miles southeast of Chivenor.

There is little doubt that the engine seizure was caused by failure of the third and fourth stage stator blades. The engine in this aircraft did not have the strengthened stator blades (mods 3330 and 3519) fitted because these were being done on an engine hours basis at Chivenor and this was the next engine that would have been done on that programme. Though these mods are classed B2 their prime intention was to increase engine life; the lack of emphasis on flight safety is reflected in the fact that engine life is the same for modified or unmodified engines, and furthermore that the modification instructions to units require the mod to be embodied on 'new engines before installation, and on engines removed from aircraft subject to 200 hours of life remaining'.

Wreckage site looking west

1. Main wreckage

2. Aircraft canopy on water's edge

3. Ejection seat

Parachute, showing the dinghy pack lowered and the line from it to the life jacket hanging beneath

4. Initial impact point on the top of the cutting where the man is standing.

XF 443 – APPROXIMATE FLIGHT PATH

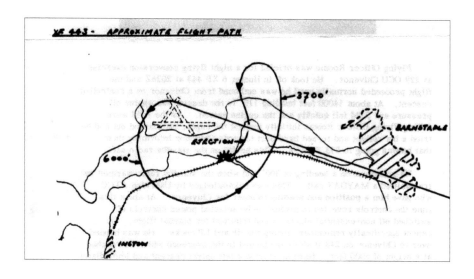

The makers consider that damage to the unmodified engines was only likely to occur on the run down when the loose shroud dropped down between the blades. In fact, only one previous engine failure could be attributed to this defect occurring in the air; another fifty occurred during engine run down on the ground. So the Flight Safety considerations were not paramount and units were not instructed to modify oldest engines first and no restriction was placed on hours to run. All Avon 207 series engines now have mods 3330 and 3519 embodied. These mods also apply to Avon 200 series engines which remain in use in Lightning Mks 1, 2 and 4 and modification action is being hastened.

Flying Officer Roome was faced with a major emergency at night on a conversion exercise and in the circumstances he acted very sensibly. He would be the first to agree that there are some general lessons to be learnt from his experience. The position of the crash debris, ejection seat and parachute after the aircraft crashed show that he ejected very late, probably leaving the aircraft between 200 and 500ft above ground level. Air Staff Instructions give 3,000ft as a 'direct the aircraft away from built-up areas and bale out' height. This would only have given Roome 700ft in which to do a lot of manoeuvring, thinking and talking, as he broke cloud at 3,700ft. The point holds good however, and he did eject at a dangerously low altitude when considering the probable attitude of the aircraft.

When the pilot went over to 243.0Mc/s so close to base he threw away the chance of a one to one approach under radar control and was left with the less satisfactory spiral type descent. He did what he had been trained to do and what Air Staff Instructions advocate. A more experienced pilot might have stayed on the approach frequency, and in the short time and distance available been able to make a one to one approach. ASI D6 paragraph 5, which says that frequencies 121.5 or 243.0 are to be used for all actual flame out recoveries, is being amended to be less mandatory according to circumstances. As a matter of interest, as Roome's engine seized he was, in fact, being handed over to radar but he suddenly became seriously distracted and went to 243.0Mc/s instead of Chivenor Radar for reasons already mentioned.

When his engine seized he thought at first that he was faced with a flame out and so tried a hot relight, an understandable mistake the way he saw things. So perhaps we had all better go through the differences between flame out and seizure symptoms for our own particular engines and make sure we have them clearly buttoned up.

And elsewhere in the same magazine was my own account entitled:

NO ROOME FOR MANOEUVRE

There had, of course, been no indication that IT was going to happen to me that evening. Just a normal Hunter 6 trip, only 25 minutes duration with empty drop tanks. All I was going to do was a QGH/ GCA and a couple of circuits. Aircraft fleet number 51, at the far end of the line as usual, furthest to walk. Everything looks normal, three wheels, two wings, one fuselage, nothing down the engine intake, so might as well get going. All checks completed and I'm cleared to go. I give ATC another demonstration of amateur taxiing as I go past down to runway 28 and from there into the sunset. Very romantic.

Gear up, lights out, flap up, pressurisation and DME on and we're away. Level at FL200 for a quick look at the countryside and the sunset before calling for the QGH/GCA. Homing in, not much cloud, just some scattered cumulus at about 4,000-6,000ft and getting darker. Into the overhead, one quick orbit for separation and down the slope we go. 300kt, 2 notches of flap, airbrake, all's fine bar the power which has crept up to 6,750. Let's have it right, then, back to 6,500. Did I see that oil pressure gauge flicker just as I brought the power back? Now that the RPM is right, let's have another look. My eyes are deceiving me, the oil pressure is not meant to fall to zero until I shut down, and why is the RPM winding down so quickly, when I have just set it? This is definitely not right, 'tis the nasty simulator instructor giving me a flame out (if I ignore the oil pressure gauge, it'll go away, hidden as it is behind the stick). Still not right, the relight switch should always work and the engine should wind up again.

Select brain to PANIC mode. Pull back, speed to height, glide at 210kt, turn back towards Chivenor, tell them I'm going to 243. Standby radio taking an age to warm up, meanwhile shed all those non-essential electrics. Put out the MAYDAY, telling them I have an engine seizure, 14,000ft, 7-8nm on the DME, want to go to Chivenor for a spiral. My voice about 3 octaves higher and Uxbridge sound as surprised as I do. Ask them to hand me over to Chivenor and feel much better immediately with a familiar voice at the other end. Oh no, not manual controls as well, both hands on the pole now, trim it in manual and the cockpit looks like a Christmas tree with almost every light on.

Into the overhead at 6,000ft and start the turn to port towards low key abeam the runway caravan. Straight into cloud, that's all I need, on instruments as well, so just hold a steady turn for what seems like half an hour and is probably less than 15 seconds. Clear of cloud now and in what a position. 1-2nm from the threshold, gone through the runway centreline and heading almost 80° off the runway heading. 3,700ft. What to do? Only thing is an S-turn to try to line up. But must lose height. Emergency air brings the gear down and I am finding new reserves of strength to fly the brute in *manual, must be all the adrenaline. Airfield still looks very close so blow the flap down, 180kt now, start hauling it back round onto the runway. Come round, come round you bitch but no, I'll crash on the estuary if I go on with it must eject no time to tell them got to get out roll level quickly pull back with both hands trim up speed now back through 140kt let go of the pole and reach for the face blind the houses look very close both hands on the blind and PULL, did I see 400ft on the altimeter, you fool you've left it too late there isn't sufficient time there goes the canopy feel the wind and wait for the second's delay wait for the second's delay wait for the second's... F*** what a kick, out, tumbling and another sharp jolt. Thank heavens, the parachute has opened, grab the lift webs and have a look down. There's the aircraft beneath me, almost level and... why has it disappeared in a cloud of dust or smoke? The railway line is beneath my feet, don't want to land on that so pull on the front lift webs and move toward the grass. No, they're trees, feet together and in we go...*

This is quiet, lying horizontal in the trees, if only I didn't feel slightly sick it could be pleasant. Must get down. Out with my knife and cut through the rigging lines under my knees and hang vertically. Odd, that's quick. I've just landed in the trees on the edge of the railway cutting and already there's a man there with an incredulous look on his face. Bang the QRB and lower myself to the ground. Yes, thanks, I'm perfectly fit... where is the aircraft? 100 yards away on the line? No, don't go near it, it may burn and there's no one else in it. Ah, there is the sound of the rescue chopper, so back up to my dinghy pack, which has come out of the PSP but not inflated. Rummage around and find two day/night flares.

Down onto the line again and fire one flare, and the chopper comes over me but he can't pick me up here in the cutting, so I walk down the line away from the wreckage and onto a steel bridge over a creek. Fire off the second flare and the chopper hovers over me directing me onto the beach 20 yards away by use of its spotlight. A last word to the man, remind him not to go near the wreckage and to dissuade anyone else from doing so until the crash crews arrive. Then down onto the beach, get winched up and back over the estuary to the airfield, still not believing that IT had really happened.

Needless to say, like many an ejection story this has an amusing side. When I ejected I was very close to the ejection seat limits and am very lucky to be around to write this. I believe that I had about four seconds in the parachute and when I crashed into the trees on the edge of the railway cutting I was knocked out after hitting my head on a tree trunk. My bone dome did its task but was smashed like an eggshell when I saw it the following day. The shell had popped back out and it looked fine, but push with a finger on the crown and it simply gave way. When I came to I was lying as if in a hammock with the parachute lift webs supporting my knees, so I used my dinghy knife and cut through them. Once hanging vertically on the edge of the cutting I was aware of a man running along the path beside the railway line pulling up his trousers (for some reason this did not trigger a question in my mind). When I had let go of the control column to pull the firing handle, I saw the altimeter unwinding rapidly through 350ft and firmly believed that my life was about to end abruptly, so as I released myself from the parachute and slid down the line connecting my harness to my dinghy I fell to my knees on the path for a moment. Having asked if I was OK, the man said that he would check the aircraft, which was about eighty yards further up the line and right across it, but I told him not to bother as I had been the only occupant and there was still 2,000lbs of fuel in it. At about that time I became aware of the rescue Whirlwind helicopter coming across from Chivenor on the other side of the River Taw. I fired a flare and was picked up by the chopper and brought back across the river to base.

It turned out that the man I met was an Army cook from the camp at Fremington, on the other side of the railway line, and after I had been lifted back in the helicopter he had run up to the guardroom there to ring British Railways and tell them of the obstruction on the line. He was later summoned to appear before the RAF Board of Inquiry to give his view of the accident. I have read the transcript of this Board and the questioning goes like this:

Board President: 'Where were you at the time of the accident?'

Cook: 'I was under the tree with the parachute hanging in it.'

President: 'What were you doing under the tree at 9.45 at night?'

Cook: 'I was with my girlfriend and we were enjoying ourselves.'

President: 'In what position?'

Cook: 'I told you, we were enjoying ourselves and when the pilot hit the tree above us, I went down onto the path, saw the pilot and then went up to the guardroom to advise British Railways.'

President: 'Well, can you tell us the young lady's name, because she probably had a much better view of the proceedings than you did?'

Cook: 'I don't know, I only picked her up in a pub in Barnstaple that night and when I got back to her she'd f***ed off!'

To complete the tale, three years later I was sitting in the crewroom on 74 Squadron in RAF Tengah, Singapore, when the squawkbox went asking if a pilot could show some Army guys around a Lightning. I agreed to do it and found myself telling the same cook about the Lightning cockpit and how an ejection seat worked. 'I know about them,' he said, 'cos I were at Fremington Camp in '67 when a Hunter pilot ejaculated.' I pointed out that no ejection was that exciting and that I knew it was '9.45 on the evening of 3 August and you were screwing your bird under the tree' which startled him! Long odds indeed.

Luckily for me, the ejection did no lasting damage to my back and I was cleared to resume flying on the following Tuesday, five days after the accident. After another three air-to-air gunnery trips the time came to complete the night flying phase, and I flew a dual trip with none other than Chunky I'Anson who, without warning, simulated a seized engine at exactly the same point in the descent as had happened a week before: this time I made a successful forced landing and laid to rest the ghosts of failure which had plagued me in my dreams for a week. As Chunky said afterward, if a single-engined aircraft suffers a catastrophic engine failure it must be expected that the aircraft will be lost, but with the hope that the pilot will be saved; if the aircraft is also saved it is a big bonus.

One month after that tumultuous night I flew the final trip of the course and walked out to the flight line with a fellow course member, Trevor Sharp. He and I had been on the same course since Syerston and he was also off to do the final trip, to include air-to-ground firing on Pembrey Range in South Wales, while I flew a low-level navigation exercise. When I returned to Chivenor I learned with shock that Trevor had crashed at Pembrey and been killed. This was the second flying death I had experienced and now saw how the RAF flying fraternity dealt with such accidents: we went to the bar and all got roaring drunk in a wake, led by the OCU staff pilots of 63, 79 and 234 Squadrons, the Flying Wing supervisory staff, Wing Commander Flying and even the Station Commander, Gp Capt Calder-Jones. The next morning everything was back to normal, although the first take-off was re-scheduled for noon! Such a wake following an accident might seem callous but was actually the reverse; it allowed emotions to run high and to be worked off so that such emotions were not carried into the air the next day when it might be necessary to carry out the same manoeuvre that yesterday's casualty had failed to complete. I would see many more wakes in the remainder of my Service career, but then, having finished the course at Chivenor I drove up to Norfolk for the final phase of my flying training, to learn to fly the most advanced fighter in the Royal Air Force, the Lightning.

7

AGGRESSIVE DEFENCE

WORK ON RAF COLTISHALL was started in February 1939 and the airfield, then known as Scottow Aerodrome, was initially built as a bomber station on land near Scottow Hall. If the established tradition had been followed the station would have been named after the nearest railway station which would have made it RAF Buxton, but to avoid possible confusion with the town of Buxton in Derbyshire it was named after the local village of Coltishall instead and adopted the motto 'Aggressive in Defence', appropriate for a unit soon to be engaged in one of the greatest of all defensive battles. By the time the airfield was completed and entered service in May 1940 England was facing defeat in France, and the defence of the country – the Battle of Britain – was soon to start; Coltishall became a fighter base within No.12 Group of Fighter Command. The very next month saw the arrival from France of a demoralised squadron of (mainly) Canadians. 'Laddie' Lucas, who wrote what many believe to be the definitive biography of Douglas Bader, paints the picture very well:

'... (242 Squadron) had been forced to withdraw, first from Châteaudun, where it had been operating with No 1 Squadron, then from Le Mans and finally from Nantes, hard by Saint-Nazaire, on the Atlantic coast. When it reached its most westernmost point, it was without effective direction, without cohesion and without its ground crews. The leadership was deficient. The pilots were servicing their own aircraft. The adjutant had become separated from the aircrew. Peter Macdonald – 'Boozy Mac' to the *pilots – was busy rounding up the ground personnel somewhere between Le Mans and the coast, hotly pursued by the advancing German forces. In such a situation, there were bound to be tales of individual courage and resource but, if the rough truth be told, little worse could have befallen the Squadron at that juncture save to fall into enemy hands and become a total loss. In the event it was something of a miracle that, after flying a few last-minute patrols over heavily laden Allied shipping making a final dash for the open sea, it was able to gather its pilots and Hurricanes together for the flight back to England.*

The squadron commander did not lead the unit on the last stage of its withdrawal from France to Tangmere on the Sussex coast. He was in no position to do so. As the rest of the pilots took to the air, he was still lying prostrate beside the flight hut. A sparkle of humour was to be found on the note left pinned to his battledress: 'When you surface, you'll find a serviceable Hurricane expecting to be flown home. Try vector 030° for the English coast, then turn right for Tangmere.' The CO was a French Canadian who had earlier been lifted out of the remoteness of Training Command in Canada and pitchforked into the hot seat at the head of 242. The appointment owed something to politics and was close to being a fatal mistake, but it cannot be laid at the door of the victim. Up to the time of taking over, he had had no operational experience whatever. He was thus quite unsuitable for the task. The responsibility lay squarely with Ottawa. It was a straightforward error of judgement, born of ignorance. In the circumstances, the result could hardly have avoided being devastating. The rest of the unit was made up mainly of Canadians with short-service commissions in the Royal Air Force, with a leavening of English and others to fill the gaps. Its potential was unquestionable; but experienced and determined leadership would have been needed to realize it. Neither the CO nor the original flight commanders had been capable of providing it.

Leigh-Mallory (Air Vice Marshal Trafford Leigh-Mallory, the Air Officer Commanding No 12 Group) had visited the squadron soon after its arrival at Coltishall from Tangmere. Having flown himself down from his HQ at Watnall near Nottingham, he went straight to the dispersal hut to see the pilots and groundcrew. As he sat on a table in the Crewroom, his legs dangling back and forth beneath it, he listened intently – and with understanding – to the squadron's story. The audience was impressive in its simplicity. It was the first contact the pilots had had in weeks with real live authority. In a few crisp plain, but sincere sentences, the Group commander brought an unadorned message of encouragement and purpose. There had been precious little of that sort of leadership of late.

What he found had shocked him. There was no commanding officer. The so-called flight commanders had not been confirmed in their appointments and were tinged with the traumas of the past month. Stanley Turner, a Canadian in the Royal Air Force, who was to serve with lasting distinction during the next two years in the great battles for command of the daylight air over Britain, France and Malta, appeared on the face of it to be the senior officer present. But Stan Turner could be obstinate and rebellious if provoked. After being tested to the limit – and beyond – in France, he was close to being exasperated by 242's lot. Blunt and direct, he employed few words to express his rudimentary views.

It hadn't taken Leigh-Mallory half an hour to size things up. The paramount need was clear. A tough, experienced and spirited leader, who could fly aeroplanes and would command personal respect, must be found quickly to take over. He would require both the knowledge and perception to understand immediately what was needed and what changes should be made. He would then have to be given full authority to grip the Squadron tight, drive the action through and mould the unit into a confident, coherent fighting machine. It would probably take a good man a fortnight to sort things out. By the time Leigh-Mallory had returned to his office at Watnall, his mind was made up. He was resolved that Bader was the man for 242.

---

* *Flying Colours*, by P B 'Laddie' Lucas, published by Hutchinson and Co, 1981

So it was that Douglas Bader came to RAF Coltishall to assume command of 242 Squadron.

Twenty-seven years later in early September 1967 I arrived there to join 38 Lightning Course. Before starting the course, however, all prospective Lightning pilots had to undergo a week at RAF North Luffenham in Rutland at the Aviation Medical Training Centre (AMTC). The centre was commanded by a senior RAF Medical Officer who, together with his medical and technical team were responsible for fitting and instructing aircrew in the use of protective flying clothing and equipment, including partial pressure suits to keep the pilot conscious in the event of loss of cabin pressure at high altitude. Instruction in medical aspects of high performance aviation included experience of hypoxia and exposure to sudden explosive decompression of an aircraft cabin. This was carried out in a complex of RAF decompression chambers installed on the site for aircrew training and research purposes. We had all undergone hypoxia training at South Cerney to familiarise ourselves with our own responses to a lack of oxygen at altitude but this was very different. Several of us would enter one of the decompression chambers and the chamber pressure would be decreased until we were at a pressure equating to an altitude of 27,000ft. At the end of the chamber was a hatch to a smaller chamber with only one cockpit seat in the centre; it had several observation windows around the end which gave the all too realistic feel of an execution chamber! One at a time we would enter this end chamber and strap into the seat, connect our personal equipment connector to the RT, oxygen supply, anti-g suit and pressure jerkin ports, and the hatch door would close. Faces appeared outside at all the windows and after confirming that we were 'ready', a rapid decompression would be initiated: with a loud bang the cabin altitude jumped to 56,000ft in a couple of seconds. The small cabin immediately filled with condensation and the pressure jerkin and anti-g suit inflated hard to compress the blood vessels; meanwhile oxygen was now fed to the mask at an overpressure of seventy millimetres of mercury. This reversed the normal breathing process: relax and the lungs filled immediately, followed by hard straining to expel the breath. The slightest relaxation then caused the lungs to be refilled immediately and this went on for thirty seconds. Speaking was so difficult that we were told to raise a thumb if we were coping; when I looked at my hand as I did so I saw that my veins were standing out like balloons! After thirty seconds the altitude was gradually lowered until we were back at 27,000ft and it was time to swap with one of the other students from the main chamber. Although this sounds very dramatic, it was good training and when I actually suffered a canopy seal failure in a Lightning at 44,000ft a couple of years later I was ready for it.

One of the by-products of the AMTC Course was that we were each issued with a No.2 uniform designed to be worn under a flying suit. The breast pockets were no longer patch pockets but were zipped, the zip matching those on the flying suit, and the epaulettes were stitched down. This 'zip suit No.2' conferred kudos upon those who wore it, a sort of 'we survived North Luffenham' cachet, and was only issued to the V-Force, some photo reconnaissance Canberra crews and Lightning pilots. The Lightning Course, like all such courses, commenced with ground school lectures on the aircraft and its systems, and in the Lightning flight simulator, initially to learn how to cope with any emergencies in flight. However, to whet the appetite, each of us was given a dual ride in one of the two-seat T.4 aircraft, purely to see what we were going to be flying, and I was flown by Sqn Ldr Terry Maddern, OC 1 Squadron of 226 OCU and who had been the President of the Board of Inquiry into my Hunter accident at Chivenor. There was no instruction on this trip, it was a chance for the instructor to show off the performance of this magnificent aircraft, so a reheat take-off followed by a reheat climb to 35,000ft took just two minutes from releasing the brakes, faster than the Hunter could climb to 10,000ft! Then he took the Lightning supersonic whilst in a climb, so different to the Hunter which required the pilot to select what was termed 'the manufacturer's shallow dive' of about 40° nose down. It was then back to the circuit and a couple of approaches at what seemed ludicrously fast speeds, 175kts reducing to 165 at the runway threshold and touching down at 155kts. However, because the Lightning's tyres were of extremely narrow cross-section to fit within the wings and were pressurised to around 300psi, the only time the runway was touched was on the final landing. The rest of the time all pilots flew to a 'low overshoot' and with experience could put the wheels within six inches of the runway surface every time. Finally, my new Boss put the aircraft down and streamed the braking parachute, an essential aid to stopping the Lightning safely. That evening in the bar we were all full of stories comparing our trips of the day – our appetites had been well and truly whetted!

The ground school and simulator passed reasonably quickly and on 9 October I started to learn how to fly the aircraft. There was a lot to learn. As one of our number said one evening as we compared notes in the bar, 'I'm only ahead of this aircraft until I do this,' and indicating a circling motion with his index finger he gave the sign for starting the No.1 engine, 'after that it all goes downhill!' We all knew how he felt. My problem was not how to fly the aircraft but how to land it. The technique employed by my instructor, Alan Morgan, was that at about one mile out from the threshold at 175kts on about a 2.5° glidepath, he reduced power and lowered the nose slightly, before adding power and raising the nose again to be at 165kts on a 1.5° glide as he approached the runway threshold. I seemed never to get the two adjustments correct and became more and more despondent as time went on. Although I went solo in the T.4 on 12 October and gained my 'Ten Ton Club' membership during the sortie by exceeding 1.65M or 1,000mph, and flew the single-seat F.1A the following day, I kept having problems until, after a further ride with Terry Maddern I was switched to a new instructor, 'Barney' Bullocke. He watched my first attempt at an approach before saying 'no, no' and taking control. As we rolled out on finals the next time he just trickled a bit of power off and the aircraft sank gently, losing the 10kts as it went – I never had another problem on the approach to land.

The end of October also marked the end of the convex phase and we transferred across to the other half of the hangar and joined 2 Squadron, 226 OCU, here to carry out the radar phase and learn to fight the aircraft, not simply fly it. Firstly, there was the radar ground school to complete, with its attendant exam, and we didn't fly again until the middle of November, when Flt Lt 'Davy' Jones took on the task of imparting the secrets of the 'green television screen', the Airborne Interception 23 radar, or AI23 for short. This was the time of buzzwords such as 'blip track analysis', and phrases like 'smash it to the edge and track it down the side (before losing it off the bottom)', 'short range it' and 'turning circle'. The radar was controlled by an ingenious hand controller, mounted just aft of the throttles and naturally found by the pilot's left hand; this controlled all the functions of the radar with over a dozen actions. Ask an ex-Lightning pilot how it worked and watch as his left hand starts to make all the movements – gain, range scale, acquisition and lock modes, radar head elevation and so on!

Inevitably we spent some time flying the aircraft by night, as this would be a large proportion of our task as all-weather fighter pilots. Here we heard of the old lady who lived near Coltishall and who complained without fail every time there was any night flying. One of the staff pilots came into the mess bar after flying had finished for the night and told how he had taken another call from her earlier that evening. 'Young man,' she had said, 'there is a Lightning circling over my house at fifty feet!' He assured her that the aircraft was, in fact, flying circuits and not circling, and was at 1,000ft and not at fifty feet. She was not to be pacified. 'I know that he's at fifty feet,' she snapped, 'because he's so low I can see the nails in it!'

As part of our introduction to the UK Air Defence System we were scheduled to visit the nearest Sector Operations Centre (SOC) at Neatishead, just five miles from Coltishall, but on 16 February 1966 a fire had broken out in the bunker. Station fire teams were unsuccessful in putting the fire out and so civilian fire crews were called but three civilian firefighters lost their lives. Later that year a disaffected airman was sentenced to seven years for starting the fire and causing the deaths. As Neatishead was still out of service we were dispatched to RAF Bawdsey near Felixstowe, the station where Robert Watson-Watt developed his ideas for using radar as an air defence tool. Even into the 1970s one of the original 'Chain Home Extra Low' towers remained on the Bawdsey site. We were taken down into the 'R3' or 'The Hole', as the underground bunker was called. After the instructional tour we repaired to the mess for lunch and this was our first sight of one of the most unusual officers' messes, Bawdsey Manor, a large house which looked as if it was hundreds of years old but in fact dated from 1886. We all headed for the bar, to be met by one of the most masculine women I have ever met. She was perched on a bar stool, legs crossed in the masculine way and was drinking from a pint pewter tankard. When one of our number went to the darts board and picked up some darts she immediately challenged him to a match, reached over the bar to pick up her own darts and promptly thrashed him!

We were to receive our postings early in December. Although our course was twelve strong, two were master pilots who were due to become simulator instructors. Also on the course was Sqn Ldr 'Bush' Barrey who went to command the RAF Wattisham Simulator Flight, and a Hunter pilot called Pete Highton who was getting some fast jet time prior to going to the USA to convert to the Phantom before helping to form 228 OCU at Coningsby on that aircraft. Finally, there was a squadron leader who was planned to become a flight commander on 23 Squadron but who failed the course and went instead to 58 Squadron on the Canberra. That left seven of us first tourists, and when the slots were announced there were three postings to RAF Germany and four to RAF Leuchars. Unfortunately, six of the seven wanted to go to Germany and so that afternoon we drew straws, after which Merv Fowler, Dai James and Rick Peacock-Edwards took us all to the bar where they put on a barrel to celebrate selection for Germany. Of the four of us destined for the shores of Fife two, Graham Clarke and Dave Hemmings, accepted it without argument but Derek Nicholls and I were very disappointed. A little while later on, Derek came up to me and suggested that we two draw again. The winner would have the chance of any odd posting that might – or might not – come up, while the other would then be certain of going to Scotland. I won the toss of the coin and then promptly forgot all about it as the evening went on. A few days later, OC 2 Squadron, Sqn Ldr Terry Carlton, stopped me in the Ops Room with the words 'I hear you won the toss of the coin, Dave. How do you fancy going to 74 Squadron in Singapore?' I floated for the rest of the day (and naturally put on a barrel that evening). It transpired that one of 74's pilots, who had deployed with the squadron to RAF Tengah in Singapore in June, had suffered a broken pelvis in a car crash and been brought home for hospital treatment: a replacement was needed and it was to be Fg Off Roome.

All UK Lightning squadrons operated either the F.3 or F.6 versions, and only the two RAF Germany squadrons retained the F.2 with radar and weaponry similar to the F.1As operated by 1 and 2 Squadrons of the OCU, so at the start of the new year Graham Clarke, Dave Hemmings, Derek Nicholls and I transferred down the flight line to 3 Squadron and the T.5 variant. Here we learned about the AI23B, and got used to the OR946 instrumentation used in the F.3, T.5 and F.6. This did not take long as the Gnat had the same instrumentation and had been an excellent lead-in aircraft for the Lightning. By the second week of February 1968, I had finished the course and started a month of something I had never before experienced: embarkation leave.

I had completed my flying training at last, taking just over three years to do so, but my 'wings' were still not safe: if I failed to achieve operational status on 74 Squadron they could still be taken away from me.

8

TYGER, TYGER, BURNING BRIGHT

Tyger Tyger, burning bright,
In the forests of the night;
What immortal hand or eye,
Could frame thy fearful symmetry?
In what distant deeps or skies.
Burnt the fire of thine eyes?
On what wings dare he aspire?
What the hand, dare seize the fire?

William Blake 1757-1827

LITTLE DID I KNOW as I boarded a Britannia aircraft of British Eagle Airways at London's Heathrow Airport on that Monday evening of 12 March 1968 just how long I would be bound, one way or another, to No.74 (Fighter) Squadron, alternatively known as No.74 (Trinidad) Squadron after the people of that island donated money in 1940 for Spitfires to aid the defence of Great Britain. The Britannia slowly made its way out to the Far East, stopping at Istanbul (in -15°C) and Bombay (+30°C). We reached Paya Lebar, then the civilian airport for Singapore, at 0430 on Wednesday 14 March on schedule, forty-eight hours after leaving London. I joined the other RAF passengers on an old RAF coach (the long supply chain meant the Far East Air Force was always the last to get more modern replacements for anything) and we drove for what seemed hours in the night-time 27°C temperature and 95%+ humidity before, as the last remaining passenger on the coach, I was deposited at the officers' mess RAF Tengah some time just before 0600. A receptionist showed me to my room, dim and dark with slatted doors and no air conditioning. I turned the fan in the centre of the room up to just about supersonic, dropped the mosquito net around my bed and fell into it.

I may have slept a little but at 0700 the first Javelin formation from 60 Squadron took off. I opened the doors on the far side of my room to find that I looked out over the runway. The Javelins were followed by Hunters of 20 Squadron, Canberras from 45 and 81 Squadrons, and finally two 74 Squadron Lightnings plugged in their burners and I gave up any hope of sleeping. At 0900 I was met by Rick Lea, who had been the Junior Pilot on 74 until my arrival and was carrying out his 'JP' duties to help the new pilot 'arrive' on the station. Rick took me to the camp tailors where a Chinese man took my measurements and promised one set of KD (khaki dress) uniform comprising short-sleeved shirt and shorts by the end of the day, the remainder of my tropical uniforms to follow before the end of the week: he was as good as his word. Then followed the familiar rigmarole of 'arriving'. Drawing my arrival card from Supply Control and Accounting Flight (SCAF) I dutifully visited the bicycle store ('no thanks'), the padre

No 74(F) Squadron Standard

72

('yes, I promise'), Accounts Flight to confirm where my pay would go (to the Hong Kong and Shanghai Banking Corporation, which is where the well-known 'HSBC' originates from), to Flying Wing HQ. Then on to clothing store for items peculiar to the tropics, such as the jungle boots, which were canvas-sided, rubber-soled, lightweight flying boots, better if walking in the jungle (more of which later), air traffic control and a myriad of other places to let them know that Fg Off Roome had now joined the strength of RAF Tengah.

On the walls of the OCU at Coltishall were photographs of all the earlier courses to have progressed through the OCU and, once I knew my posting, I had studied them to identify those who were on 74 Squadron, which had undergone quite a large change of pilots prior to leaving Leuchars for Tengah in order to give everyone a decent tour length in Singapore. The squadron comprised the CO, Wg Cdr Ken Goodwin and two squadron leader flight commanders, Derek Burrows (OC A Flt) and Norman Want (OC B Flt); the remaining thirteen pilots (prior to my arrival) were not difficult to memorise. This proved useful, because many new pilots arriving on the Tengah squadrons were subjected to elaborate and detailed 'spoofs', where ranks and jobs were changed to confuse the

RAF Tengah Officers' Mess Frontage 1968

poor new boy. The masters of the art seemed to be 20 Squadron flying the Hunter, and the three new pilots who arrived in the same week as me to join 20 were subjected to hours of uncertainty and confusion. Brought down to the squadron crewroom on the same Wednesday morning they witnessed a very stroppy airman, clad in the standard old, oil-stained khaki shorts, come rushing in and proceed to rant and rave at the squadron commander, who took it all quite meekly. Then a civilian in white shirt and shorts from MPBW, the Ministry of Public Buildings and Works (who were responsible for the station's infrastructure), came in complaining about the runway surface (he held a piece of it in his hand to make his point about leaking fuel on the tarmac). He was interrupted by the squawkbox asking for the Boss to go to his office as one of the squadron's Hunters was overdue on a flight back to Tengah from Labuan in Borneo (the Boss was philosophical about this serious news, saying that the particular aircraft had had fuel leaks in the past). As the new boys wondered just what they had joined, the 'gay' padre would seek to get them to visit him that evening, (accompanied by a squeeze of the knee!) The next morning worse was to follow: the three were told that a mistake had been made in sending out three pilots when only two were needed. However, no one would have to go back to the UK as 60 Squadron (the Javelins) needed a pilot. As the role of that aircraft was air defence the three would sit a written aircraft recognition exam with the winner going to the Javelin! No matter how hard they tried someone had to come top (probably he who spelt his name correctly) and one reluctant young man was sent down to 60, where he was given a set of pilot's notes for the Javelin and told to expect to do his first trip on the Monday. This mayhem continued through to the Friday afternoon when the Stag Bar at Tengah opened at 1615 for POETS night (piss off everyone, tomorrow's Saturday). As the confused newcomers were brought into the bar they became aware that many rank tabs had been changed once more: the stroppy airman reverted to being a flying officer pilot, 'the Boss' was now a flight lieutenant, one of the flight lieutenants turned out to be the squadron commander and 'the MPBW man' was none other than the station commander, Gp Capt Philip Lagesen! 60 claimed their Javelin pilot's notes back and three very relieved guys were welcomed into the 20 Squadron fold! Variations on this theme were played out in many squadrons as new pilots joined, but it didn't always go to plan. One pilot returned to the crewroom after a particularly odd arrival chat with his squadron commander and sat down with a coffee alongside another squadron pilot. 'How did your interview go?' asked the other. 'I have to say that it was quite odd,' said the new pilot, 'but then again, I had heard some odd rumours about this officer before coming out here.' The 'spoof' was terminated abruptly as the other squadron pilot suddenly took on his real rank (that of the CO) and invited the new pilot back to his office for a second, in-depth, arrival interview!

The routine followed by 74 Squadron during its time at Tengah was that in any week one flight would fly 'days' (0800-1600) and the other 'nights' (1500-2300). This would be the case for Monday to Thursday, but as there was no station night flying on Friday and generally no flying whatsoever at the weekend, the 'night' flight would come in at 1300 on Friday and the afternoon would be spent on ground training, lectures on the aircraft or weapons systems, perhaps some aircraft recognition and this generally ended around 1500 for a pilots' meeting. This was the time for the CO to address everyone and for the dissemination of information from higher authorities such as HQ Far East Air Force (FEAF) at Changi. Now and again Ken Goodwin would turn to a particular subject he used to favour. Following the tradition of fighter squadrons since the war, each aircraft carried the name of a pilot on the left-hand side of the nose below the cockpit (with only fourteen aircraft there were not enough to go around). The CO would pick one pilot and ask him to give the assembled company a few minutes on the state of 'his' aircraft, whether it was on the line serviceable or in the hangar on servicing and whether that servicing was scheduled or awaiting parts. The unspoken threat was that if the 'owner' could not give an accurate summary, his name could be erased and a more junior pilot be allocated that aircraft! This ensured that everyone took a very keen interest in their aircraft and the whole squadron benefited too, as engineering personnel working in the hangar were regularly approached to update a pilot on what was going on in the bowels of 'his' Lightning. At the end of the pilots' meeting there would be a general move back to the mess and POETS night, but in those days there was no permission to wear flying kit in the mess; everyone would change into KD shirt and shorts, long khaki socks and black shoes. That 'rig' was permitted until 1900 when everyone had change into 'planters' – a long-sleeved shirt, tie and long trousers – and fines would often be awarded by the station commander, known to one and all (but NEVER to his face) as 'Largy-baby' if he (correctly dressed of course) observed anyone still in shorts after 7pm.

Philip Lagesen was an impressive station commander. Born in Johannesburg, he joined the South African Air Force during WWII, training initially as an air gunner before transferring to pilot. In 1945 *The London Gazette* recorded the award of a Distinguished Flying Cross:

'This officer was the second pilot in a Liberator aircraft detailed to attack the Parona rail/road bridge at Verona. Soon after leaving the target area the aircraft was attacked by a fighter. Evading action was taken but the aircraft was hit by a burst of machine gun fire. Much damage was sustained. A fire commenced in the rear of the aircraft. Being unable to communicate with other members of the crew, owing to the unserviceability of the inter-communication system, Lieutenant Lagesen went aft to investigate. He found the rear gun turret on fire. The rear gunner lay wounded just outside the turret. Ammunition was exploding intermittently. Despite this, Lieutenant Lagesen fought strenuously to overcome the flames and finally subdued them by means of extinguishers. He then turned his attention to aiding his wounded comrade. Just then, another fighter closed in. Lieutenant Lagesen promptly manned the beam gun and assisted the mid-upper gunner to drive off the attacker. Fire again broke out in the rear of the aircraft. All the effective extinguishers had been used. Nevertheless, Lieutenant Lagesen tore down and threw out some burning material and then beat out the remainder of the fire with his hands. This officer set a splendid example of courage and coolness in the face of great danger.'

After transferring to the RAF in 1951 and rising through the ranks, Gp Capt Lagesen took over command of RAF Tengah in 1966 and remained in command until mid-1969 when he was replaced by Gp Capt Peter Latham, more of whom in due course. 'Largy' had one particular quirk he often employed: he kept a bull whip and was quite an expert in cracking it just behind some unsuspecting junior officer. Many can quote stories of being startled by a loud crack just behind them, usually for some minor transgression!

However, in those days many senior officers had illustrious pasts and at Tengah the Officer Commanding Administrative Wing in 1968 was Wg Cdr Peter Thompson, an officer who had had a most interesting background and I make no apology for summarising it here.

Peter Thompson was born on 7 September 1920. He joined the RAFVR in January 1939 and began elementary flying training but was called to full-time service at the outbreak of war and posted to 5 EFTS Hanworth. A year later he went to 3 FTS, South Cerney and after completing the course in June he was sent to 6 OTU, Sutton Bridge on 4 September to convert to Hurricanes. Thompson joined 32 Squadron at Croydon on 21 September 1940 but was then posted to 605 Squadron on 11 October. He damaged Bf109s on 20 October, 1 and 13 November before sharing a damaged Do17 on 26 March 1941. On 27 April 1941 Thompson was one of 24 pilots who flew Hurricanes off HMS 'Ark Royal' to Hal Far, Malta, where he joined 261 Squadron in the defence of that island: he was wounded on 6 May but landed safely. When 261 was disbanded in May he went to the newly-reformed 185 Squadron and shared in destroying a Cant Z1007 on 25 July, destroyed a Macchi 200 the next day and shared a SM79 the very next day. He claimed a probable Bf109 on 29 December and a probable Ju88 on 25 January 1942. He returned to the UK in January 1942 and was awarded the DFC (gazetted 30 January 1942). In early 1943 Thompson joined 601 Squadron in the Western Desert as a flight commander, moving with it later to Sicily and Italy. He destroyed two SM79s in an attack on Ancona airfield on 3 November 1943. He returned to the UK in early 1944 and in July took command of 129 Squadron, operating from Ford in Sussex with Mustangs, from where he destroyed three V1 flying bombs and damaged two others. Thompson led the squadron until April 1945.

By the mid-1950s Wg Cdr Thompson DFC was station commander at RAF Biggin Hill in Kent, where LF363, the only airworthy RAF Hurricane IIC, was based and this gave Peter the idea for a grander plan. There was a strong belief among some in the RAF that the Service's greatest battle honour should continue to be commemorated in a fitting fashion and the best way to do that was to keep the last remaining examples of those legendary aircraft – the Hurricane and Spitfire – in the air. Wg Cdr Thompson sought the authority to form an historic flight at Biggin Hill but with no public funding all manpower would have to be voluntary. Nevertheless, it was achieved and from such a small beginning the Historic Aircraft Flight, operating three Spitfire XIXs, metamorphosed into what we know today as the Battle of Britain Memorial Flight.

RAF Tengah was part of FEAF, itself part of the tri-service organisation, Far East Command; HQ FEAF was at Fairy Point within RAF Changi on the eastern side of Singapore Island. RAF Changi was the main transport base, with 48 Squadron having recently exchanged its Handley Page Hastings for the C-130 Hercules strategic transport, 205 Squadron flew the Avro Shackleton in the maritime reconnaissance role and 52 Squadron had Andovers for medium-range transport duties. To the west of Changi lay Seletar, home to 66 Squadron operating the Bristol Belvedere twin-rotor helicopter, 209 Squadron with their Scottish Aviation Single and Twin Pioneers, and 103 and 110 Squadrons with Westland Whirlwind helicopters, 103 primarily for search and rescue and 110 for transport. Further west was Sembawang, which the RN operated (as *HMS Simbang*) and this was home to various helicopter squadrons, as elements of the RN carrier fleet visited Singapore and the squadrons deployed ashore, fixed wing usually to Changi and helicopters to Sembawang. To the west of the Bukit Timah Road which ran from Singapore City to the causeway into mainland Malaysia, stood RAF Tengah, the main fighter and attack station. Here were based the day fighter and ground attack Hunters of 20 Squadron, two squadrons of Canberras, the 'bomber' B.15s of 45 Squadron and PR.7s of 81 Squadron who flew photo reconnaissance tasks, and the all-weather fighters, Javelin FAW.9s of 60 Squadron and 74's Lightnings. Radar coverage and control was provided by RAF Bukit Gombak, high on a hill in the centre of the island. Finally, operating in the ground defence role for airfield protection was 63 Squadron RAF Regiment with its Bofors 40/70 anti-aircraft guns. In all, twelve RAF flying squadrons operated from an island almost exactly twice the size of the Isle of Wight (and in the middle of the island was Paya Lebar, the civil airport!). Far East Command had many army and navy units within its sphere; indeed, the RN Naval Base at *HMS Terror* covered a large swathe of the north shore of the island, but as I took stock of Tengah I realised that I had never seen such a collection of fighting hardware. There was more. Three hundred and thirty miles up the Malaysian peninsula was Butterworth, where the Royal Australian Air Force (RAAF) based 77 Squadron, flying probably the best version of the F-86 Sabre, re-engined to take the Rolls-Royce Avon, and 75 Squadron operating Dassault Mirage 3 fighters. The Royal New Zealand Air Force (RNZAF) maintained 41 Squadron at Changi with the venerable Bristol Freighter and regularly deployed 14 Squadron and its B.12 Canberras from Ohakea in the north of New Zealand to Tengah. Finally, Tengah also hosted regular detachments of Vulcan bombers from the UK and Victors, both the strategic reconnaissance SR.2 Victor of 543 Squadron and the K.1 Victor tankers, who came out to ensure that 74 remained current in air-to-air refuelling (AAR).

This was, therefore, the very busy RAF station that I joined and very lively it was too, as I was to find on my very first weekend, as a squadron party was held at one of the married quarters just off the Bukit Timah Road about six miles from Tengah. The theme was simple: a shirt party! I wore a shirt and, like the rest of those attending, omitted any trousers (I *was*, however, wearing underpants!). As I had been in Singapore for a total of three days, my legs were still as they had been in the UK, very pale, and I was immediately christened 'Lily Legs' by one of the squadron wives. The party was great fun and I had a most enjoyable time, partly because I met a lady who had come to the party from elsewhere and I had not met her before. We got on extremely well and at the end of the evening she offered me a lift back, as I had no transport of my own. One thing led to another and we actually went back to her place. Then, at about six the next morning she said that I had to leave, because her husband would be arriving back in a couple of hours! I had assumed that she was single and one of the school teachers at Tengah, but I raced out of the house, clad once again in my shirt, only to find that I was not at Tengah but at RAF

Seletar, about ten miles away. I can assure the reader that standing at the main gate of Seletar in shirt tails very early in the morning while trying to hail a taxi meets all the criteria for a 'walk of shame'. Even so, whenever I hear the Four Seasons song, 'Oh, What a Night' it brings back some pleasant memories as well.

For 74 Squadron March 1968 was also the fiftieth anniversary of its formation and I was (a very small) part of the celebrations. On 21 March, exactly one week after arriving and wearing my brand new tropical mess kit, I attended a formal 74 Squadron Ladies' Guest Night. The next day a parade was held, reviewed by the Air Commander, Air Marshal Sir Rochford Hughes, followed by a flying display and also a cocktail party. On 29 March the squadron held an all ranks dance in the McGregor Club on the station to round off the celebrations, so it was a busy two weeks. It was similarly busy in the air as well and by the end of April my logbook shows that I was qualified on the Lightning F.6 by day and night and had flown thirty-five hours since arriving. At the end of April, I witnessed the disbandment of the last operational Javelin squadron in the RAF, 60 Squadron. As the commander of an all-weather air defence squadron, Wg Cdr 'Dusty' Miller decided to hold the disbandment parade at dusk, something which in those latitudes (Singapore is only eighty miles north of the equator) lasts only five minutes or so. Following a diamond nine flypast over the parade, a formation which suited the Javelin's triangular shape, five aircraft flew straight-in approaches to land, but the last four flew over exactly as the Squadron Standard was being marched off the parade. By now it was night and the four selected reheat for effect, though that was all it did, as the lack of a reheat fuel pump in the Javelin meant that reheat selection at low level resulted in a decrease in thrust but nice, visible flames. They then all landed and taxied in together. The Javelin was powered by the Bristol Siddeley Sapphire, as was the Mk.1 Victor, and this engine had a great tendency to resonate at idle on the ground. With nine Javelins lined up together and the squadron commander's aircraft as the middle aircraft one length ahead, they all cut their engines for the last time on a radio call and as the reverberations died away those of us watching from the top bar stood in silence. Eventually, someone said quietly, 'Bye, bye, Javelin,' and another chapter of Royal Air Force history was closed.

Much of our flying was carried out over the sea, either the Malacca Straits to the west or the South China Sea to the east, but obviously a portion was over land – the jungle. It was essential that we knew how to survive in that environment and so in June I was sent across to Changi to attend the FEAF Survival and Parachute School's Jungle Survival Course, two weeks of learning how to survive in and, if necessary, to walk out of, the jungle. The first week was spent in the school compound on the seafront to the east of Changi airfield (now somewhere under Terminal 3 of Changi International Airport). Here we learned how to make fires, if necessary without giving away our position, how to recognise which insects, reptiles or animals were dangerous and which were not, and how to make progress on foot in the difficult jungle terrain. The week included trying to make progress in some of the most inhospitable terrain I had experienced to that time, when we were taken out to the Mandai swamp and expected to walk a fair distance within this mix of mangrove swamp, water and unpleasant plants. The Mandai, in the very centre of Singapore Island, was what is known as secondary jungle, where the jungle canopy has been cut down and the undergrowth been allowed to re-grow in the

Orchard Road, Singapore

full sun. This permits rapid and massive growth of such plants as ferns which stand over two metres high and have large and strong barbs on the underside of the leaves. Unsurprisingly these are known as 'Wait-a-while'. There was also a lot of mangrove swamp. Progress in such terrain was agonisingly slow, often in fetid water and mud up to our chests, and our feet had to feel for purchase amongst roots (and occasionally something which moved underfoot!). The teaching was that the leading man in any group would be responsible for clearing the path, using the long Malay machete called the *parang* to slash undergrowth. Further back was the compass man who took a bearing on a feature and tried to ensure that the intended track was maintained, for it was very easy to walk in circles if this was not rigorously followed. Further back were the 'pace' man and the 'stick' man; every one hundred paces the pace man would call and the stick man cut a notch into a stick he carried. In this way, progress through the jungle could be estimated with some degree of accuracy, one hundred paces counting as fifty yards. Walking in single file, as the man ahead moved forward the mud would part, releasing gases, and we each had our own personal swarm of midges and mosquitos: it was hardly 'a walk in the woods'! When we came face to face with these huge ferns, the best way to get through was for one man to place a branch across his back and under his arms, and then to walk backwards, pushing the ferns down as he went, and this often included the ferns falling because the man fell backwards too.

When our group finally came out of the Mandai onto a road to await collection, there was an almost surreal event when toward this motley group of six, covered in mud and stinking to high heaven, came a Magnolia Man! The Magnolia company made and sold ice creams, lollies and cold drinks, and many of the outlets were men on a tricycle with the two wheels at the front, one each side of the cold tub containing the refreshments. They advertised their approach by the tinkling of a bell and this was what we heard at the roadside. However, knowing what we were to undergo that morning, not one of us had carried a wallet and so the Magnolia Man pedalled on, searching for someone who could pay for his ice cream!

After a weekend back in civilisation we reported back to the school on the Monday and were loaded into transport which then took us over the

Overhead Tengah

causeway into Johore and up to near Jemaluang on the east coast. Here we were split again into our teams of around six, my team being selected as the 'single-seaters', those who would in all likelihood arrive in the jungle on the end of a parachute and alone. There was a pilot from 1574 Flight whose Meteors towed gunnery targets from Changi, two Australian Mirage pilots from Butterworth and two Tengah Hunter pilots, Julian Leigh and Ian Ord, who I had known since South Cerney days and who had arrived in the Far East at the same time. Although we formed a team of six for the week, each night the staff required us to make single-man shelters known as *bashas* while those others on the course, which numbered more than thirty, including another six from the Canberra squadrons at Tengah, were all from aircraft carrying more than one person and who, it was hoped, would be able to join up and survive together; they were therefore allowed to make multi-occupancy *bashas*! Unlike some areas of the world, where water, or lack of it, is a great threat to successful survival, the jungle has plenty, much of it falling from the sky and plenty of it underfoot. Indeed, we found that following a stream or river was usually done best by walking in the river, as there is often less undergrowth to impede progress, and drinking water can be found in vines and pitcher plants, whose flowers are similar to a cup. Into these cups fall many insects which then cannot escape and are devoured by the plant, but if the flower is carefully tipped up, water may be drunk without getting the solids at the bottom! One of the less attractive bugs to be found in the jungle is the leech, which drops off vegetation and then searches for warm and damp areas such as underarm or groin, or is trapped by items such as a belt. They then bite into the body and suck the blood, growing in size from a thin worm to something thicker than a thumb. Brushing a leech off is inadvisable, as the teeth remain behind and fester, so we all carried some iodine, usually in a nasal spray bottle or similar: one drop on the head of the leech was enough to cause it to drop off and the iodine had the additional benefit of sterilising the wound. One day during our week there we came across a tortoise that had a leech embedded in its neck just behind the head, preventing the tortoise from doing its usual disappearing act: one drop of iodine got rid of the leech although we got no thanks from the tortoise. The course finished on the Thursday of the second week and we all returned to our bases much the wiser and better prepared, with fear of the jungle overcome; indeed, I always felt that it was a more benign survival environment than many others. It did not change one basic difference in the way one would face an airborne emergency in the Far East, however. In Europe a pilot with an emergency over the sea will head for land: out there the reverse applied and survival just off the coast was definitely the preferred option.

1968 was not just the fiftieth anniversary of 74 Squadron but also that of the Royal Air Force itself, which had been formed on 1 April 1918 from the amalgamation of the Royal Flying Corps and the Royal Naval Air Service. During my Service career I witnessed both the RAF's fiftieth and seventy-fifth anniversaries from within and then watched as its Centenary was commemorated.

My time as the junior pilot on 74 was short as in mid-June Frank Whitehouse joined from Coltishall to start his own operational work-up, and a month later some Victor tankers from 55 Squadron at Marham arrived to give us AAR training. This was another step on my path to being declared operational and although I found it demanding I succeeded in gaining my day qualification. Because the AAR probe on the Lightning was low on the left-hand side of the aircraft's nose there was nothing to be gained by flying dual in the side-by-side T.5. Instead, a pair of aircraft would go to the tanker and the experienced pilot would make a couple of 'dry prods', making contact between probe and drogue without any transfer of fuel, with the new pilot watching closely from alongside or behind. Positions were then reversed and contact would be attempted. Tanking is reckoned to be like riding a bike and once successfully mastered it was a rewarding experience, essential for fighters to cover long distances without landing, and later I would complete sorties of well over eight hours utilising this method. In the week and over five sorties I made eight 'wet' contacts when fuel was passed, and no fewer than sixty-six 'dry'. The week culminated in a two-hour, thirty-five-minute (2:35) cross-country flying a 'tanker cross-country', the usual means by which aircraft with a relatively short range could cover great distances. Periodically the tanker would call in the receiver: '74, you're clear astern the starboard hose.' Once astern, the fighter would be 'cleared for contact, wet for 1,000lbs' or similar, or 'clear for contact, dry'. Eventually, RT would be dispensed with and when the fighter pilot saw hoses start to reel out of the underwing pods or from the centreline Hose Drum Unit (HDU or 'hoodoo'), he knew this was the signal to go astern the appropriate hose. Within the HDU were multi-coloured traffic lights and when first astern the lights would show amber and red. When the red lights extinguished it meant 'clear for contact' and once in contact, if fuel was passing the ambers went out and the greens showed. If fuel transfer finished the ambers would replace the greens and flashing ambers meant 'clear to break contact'. Various other light combinations were used and this excellent system saved much unnecessary RT. Indeed, the operational need for RT silence sometimes made the light sequence essential.

The small size of Lightning squadrons (74 only had 170 personnel, including sixteen pilots) meant that secondary duties were a large part of squadron life. By the time I had been at Tengah for four months I was responsible for the standards of the pilots in aircraft recognition; I was also the squadron's social secretary and combat survival and rescue officer (CSRO), which required me to arrange and conduct periodic dinghy drills for all pilots. At the beginning of August that year I took over as the station CSRO, which broadened my responsibilities considerably and which I retained until we all left Singapore. When we flew at low level over the jungle we were meant to carry a 'Treescape', equipment that had 150ft of nylon rope and a snubber unit which was contained in a canvas pack and attached to the chest of our flying suit. If a pilot had to eject and then found himself caught up in the jungle where the trees are often over 100ft high with very little in the way of branches below the leaf canopy itself, the idea was to get out the unit and tie the rope to one's parachute harness. The next rather daunting task was to release the parachute harness (a real leap of faith) and, using the snubber unit, allow the rope to slowly pay out, lowering the pilot to the ground. Many aircrew had little faith in this kit, declaring that it was dangerous and a waste of time, and so I was prevailed upon to demonstrate its efficacy. One Friday afternoon the majority of Tengah's aircrew came over to 74 Squadron, many convinced they were about to see Dave Roome have a major accident. There I was, at the very top of one of the gantries that held the lights to illuminate our aircraft line at night. I tied the rope of the Treescape to the gantry and let myself over the edge before successfully arriving slowly at ground level. Many of the onlookers were, I suspect, not a little disappointed that it had worked as advertised, but from that time onward my demonstration was always part of the initial briefings given to squadrons detached from the UK to operate over the jungle from Tengah, and I carried out many Treescape descents.

In mid-August another first tour pilot arrived. Pete Thompson had completed Coltishall just behind Frank Whitehouse and quickly started his operational work-up, but tragedy struck within a month. On 12 September Pete experienced a double reheat fire indication as he joined the circuit. He immediately turned downwind to land but in the finals turn the aircraft pitched up, flicked into a spin and crashed. Although he ejected he left the aircraft too late, leaving insufficient time for the seat automatics to work and was killed on impact. It was found that the control rods from the cockpit to the tailplane were made of light alloy and burned through very quickly in a fuselage fire. Once the rods were severed the tail ran away to fully nose up, though the 'feel' to the pilot through the control column was unchanged and would have confused Pete for a few critical seconds. Following this accident and pending the replacement of the alloy rods, pilots were advised not to attempt to land following a double fire of this type and if below 5,000ft at the time, to pull up and eject immediately. For the second time in just over a year I would be a pallbearer at the funeral of a friend.

Although overshadowed by Pete's death, there had been another nasty incident during the preceding weekend. I had joined a syndicate of squadron pilots to buy a share in a water-ski boat and we regularly used to go water skiing at Snake Island in the Johore Strait to the north of Singapore Island. We were in the process of putting the boat into the water at the boat yard at Ponggol when another boat came in at high speed calling for help as they had a man on board who had suffered a heart attack. We attempted to resuscitate him for over an hour but it was to no avail and eventually a doctor who arrived with a rescue helicopter pronounced him dead. He had been a rubber planter from Malaysia and I later received a very laudatory letter from HQ Far East Fleet, as another in the party had been a Royal Navy captain. However, on the plus side, we had a visit from a bunch of USAF pilots flying the F-105 Thunderchief – the 'Thud' – from Udorn Air Base in Thailand. Any suggestion that an exchange might involve us taking our Lightnings to them had been quickly squashed, as a picture of the RAF alongside F-105s bombed up for attacks into Vietnam would have gone down badly in Whitehall and, for similar reasons, they were forbidden to fly their aircraft into Singapore. Instead, they came down by C-130 Hercules and certainly made the most of their 'holiday'. These guys were heavily involved in attacks into Vietnam, where over 20,000 Thunderchief sorties were flown (and 382 aircraft were lost) and told some very hairy stories, including one which bears re-telling. The aircraft had a very high airspeed limit at low level of 810kts, which equates to 1.2M, well and truly supersonic, and they told of regularly coming out of North Vietnam by means of a valley called 'Banana Valley', which had a considerable number of enemy anti-aircraft guns along the valley sides. However, North Vietnamese early warning consisted only of acoustic chambers cut into the hillsides with a man sitting in the chamber. When he heard the sound of an approaching aircraft he would warn the gunners who would then put up a curtain of fire. The lead 'Thud' would race down the valley as low as he could go at 800kts or so and the shockwave would be the first thing to enter the acoustic chamber (and probably pass through the head of the 'early warner'), giving the remainder a good chance of getting through the valley without loss. During their time at Tengah the Americans introduced us to the fun of the 'bar bazooka', made by hollowing out about five beer cans and taping

Pairs Take Off – Self and OC 74

88

them together to form a barrel. Then a further can would have four holes made on one end using a triangular punch while the other end had only a single small hole in the centre. This can was now taped onto the others as the firing chamber, lighter fluid sprayed into the chamber and a tennis ball inserted in the open end. Once the firing chamber was warmed up the tennis ball could be fired over about twenty feet with no appreciable gravity drop. They also told us of one of their number back at Udorn who had developed the ultimate version using the smaller diameter tins that held fruit juice. These, he found, would take a billiard ball and he then made up a multi-chambered version of this 'gun' with the 'rounds' fired electrically in sequence! Apparently he could clear the food hall within seconds of entering!

Soon after the F-105 guys returned to their war a most unusual visitor arrived at Tengah when two rare aircraft arrived for a couple of weeks. Prior to Concorde entering service with the airlines, much work had been expended deciding which routes could be made viable: one was the London to Singapore route, stopping at Bahrein. As part of this preparation a Canberra from the Royal Aircraft Establishment at Bedford, capable of flight at the levels Concorde would fly (in excess of 60,000ft), was joined by a USAF RB-57F from Yokota Air Base in Japan. Both aircraft were there to study the high altitude turbulence that could cause problems for Concorde. The RB-57F was a very specialised aircraft, a modification of the Canberra which had been built under licence by Martin/General Dynamics, but this version had a wingspan of 122ft, and had two turbofans and two podded engines which together produced 36,000lbs thrust, a lot more than the 20,000lbs of the most powerful British PR.9. In addition to carrying out their assigned tasks, the RB-57F crews agreed to fly some target sorties at very high altitudes for the Automated Air Defence System installed at the Singapore Ground Controlled Intercept (GCI) site at RAF Bukit Gombak. This GL161 Linesman system controlled our Lightnings to an intercept, at least that was the plan. With the target at altitudes between 60,000 and 80,000ft we had a difficult job achieving a firing solution and the GL161 regularly demanded that the Lightning fly at 2.0M on a stern intercept and finish up behind the target. With the target flying very slowly the fighter's overtake was so great that the firing bracket (the time between maximum and minimum firing ranges) was very short indeed.

USAF RB-57F at RAF Tengah Open Day 1968

The American aircrew on this aircraft obviously enjoyed their break from normal duties (the aircraft was regularly used for very high altitude reconnaissance of the Soviet bloc, doing the same sort of job that Gary Powers was doing in his U-2 when he was shot down by a Russian surface-to-air missile). They delighted in doing their impressive take-off and departure, with a ground roll of only 2000ft. Once airborne and with the gear up, the throttles were advanced to full power and the aircraft stood on its tail just short of the vertical at 85° of pitch. At this angle it proceeded to climb out of sight on two columns of thick brown jet efflux. I was most impressed with the machine and was delighted, after a bit of pleading, to be offered a trip in the back seat. This required me to don a full pressure suit similar to that worn by the Gemini astronauts and to pre-oxygenate. Because of the altitude it was important to get rid of all carbon dioxide from the body and so, fully suited, the pilot and I sat on reclined couches for two hours breathing 100% oxygen. Meanwhile a 'buddy crew' carried out all the pre-start checks on the aircraft, with the intention that we would transfer direct to the cockpit carrying our small oxygen supply to maintain the 100% oxygen, be strapped in and have nothing more to do than press the starter buttons. It was a severe let down when the buddy crew came in to tell us that the aircraft was unserviceable and we would not be flying. I never got another chance.

In early November I took (and passed) the 'B' promotion exam, the requirement for promotion to flight lieutenant, though subsequently this requirement was removed and promotion simply depended on serving the appropriate time in rank. Some years later the same happened: having passed the 'C' promotion exam to become eligible for promotion to squadron leader, that exam was removed. However, much more important in November was that Wg Cdr Goodwin declared that I was now operational. This is the most important milestone on any pilot's first squadron, as it is only then that his pilot brevet is confirmed and can no longer be taken from him. Although unusual, failure of any preceding course and transfer to another branch can lead to the brevet being removed. Much later in my career I became the officer responsible for deciding whether this draconian step should be taken and had to take that very action in one man's case.

It was not all work by any means. Soon after arriving I had bought a car, an open-top Triumph TR3A, from a navigator on 60 Squadron as he returned to the UK. During his ownership he had run it under the tailgate of a truck, losing the windscreen and bending one of the windscreen stanchions. It took a while to get a replacement so in the interim I drove it with just a semicircle of Perspex screwed in front of the steering wheel, and I wore a pair of old motorcycle goggles to protect my eyes from the dust. There was nothing to enhance the passenger's comfort and so almost all my driving was done solo and in the dry, as it was impossible to put up the hood! The local garages were good at restoring cars though, and eventually my TR3A looked much as it would have done on leaving the factory. It was one of my success stories in that I bought it for $1,800 (Singapore dollars were valued at eight to the pound, so about £225) and sold it three and a half years later for $2,400. I ranged all over the island in that car, to places such as The Gap, a British Army rest and recuperation hostel which did the best Sunday curry lunches anywhere, or to Pasir Panjang, where there were other excellent restaurants like The Seaside and The Paradise, superb for chilli crab, and to downtown Singapore on many an evening spent in various bars, clubs and at roadside stalls for local food such as satay. In the late '60s, the cars were generally British of late '50s vintage, many of which would now command premium prices, but then it was common to find parked outside the officers' mess MG TC and TDs, or large Ford saloons such as the Consul and Zephyr. One amusing episode to do with cars occurred when Mike Rigg, one of our pilots, was giving a lift downtown to a couple of visiting RAAF pilots on detachment from Butterworth. The two visitors were in the back while in the front passenger seat was Mike's wife, Helen. As Mike went around a roundabout with his tyres squealing Helen turned to the two in the back and in one of the funniest spoonerisms I have ever heard, said, '… and he wonders why his balls are tired!'

Many evenings ended up at the infamous Bugis Street, which had become popular after the war. Many will recall that this notorious drinking section ran from Victoria Street to Queen Street and halfway between the two there was an intersecting lane parallel to the main roads and lined with al fresco bars. Here there was a well-patronised public toilet with a flat roof of which there are archival photos, complete with jubilant rooftop occupants. One of the hallowed traditions bestowed upon the area by sojourning sailors (usually from Britain, Australia and New Zealand) was the ritualistic 'Dance of the Flaming Arseholes' on top of the infamous toilet's roof. Compatriots on the ground would chant the signature 'Haul 'em down, you Zulu Warrior' song whilst the matelots performed their act and stripped. When transvestites, commonly called *kai tais*, began to rendezvous in the area in the 1950s, they attracted increasing numbers of Western tourists who came for the booze, the food and the 'girls'. Business boomed and Bugis Street became an extremely lively and bustling night-time area, renowned internationally for its nightly parade of flamboyantly-dressed *kai tais* and for the hordes of caucasian gawkers who had never before witnessed these Asian queens in full regalia. The latter would tease, cajole and sit on visitors' laps, or pose for photographs for a fee. Others would sashay up and down the street looking to hook half-drunk sailors, American GIs and other foreigners on R&R, for an hour of profitable intimacy. Not only would these clients get the thrill of sex with an exotic Oriental, there would be the added spice of transgressing gender boundaries in a seamy hovel. The area was a must see for those on their first 'run ashore' after arriving, when beer could be obtained free by betting the newcomer that he couldn't pick out a real woman from those parading. We could easily tell who was a real female and who was not, for the *kai tais* were always drop-dead gorgeous. As the skimpy dresses left very little to the imagination and the figure on display was superb, the new arrival would eventually be certain and point to one, who would come over and be asked to speak: the male voice which emanated meant that the bet was lost and the next round was free for the rest of us!

Bugis Street beauties

We also used to plan weekends on 'The Islands'. These were two small islands about seven miles out to sea from Mersing on the east coast of Malaysia, itself about ninety miles up from Singapore by road. A trip would be planned for a long weekend of three to four days and would not usually include more than ten people, as more than that made logistics a nightmare, particularly in supplies. Forward planning was essential for there was nothing on the islands and everything had to be carried. We would leave Tengah very early in the morning and after crossing the causeway into Johore carry on up the east coast road to Mersing. The road was for the most part tarmac, though with no verge to speak of and often with a sharp drop off the tarmac surface into mud. Rivers were bridged by Bailey bridges, single carriageway metal bridges with a wooden planked driving surface and erected by the Army after the war, but traffic was generally light and posed no problems, except for the dreaded logging trucks. These were old, large-engined trucks of just post-war vintage, with a flatbed carrying between four and six huge tree trunks to timber yards. The trees were secured by chains, though not sufficiently well to preclude all movement and they would slide sideways alarmingly on any bend. Overtaking involved a degree of 'heart in the mouth' driving and as the cab was passed you could see the driver with his foot flat to the floor while striving to control the truck as he played with the half-turn of slack in the steering wheel! On arrival at Mersing a boat and boatman would be hired to take us out (not forgetting the important agreement that he would return at the appointed day and time to bring us back), while others would go to the ice factory in the town and get two large blocks of ice each about 3ft by 1ft by 1ft. These would be placed in sacks and on arrival on the island dropped into holes dug at the top of the beach. Around each block would go the fresh food, carefully wrapped, and all the drink, much of which was water, which was more important than beer! Even after four days there would still be ice remaining in these sacks and anything around them would still be very cold – they were great fridges! Sleeping arrangements were left to the individual: some took small camp beds and mosquito nets but I found that a parachute was ideal. Each evening I would dig up a length of sand to ensure it was soft and free from sharp objects, then wrap myself in the parachute and fall onto my 'bed', pulling a thin layer of nylon over my face to keep out the bugs. These stays were truly idyllic and all who went remember them with great affection. The days were spent relaxing, often in the clear turquoise water with a snorkel and fins, for there were a great many fish. One unforgettable occasion was when I swam alongside a ray with around a five-foot 'wingspan' until it finally got bored with me and swiftly accelerated away from me into the blue. In the evening a fire would be lit over which we cooked and around which we sat and ate, and later chatted and drank until drifting away to our beds. The most northerly of the three islands, Pulau Babi Ujong, which in Malay means 'the small island on the end' and which became our favourite, had a small shack just at the top of the beach and about twenty yards into the jungle there was a small stream which, though unsuitable for drinking, was dammed and we used the resultant pool to wash off the salt at the end of each day. Just down the path was even placed a 'FREE/ IN USE' sign to give the girls some privacy.

These trips to the islands were really magical times, remembering that in those days before mobile phones and the internet we were truly unreachable, out of contact until our return to the mainland. There were few dangers, although as the station CSRO I used to take up a SARBE (Search and Rescue Beacon Equipment) beacon from our safety equipment. Each of our flying lifejackets, known since the war as a 'Mae West' after the Hollywood film star's large chest, carried one. Following ejection, the SARBE would be used to transmit a signal on the distress frequency and any aircraft with the correct equipment could home onto the beacon to locate the pilot. As part of preparation for these trips I used to phone 205 Squadron at Changi, the Shackleton squadron responsible for long-range search and rescue, advising them of our whereabouts and of the duration of our stay. In the event of some form of accident or emergency I would have operated the SARBE in the hope that it would be picked up and rescuers appear over the horizon! Thankfully we never had to use the SARBE in anger but it was not unknown for a Shackleton to pass low down the beach sometime over the weekend, giving us a flypast.

Later in the year and after seeing the sorts of altitudes that the Lightning could attain, there came the chance for me to find out just how high it would go. On the OCU at Coltishall we had each gone to around 67,000ft in the F.1A as part of the sortie to determine the service ceiling in cold power and in reheat. In a cold power climb, the F.1A reached its service ceiling (when the rate of climb falls below 500ft/min) at about 42,000ft. Select

'The islands were truly idyllic'

reheat and continue the climb at 0.9M and the ceiling was reached quite quickly at only 48,000ft. But then the aircraft was held level and allowed to accelerate to its maximum permitted Mach number of 1.7M and a zoom climb easily passed 65,000ft. However, the F.6 was cleared up to 2.0M and one morning I was tasked to fly a singleton sortie out to the far northeast, almost to the Malaysia/Thailand border, there to intercept a Victor tanker returning to Singapore from Hong Kong. After carrying out some tanking I would return to Tengah. After joining the tanker and carrying out about half a dozen practice 'dry' contacts the tanker crew, who no doubt wished to land as soon as possible, told me that I could 'fill to full' and then leave. Having done so I found myself far up the Malaysian east coast where we were permitted to fly supersonic and I also had completely full tanks. I climbed the aircraft to 50,000ft, accelerated to 2.0M and zoomed at what we believed to be the optimum angle of 16° before levelling out at around 68,000ft and once again allowing the aircraft to accelerate, this time to 2.2M. Now came the chance to see what I could reach and once again I pulled the nose up. As I climbed, the reducing downwash over the aircraft's low-set tailplane meant that I had to pull the control column further and further back to hold the climb angle and eventually I reached the stick backstop. Slowly the aircraft nose lowered until I topped out with the altimeter reading 87,800ft. I felt as if I was on the ferrule of a very long umbrella and looking back over my left shoulder I convinced myself that I could see Vietnam. Borneo was ahead and to the left, while to my right were both Malaysia and Sumatra. Then both reheats extinguished and I brought the throttles back gently as we started to descend. Suddenly I was startled by the 'bells and clangers' as the attention getters drew me to the warning panel on the left side of the cockpit. The red warning for cockpit pressurisation shone accusingly at me and for a split second my heart was in my mouth, for although I was wearing my pressure jerkin over my flying suit we had no pressurised helmets anymore and 85,000ft plus was not a good height to be lacking cabin pressure. Then I realised that the cockpit altitude which, with normal pressurisation, would be maintained at about half the actual height plus 2,000ft, was above that differential but not dangerously so and although I felt some pressure breathing at my mask it was nothing like the 70mm of overpressure I had experienced in the decompression chamber at North Luffenham. With the throttles at idle I glided back toward Singapore, responding to questions from Singapore Radar interested in my height with the standard call of those days: 'I'm above FL450 (45,000ft).' In those days all controlled airspace ended at that altitude, and I remembered the story of a USAF U-2 who, when strenuously questioned as to his actual height was reported to have said, 'Look, buddy, if you have anyone else up here, let me know and I'll get out of his way!' I reached the overhead of Tengah still at 56,000ft and my overhead call was the first to state my altitude, to the Tengah ATC controllers' disbelief! Years later I read the story by another Lightning pilot which was so similar to mine that I suspect plagiarism: I know what I saw and I claim the Lightning world altitude record.

At the end of 1968 the officers' mess held its usual New Year's Eve Ball, during which there took place an event seen every six months in those days, the Feast of the Passover. However, this had nothing to do with the Jewish festival but everything to do with promotion and honours. Prior to midnight, the biannual promotion list, published on 1 January and 1 July, remained a closely guarded secret to all but the station commander. As the clock approached midnight, everyone would gather in the top bar of the mess and the group captain would read out the names of those flight lieutenants who were to be elevated to squadron leader and occasionally those squadron leaders and wing commanders who were also to be promoted to the next higher rank. On New Year's Eve there might also be names of officers from Tengah who were mentioned in the Honours List. There would be much cheering for those whose names were mentioned and a bottle of bubbly would be given to each of the lucky officers. Then the celebrations would go on into the night, often until breakfast started in the dining room.

The start of 1969 brought the Royal Navy's carrier *HMS Hermes* to the Far East and we found new playmates in the Sea Vixens of 893 Naval Air Squadron. The Vixen was quite a formidable fighter, developed from the Vampire and Venom but with two engines and two crew, and four Firestreak or Red Top missiles (double the number carried by the Lightning). With the navigator (observer in RN parlance) buried in the 'coal hole' alongside the pilot working its radar and other electronics, it was a very capable opponent, with a very good turning performance from its large wing and with plenty of power from its two Avons (though they had no reheat). The Vixen could also carry a refuelling pod, allowing the aircraft to act as a tanker. However, although the hose could be trailed from and wound back into the pod, unlike the Victor tanker the Vixen could not set how much fuel was to be given: in effect, if a receiver remained 'plugged in' he could drain the tanker aircraft! Early in January I found myself working against just such a Vixen, who offered at the end the sortie to give us some fuel. While my No.2 sat off to the starboard I made contact and was just settling down comfortably when the Vixen pilot said, 'You've had 200lbs, you're clear to break,' and as I slowly started to back out of the hose, he followed this up with, 'You've had 300lbs. Get out!' The Lightning had probably used 300lbs of fuel in the time it took to join, make contact and break, but it was an interesting diversion.

The move of 74 to the Far East had been part of a planned modernisation of assets in that arena and 74 had replaced 64 Squadron's Javelins. In January 1969 Tengah welcomed another Lightning Squadron, No.11, from RAF Leuchars. They had been planned to move out permanently to Tengah to replace 60 Squadron but the Wilson government had in the interim announced that UK forces would leave the Far East by the end of 1971. As a result, 11 Squadron came out for a month only on what was called Exercise Piscator. Nevertheless, we all enjoyed their time at Tengah and one advantage of the detachment was that they left us an extra airframe to replace the one lost when Pete Thompson crashed.

Obviously we all tried to get along with other squadrons and units but one outfit who seemed to enjoy making life difficult for us whenever our paths crossed was RAF Changi Movements Squadron. We used to joke that they were fully paid-up members of the Unipart shop – 'The answer's no, now what's the question?!' I was flying an aircraft one night in late February doing supersonic intercepts in the South China Sea area and when I returned I was informed that there had been complaints from Changi that I had 'dropped a boom' and caused some broken windows on that station. Examination of the radar tape showed that I had been about thirty-five miles off Changi at the time a hard turn had created what is called a 'superboom' when the shockwave travels further on the outside of a turn. I was apologetic until we learned that the windows broken were those of the air-conditioned offices of none other than RAF Changi Air Movements: I was then a minor hero instead!

February also saw a change of squadron commander for us. Ken Goodwin, who had led the Squadron since 1966 in his own inimitable fashion, had come to the end of his tour and was to be replaced, but a problem developed when his replacement withdrew from the conversion course at Coltishall. The decision was made that our A Flight Commander, Sqn Ldr Peter Carter, was to take over the squadron *pro tem*. For most squadrons an acting squadron commander could have been promulgated without any special event, but 74 had been presented with the Malan Sword in memory of one of the squadron's most famous commanders, Sqn Ldr Adolph (Sailor) Malan, who had joined 74 as his first squadron in December 1936 and then commanded it in August 1940 at the height of the Battle of Britain. He led the Biggin Hill Wing, which included 74, from March 1941 and in 1943 commanded RAF Biggin Hill itself. Indeed, 74 was the only squadron on which Sailor Malan served. In 1966 the Malan Memorial Sword was presented to 74 by no fewer than twenty-eight former squadron members in his memory, to be carried by OC 74 Squadron on parade and to be permanently displayed on the squadron. Accordingly, a parade was held in February at which Wg Cdr Ken Goodwin handed over command of the squadron – and the Malan Sword – to Sqn Ldr Peter Carter. This was also my first appearance as the squadron standard bearer, carrying the standard on which 74 Squadron's Battle Honours are displayed and which had been presented by HRH Princess Margaret in 1965.

In 1969 the US Navy was still coming into Singapore for R&R and in February the carrier *USS Coral Sea* arrived from its station in the Gulf of Tonkin operating in the war with North Vietnam. The 45,000ton ship was the first US carrier to be fitted with PLAT (Pilot Landing Aid Television), designed to give a videotape of every landing, and when we were invited on board the aircrew of one particular F-4 Phantom squadron used it to show us what their operations were like. The tape was played in the squadron 'ready room' and showed the recovery to the deck of many aircraft returning from a raid on North Vietnam. The film was taken from a cat's eye in the centre of the deck and as one aircraft landed and rolled over the lens as it 'trapped' the arrestor wire, another was already visible some three miles out on the approach. Suddenly we were all aware that the next approaching aircraft had suffered damage: its left-hand underwing tank was missing and sky was visible through a hole in the left wing. On impact with the deck, although the hook caught a wire, the left main undercarriage leg failed outward, immediately followed by the nose and right legs, and the aircraft came to a halt on its belly. We watched in amazement as the aircrew remained in their seats with the canopies closed, while a large bulldozer appeared stage left and pushed the whole aircraft straight off the side of the deck! As the aircraft hit the sea, the aircrew escaped the wreck and were picked up by the 'planeguard' helicopter, while recovery of the remaining aircraft continued without a break. As was pointed out to us, recovering aircraft at one per minute didn't allow for any delays, or the man at the back would probably run out of fuel in a serviceable aircraft and another would be lost. Hard rules though.

On 18 March 1969 after I had been on the squadron almost exactly a year, proof came that a moment's lack of concentration was all it took to claim another life. This time it was the commanding officer of 75 Squadron RAAF from Butterworth near Penang, Wg Cdr Ted Myers, who crashed into the Malacca Straits while carrying out night intercepts. His body was never found. But, on a lighter note I finally got to have my name painted on the nose of one of our Lightnings, by which time most of our aircraft had also received a coat of black paint on the fin. Brightly coloured aircraft had been the norm in RAF Fighter Command, and 74 Squadron had adopted a black fin and spine on its aircraft for some years. Unfortunately, in 1963 56 Squadron had gone 'over the top' by painting their Lightning fins with a red and white chequerboard pattern and the C-in-C of Fighter Command had directed that all aircraft were to revert to bare metal finish. But Fighter Command had ceased to exist in April 1968 and we obtained FEAF's permission to 'go black' once more. The high temperatures of the tropics meant that it was not sensible to paint the spine black, as under it were housed the recorder camera and the highly volatile AVPIN starting system, so just the fin was painted a gloss black once more. 'My' aircraft, XR773 'F' Foxtrot, emerged in late May from a long stay in the hangar undergoing one of the many modification programmes suffered by the Lightning and I carried out its acceptance air test on 29 May: I was pleased to sign back in from the trip with the aircraft fully serviceable. Another first for me came in early June when I went to fly with C Flight of 20 Squadron. This was formed when 209

Squadron disbanded at RAF Seletar and four of their Scottish Aviation Single Pioneer aircraft were given to 20 Squadron to use for forward air controlling (FAC), which had come into its own during the Vietnam War. A couple of Hunter pilots would transfer to 20 Squadron C Flight for a month or so and I got four trips in this amazing aircraft, capable of flight at 18mph and of landing and taking off in ridiculously short distances on jungle strips. As one of the Hunter pilots said: 'I don't bother with a map when I'm in the Pioneer, I just go down and read the road signs!'

9

GETTING AROUND

THE FIRST TIME THAT RAF Lightnings visited Australia was in June 1969 when a detachment of 74 Squadron left Tengah for Darwin and Exercise Townhouse. For the Lightnings it was a four-hour trip with a Victor tanker, but for me it was over six hours in the back of a C-130 Hercules, as I had been selected to be in charge of the squadron advance party. My arrival was less than welcoming as after landing we all had to remain seated in our paratroop seats while an Australian health official came along the cargo hold spraying some form of insecticide everywhere including (perhaps especially) into our faces! Then we faced Australian Customs. 'What's this?' said the official, examining the rations we had brought out for the pilots' coffee bar. I showed him the 'slab' of evaporated milk, which was what we put in coffee and tea in those days, which had come from Australia and was unopened. 'You can't bring that into Australia' was his statement and he would not budge, so it went into 'bond' and one month later we took it back, still unopened, to Singapore! I had gone out one week before the aircraft arrived and found the most basic accommodation I had seen since officer training at South Cerney. Our sleeping accommodation was to be in dormitory huts close by the officers' mess which as a metal-framed building on stilts was itself unlike any mess I had seen previously, for the RAAF element of Darwin's international airport was a bare base, activated only for exercises: aircraft would fly in from elsewhere in Australia and beyond. Working accommodation was even sparser, being a runway controller's caravan, some tin sheds and a length of taxiway for the aircraft. There was nowhere under cover and I asked if any would be provided elsewhere on the base. 'No chance!' was the reply, everything was to be done in the open air. 'But what if it rains in the middle of say, an engine change?' I asked. 'This is Darwin in the Dry (season), mate, if it rains before September it'll be a world record!' Of course it didn't rain and the greatest problem was the heat of the sun slightly melting the surface of the taxiway leaving one of our aircraft threatening to sink through the tarmac! There was also a detachment of Vulcans from the UK for the exercise and a squadron leader had been sent out as their advance party. He and I quickly made friends and also got to know the 76 Squadron RAAF guys who had come up from Williamtown in New South Wales with their Mirages. Inevitably much of the socialising took place in the mess bar and here I first met the quaint Aussie custom of serving beer through a nozzle similar to a petrol pump. The usual glass size was a 7oz glass (or thimble as we two 'poms' immediately christened them), though hardened drinkers were occasionally seen drinking from 'schooners' of around 13oz. My Vulcan compatriot immediately asked the barman if they kept any pint glasses and he delved into the recesses of the bar cupboards before emerging with two dusty pint tankards which were ceremonially washed and served full to us. This caused much mirth amongst the Aussies, as they were convinced that we would be drinking our beer warm (they said the reason they drank small glasses from the nozzle was that it was the only way to get cold beer), but we matched their drinking rate with our pints one for one and after about three or four of these they admitted that our beer wasn't getting very warm at all!

It was also in the mess that I met an Australian air traffic control officer who had just arrived on posting from RAAF Williamtown, 1,700 miles away in a straight line and 2,400 miles by road! As was quite common, he had placed an advert in the New South Wales papers stating that he would be driving this route and was willing to take anyone who wished to share the journey (and the fuel). A man had rung him up and they eventually came to an agreement, but when he arrived at the meeting point some days later he found to his surprise that his passenger was a very attractive young woman, whose father had wished to vet the person who would drive his daughter to Darwin. Unsurprisingly, by the time they had reached Darwin they were well acquainted and were 'an item', so it came as a slight surprise to be invited to join them that evening to go out to a local pub and restaurant at Fannie Bay, just up the coast. What surprised me even more was that when we arrived at the pub and sat at a table outside, the guy got the two of us a drink and then sauntered off to spend the entire evening standing at the bar chatting with some mates. He was not a little angry to eventually return to find that he now had an ex-girlfriend who was now leaving with me for the caravan she was sharing with another girl just behind the beach. She and I got on very well and I continued to see her throughout my time in Darwin.

Exercise Townhouse was quite an eye-opener for me. Before the exercise got going the RAAF base commander appeared on local TV to warn the people of Darwin that they could expect supersonic booms during the exercise because, as he put it, 'We're trying to defend Darwin and need the freedom to do so realistically.' There was also no minimum height limit on our flying and more than once I took my Lightning virtually down Smith Street, the main road in the city, while chasing some attacking aircraft. Our Lightnings and the 76 Squadron Mirages were the defenders and faced the Vulcans, the Canberras of 2 Squadron RAAF, 14 Squadron RNZAF and some 81 Squadron RAF aircraft from Tengah, all of which flew out of RAAF Tindal for the duration. I asked someone familiar with Tindal what it was like and received the answer (to be spoken in an Aussie accent), 'Well, mate, if Darwin's the arsehole of the continent then Tindal's 150 miles up it!' I got the picture. Tindal was another bare base some 150 miles southeast of Darwin and there was almost nothing in between, which meant that low flying could really be low flying: it was not unusual to pick up a low-flying attacking Canberra from the dust trail he was leaving behind him. Another good example of realism in this exercise was that the likelihood of a missile kill had been estimated and when one of us called a 'kill' in to the radar site at '2 CARU', the controller would reach for a pack of cards. If the chance of a high-level missile kill by a Lightning was believed to be, say, 55%, then fifty-five of the cards showed 'success' and forty-five 'fail'; several of us fired more than one missile to get a successful 'kill', a touch of realism not often seen. The flying was certainly different to that I had experienced up to now and a good example of this was the manoeuvre adopted by an Australian Canberra being chased across the airfield at Darwin as a BOAC Boeing 707 took off, for the civilian movements continued throughout the exercise. Behind the

Darwin - Exercise Townhouse 1969

Canberra came a Mirage and also me in my Lightning, each of us trying to get a missile kill on the Canberra. The Canberra overtook the Boeing and then turned across in front of its nose, obscuring our sight of the 'target'. The 707 did not find this amusing and registered a complaint on the radio but didn't get much sympathy from the RAAF ATC controller, who simply said, 'There's an exercise in progress and you were asked if you wanted to delay your departure because of the raid inbound. You refused to delay!' It wasn't all work and no play, however, and one day Darwin laid on a Dakota of the RAAF to take those of us unfamiliar with the Northern Territory down to Katherine, just to the northwest of Tindal, from where we were taken on a trip down Katherine Gorge where the river has cut down through the sandstone to leave deep gorges. We were shown engravings in the stone carved by early aborigines so long ago that they were now out of reach above our heads, as over time the river had continued to cut away at the rock. A fascinating day out culminated in a stop for lunch in Katherine town. In those days the main street resembled that seen in a cowboy western, almost down to the dust balls blowing down the road, and the general store had a sign placed at the entrance: 'All person (sic) entering this establishment must be dressed and behave.'

After the exercise was complete and we had returned to Tengah we went through a period when the aircraft were fitted with their overwing ferry tanks (fitted periodically to aircraft in rotation in order to prove the workings of the system). This increased the overall fuel capacity of the Lightning F.6 to 15,000lbs and we enjoyed the ability to go further than usual as we flew some high/low navigation exercises up to the Malaysia/Thailand border at height and then descending to 250ft over the jungle for the return all the way back to Tengah. The jungle canopy does not exactly abound with easily identifiable features, being in the main a green carpet, so accurate flying and timing was essential if we were to follow the planned route: it made for some demanding flying for those of us out of practice at that game, though as all pilots do, we rapidly picked up the techniques once again. Then in August I renewed my association with the RAAF as I went up to Butterworth on my first 'Tiger Rag' detachment, when one flight of 74 Squadron detached to Butterworth and one of 75 Squadron flew down to Tengah to operate alongside the other squadron for a fortnight. We had quickly formed a close working and social relationship with the Australian squadrons based at Butterworth. 75 Squadron had been operating on its own for a while after the last RAAF F-86 Sabres had returned to Australia at the end of 1968 but now they were being joined by 3 Squadron with more Mirages; meanwhile the embryonic Royal Malaysian Air Force (RMAF) were sold (or given) the remaining F-86s. Ever since 75 Squadron had been at Butterworth the Mirage had been flown in a bare metal finish except for national and squadron markings, but 3 Squadron had a ground attack role and their aircraft flew up from Australia in a dark matt green finish. The RMAF decided that this was obviously the colour *du jour* and asked that the F-86s be painted green too. The answer was in the negative, although the story sounds better if told (in an Aussie accent again) along the lines of 'You got them for nothing and never said any thanks, so paint 'em yourself!' On my arrival at Butterworth I was met by a RAAF pilot almost helpless with laughter, who insisted on driving me to one of the open-ended alert sheds in which there was a green RMAF Sabre, literally all over green. The ill-trained person who had been given a spray gun and instructed to paint it had covered the fuselage, the wheels, the undercarriage oleo struts, up the jet pipe and even over the cockpit canopy; it was truly a green Sabre (and a write-off).

Flying out of Butterworth was a pleasant change for, unlike the UK where there are many airfields to operate from, in Singapore there was only Tengah and Changi for us. However, my first flight from there was somewhat more exciting than I would have wished: in the midst of a sortie of practice interceptions the main air turbine, which powered the aircraft electrical supplies, failed, leaving me with only battery power, generally assumed to give about twenty minutes of essential power. I raced back to Butterworth, only to then experience a failure of my braking parachute on landing. Looking back now they were minor problems but the unreliability of the aircraft and its systems was the Lightning's main weakness, and emergencies of this nature would become quite common during my time on the aircraft. However, regardless of the various problems there was plenty to enjoy, such as when Dave Carden came to the end of his tour and chose as one of his last trips to carry out an intercept sortie on an aircraft flying at 2.0M, twice the speed of sound, with the fighter flying at the same speed. I flew the target aircraft. Tactically, to engage a target flying at 2.0M with a Lightning carrying the Red Top missile, which could fire from head on (as opposed to the limitation of the earlier Firestreak missile which could only fire from astern the target), the fighter could fly relatively slowly (at normal cruising speed of around 0.9M, or 500mph), but on this occasion we had a closing speed of Mach 4, around 3,000mph. It was breathtaking to watch the vapour trail of the fighter approaching me and then passing down one side in an instant.

RAF fighter squadrons have always maintained scrapbooks, or squadron diaries. 74's was a work of art and since the squadron took the Lightning had included some highly artistic diarists such as Vaughan Radford, Heinz Frick and particularly 'Jim' Jewell. Now came another change, as 'Jim' left on posting back to Coltishall and I was 'handed the pen'. My initial servings were woeful but I enjoyed the task and grew to like doing the diary. I was to remain the diarist for the rest of 74's time in service in the Far East and continued to look after all the books throughout the thirteen years while the squadron was out of service, before eventually handing them over in 1984 as 74 reformed at RAF Wattisham. Even that was not the end, however, for, after its final disbandment at RAF Valley, I once again took the diaries for safekeeping and did so until 2016, which must rate as one of the longest periods any one person has held such memorabilia. They are now held by the Squadron Association and brought to all reunions for everyone to peruse.

Living in the Far East opened up many opportunities for leave travel and it was nice to escape the constant high humidity of Singapore where the climate hardly changes throughout the year. I particularly enjoyed visiting Hong Kong during the winter months between October and March, when evening temperatures there were cool enough for a jacket but it remained warm during the day. I paid many visits there, staying in the RAF Kai Tak officers' mess which overlooked the joint military/civil airfield with its famous approach. Making an approach to land on the southeasterly runway (RW13) necessitated an approach around Lan Tau Island where Chek Lap Kok Airport is now, and the close proximity of mainland China – then all prohibited airspace of course – meant that the majority of the approach was flown heading almost east until 'Checker Boards'. This was a small hill marked with a huge orange and white checkerboard and was used as a visual reference point on the final approach until the runway centreline was approached, when the pilot had to make a 47° visual right turn to line up with the runway and land. At the turn the aircraft would be just 2nm from touchdown and at a height of about 650ft, rolling out at about 200ft lined up with the runway. Hong Kong had a large expat community and I made several friends there, including David Baker, then a captain with Cathay Pacific Airways, who became a close friend. Dave managed the amazing feat of sixty-four years of flying before he 'handed back his goggles', beating my forty-seven years hands down.

Most of my trips to Hong Kong were made as what were termed indulgence flights. We could submit applications for such leave flights through the RAF network, either opting for pot luck as the destination, which could then be anywhere, or stating a particular place. Visiting family in the UK was a popular choice and so these flights were almost always oversubscribed. However, there was another way to achieve a UK visit and that was to apply to be a courier. When classified or sensitive documents or equipment were to be flown back to the UK a commissioned officer was always appointed to be responsible for the items. There might be drawbacks to acting as a courier between Singapore and the UK, for it could be on a Britannia or even a C-130 and be very slow, but the big advantage was that having done so we were guaranteed a duty flight back out at the end of leave, a big plus as indulgence flights back out from the UK to Singapore were rare and one always ran the risk of not getting such a flight before leave expired. The only option then was a full fare on a civil flight – very expensive. One event on a flight between Changi and Kai Tak sticks in my mind. I was on board a C-130 Hercules of 48 Squadron and was sitting in the hold when the air quartermaster told me the captain had suggested I go quickly up to the flight deck. Looking ahead out of the cockpit I saw the amazing sight of tens of contrails crossing from right to left as a raid of USAF B-52 bombers headed to bomb Vietnam. It reminded me forcefully of similar photos of mass bombing raids en route to Germany in WWII.

Toward the end of 1969 I was selected to become an instrument rating examiner (IRE) and so I learned how to fly the Lightning T.5 trainer from the right-hand seat, where the pilot flew the aircraft with the left hand and operated the throttles (and all radar controls) with the right. This involved a couple of trips to get used to it as it was a bit daunting at first, demanding total concentration as nothing seemed natural anymore, but then it clicked and (almost) everything was fine. I tried tanking once from the right-hand seat but as there was always a qualified Lightning pilot in the left-hand seat, I left it to them, as I always feared reverting without thinking. If I had needed to reduce power and descend, and instead finished up climbing and going forward, tragedy lay waiting.

As we entered December 1969 I prepared to take a month's leave in the UK before reporting back to RAF Coltishall as a member of 47 IRE Course. My temporary farewell on my last trip was a reminder of the Lightning's problems of the time when I had my first of several airborne fire warnings. Luckily I was not too far from base and landed safely, but on inspection it was found that the lower engine bay had suffered severe damage from burning fuel.

10

MIDWAY

EVERY ALL-WEATHER PILOT MUST be confident to fly the aircraft with no visual references, known as being under instrument meteorological conditions (IMC) and what is more, in fighter aircraft a pilot must be capable of leading a wingman down to a safe landing from an instrument approach in poor weather. The wingman simply flies formation on his leader, never looking inside his own cockpit and quite literally trusting his leader with his life. Everyone is tested annually by an IRE qualified on type, and in order to become one I joined Mike Wraight and Keith Jackson to form 47 IRE Course at 226 OCU RAF Coltishall from 12-27 January 1970. Ground school came first, as it always does on courses. We had to understand the aircraft instrumentation in great depth, along with the errors to which the various instruments are prone as an aircraft is manoeuvred. We had to know the complexities of the air traffic system and, needless to say, we had to know the different types of instrument approach the Lightning could carry out and be able to fly each to a great degree of accuracy. The later marks of Lightning had a complex master reference gyro (MRG) developed initially for use in the Skybolt guided missile which the UK considered for the V-Force but eventually discarded. This MRG was virtually impossible to topple and so the days of erroneous instrument indications following periods of harsh manoeuvring had gone. Aircraft had been lost in the past after going into cloud suddenly with instruments that were haywire after, say, doing aerobatics, but the Lightning pilot could have total faith in his instruments. However, the IRE Course required us to know this MRG in great detail, so much that on the course we joked that we could build one with our eyes closed! Although the Lightning was well known for its extremely rapid reaction times it was equally well known for being short of fuel even when full. One wag once said that the Lightning scrambled in a heartbeat, went like greased weasel s**t but ran out of fuel at the airfield boundary! At the time I did the IRE Course there was still a requirement to examine a pilot's instrument flying both subsonic and supersonic and because the aircraft had such a short endurance the IRT had to be flown over two sorties so that is what our final two trips of the course were: a full IRT flown from the right-hand seat and including some fault analysis of 'errors' made by the IRE in the left seat.

I returned to Tengah with my new qualification and looked to find which pilot would be the first to need a renewal of his instrument rating. I was relieved to find that it was another flying officer like me, but my relief was short-lived when the Boss announced that he would be my first rating. Difficulties started at the Ops Desk, as he put himself into the authorisation sheets as the aircraft captain and I had to point out that the IRE is always the captain of the aircraft on tests, so things were a little frosty from the off. We strapped in and flew the first sortie, planning to remain in the cockpit while the groundcrew carried out a rapid refuel so that we could go again. As we taxied in at the end of the first trip I wrestled with my conscience as I had not been impressed and eventually I plucked up the courage to suggest that we called this sortie a practice. There was a stony silence as we vacated the aircraft and walked in, and I had to put all my new-found fault analysis skills to use to make him accept my decision. In the end it was worth it, for he later flew an excellent IRT and I never had another problem with any other squadron pilot querying my IRE decisions.

In early 1970 the rundown of UK forces in the Far East began to hit home hard with the disbandment at Tengah in January of 81 Squadron, followed the next month by both 20 and 45. Before they left we held what turned out to be a very memorable dining-in night, started by a 'Beating of the Retreat', by the pipes and drums of the Ghurkas in Singapore. As was standard, the meal passed off normally (no high jinks at the table), but afterwards in the anteroom things started to develop. One of the tricks we often did was to build a tower of bar stools under one of the ceiling fans, starting from being seated on one and being handed the next to fit on top and so on until just below ceiling height. The idea was then to slowly sit up and use one's head to press on the boss of the fan, slowing it down until it stopped. It was not as easy as it sounds but many achieved it. That evening, one of the RAF Regiment officers of 63 Squadron decided that he was going to do the same thing but very impressively. He built the tower without incident but had not noticed that someone had cranked up the fan speed to maximum, much faster than usual. Then, instead of slowly raising his head onto the fan boss, he quickly sat up straight and collected a fan blade directly into his forehead! Being a 'rock ape' it didn't appear to hurt and there wasn't too much blood! Later on, one of the 20 Squadron pilots decided to bring his MGA sports car into the anteroom and drive it round. This went without incident until the Station Commander decided that he had seen enough and told 'Wharty' to leave. Neal drove at the doors but wasn't as accurate as he had been on entry and one door was completely smashed, with wood and glass all over the floor. This did not go down well with the senior officers and an ultimatum was issued: if a door replacement could be produced (and be a perfect match) and in place by breakfast time, no disciplinary action would be taken. It was now one o'clock on a Saturday morning. Had it happened in the UK there would have been no chance of carrying this off but in Singapore almost anything was possible and a visit to 'Hong's garage' and some very hard work from them produced a new door soon after 7am, witnessed by Chris Strong (OC 20 Squadron), 'Wharty' and OC Flying, Erik Bennett! Mind you, the varnish was still wet!

A joint disbandment parade for 20 and 45 Squadrons took place just before dusk on 18 February with a flypast of six aircraft of each type and two days later many of us went across to Changi Creek, the unofficial 'departure lounge' for those leaving for the UK. In those halcyon days before luggage and personal scanning, departing passengers simply were called forward to get onto a coach directly from the bar and go from there to the aircraft steps. It was quite an emotional farewell, with a lone piper playing as the coach left for the VC10, and Tengah was a lot quieter from that date onward. Only two months later Andy Bailey from 20 Squadron was to die in a Hunter crash while carrying out the Fighter Reconnaissance Course at Chivenor and John Duckworth was killed fifteen months later at low level in Wales while a QFI on the Hunter at Valley. Yet another piece of bad news reached us in mid-March when we heard that Tony Doidge, who had been on 74 when I joined but who had left in August 1968 for a further Lightning tour on 11 Squadron at RAF Leuchars, had been killed following an ejection over the North Sea at night.

The 'Tiger Rag' detachments to Butterworth did, however, provide good times. During the Vietnam War, Australian Army, Navy and Air Force personnel fought in Vietnam and although no fighter aircraft were deployed, many RAAF fighter pilots were sent to carry out detachments as forward air controllers (FACs) with American forces. These FACs generally operated airborne, flying either the single-engined O-1 Bird Dog (a light Cessna) or the twin-engine O-2 (the Cessna 337 with its unusual power arrangement of one engine driving a conventional propeller on the nose and another 'pushing' behind the cabin between twin tail booms). Spotting enemy troops on the ground from a high performance jet is always very difficult and indeed often impossible, especially over jungle, so the slow-speed Cessnas acted as the fighters' eyes and called in fighter attacks when deemed necessary. In 1970 the US forces used Penang for R&R, and transport aircraft would often fly into Butterworth to pick up and drop off some of these US troops. It was on one of our detachments to Butterworth that I was returning to the officers' mess at the end of the working day and driving the VW crew bus when I stopped to give a couple of USAF aircrew a lift. I expected simply to take them to the main gate where they would pick up a taxi to take them to the ferry across to Penang, but when they learned that Butterworth had two RAAF fighter squadrons, one told me that his life had been saved by an Australian FAC who was usually on fighters. This USAF pilot had been shot down during an attack but had ejected successfully and hidden in the jungle hoping to be rescued. The FAC above him had established radio communication with him but the Vietcong (VC) were searching for him and were getting closer. Knowing the downed pilot's exact position, the FAC called in more fighters to attack the VC, but a rescue helicopter was not immediately available and the Australian FAC spent three hours keeping the attacks going to prevent the pilot from being captured, much of the time under fire from the enemy as well. In the end a helicopter arrived and the FAC talked it into position for a successful rescue. As I listened to this story

I realised that I had heard it before from one of Butterworth's pilots so instead of dropping the two Americans at the main gate I took them to the mess and there we found the Australian who had been the FAC: the party went on very late that night!

The periodic detachments to the Far East by the Victor tankers continued throughout our time there and we always did some tanking by night during their stay. There had been little enhancement made to the external markings and lighting as the Victor B.1 (Bomber) was modified to become the K.1 (Tanker – don't ask why it was 'K', although 'T' is reserved for trainers) other than painting of reference lines on the wing undersurface and so on, but improved lighting was not high on the agenda and the drogues themselves had only small 'beta' lights around the basket rim. After a few enthusiastic 'prods' by fighters most of these would have failed, so there was certainly a degree of luck involved in making contact at night. On one particularly dark night Neil Davidson and I were on a night tanking detail and were both 'plugged in' in cloud so all I had as reference was the underside of the tanker wing. Then suddenly the formation came out of the cloud and as the top surface of the cloud layer slowly fell away beneath us I had the strong feeling that the Victor had pulled up into a very steep climb, almost into the vertical as my 'ground' fell away out of sight below. Although I was sure this had not happened the disorientation was immensely strong and persisted until the tanker gave us permission to break contact and back off, when the night sky and my instruments could confirm that no night aerobatics had been attempted! When we got back on the ground, Neil confirmed that he had experienced exactly the same feeling – not at all pleasant!

Back at Tengah the squadron experienced the first of four events that would severely test morale. On 6 April one of our aircraft caught fire on the line, caused by venting fuel flowing over the port wing from a sticking vent valve during the starting sequence. After starting the Lightning F.6 about 150lbs of fuel was used from the wing tanks after which the pump in the large ventral tank would start to transfer its fuel into the wings and thence into the engines. On XS928 that morning on the top surface of the wing root just behind the cockpit, the vent valve had not fully closed and fuel ran down the top of the wing and onto the hot number two engine starter exhaust, where it ignited. I was in the Briefing Room preparing for a sortie and looked out to see the entire top of the left wing covered in flame and this was the middle aircraft in a line of five. By the time I got downstairs the entire aircraft was enveloped in flames, with just the jet pipes and fin visible, and flames up to twice the height of the fin. Everyone available ran out to the line and started to manhandle the adjacent aircraft away, not the easiest of tasks as the Lightning was no lightweight, but this allowed space for the emergency crews to attempt to extinguish the flames. It took a fair while to achieve this and by the time they succeeded XS928 was a sorry sight. Fuel vapour at the top of the ventral tank had exploded leaving four large holes along the ventral and visible ripples along the fuselage, wings and fin. The undercarriage doors had melted, such was the fire's ferocity and dripping aluminium had pitted the concrete of the dispersal. Paul Adams had been the pilot and had vacated the cockpit over the windscreen and down the side of the nose, fortunately suffering only a twisted ankle. The deliberations which followed this near catastrophic event were to have serious consequences, but in order to preclude any repeat of 6 April, it was decided that all Lightnings were to start with the Flight Refuel Switch set to Flight Refuel, thereby ensuring that all fuel tanks remained depressurised and the ventral pump could not run until the switch was returned to normal, which we then did after take-off.[*]

It was also in April that a new pilot joined 74, when John Webster arrived as a first tourist from the OCU at Coltishall. He was planned to be the final pilot to be posted out to us and would get eighteen months before we left Singapore as part of the withdrawal. He was working through his operational work-up when I flew a night sortie with him on 26 May, doing low-level interceptions over the Malacca Straits. We had carried out several intercepts, alternating as fighter and target as usual when on one run as fighter I rolled out behind John who should have been flying at 1,000ft. On the Lightning it was always difficult to detect aircraft at low level and the target was often too low to maintain radio contact with the GCI site at Bukit Gombak, although on this attack I had the odd radar paint of the target as he tracked toward the Malaysian coast. Eventually GCI advised John that the Malaysian coast was seven miles ahead but he

---

[*]   Because of the shortage of Lightnings, the aircraft was taken apart and flown back to the UK in a Belfast transport, there to be rebuilt. In the event, XS928 was one of the last Lightnings still to be flying at Binbrook as the Lightning went out of service.

did not acknowledge and I repeated the call: there was no response. When I reached the coast and climbed up, GCI now confirmed that there was no trace of him on their radar. John had somehow flown into the water. The weather was not bad and the cloud cover was broken, but it was easy to become disorientated, as had almost certainly been the case when 75 Squadron RAAF had lost their squadron commander early in 1969 doing exactly the same thing. Although I went back over the track looking for a flare in the hope that he had ejected I saw nothing. The subsequent search included flights over the area by a RAAF P-3 Orion with its very new and then quite secret Magnetic Anomaly Detector, more commonly used to detect submarines. This showed a large metallic mass at one point along John's final track but the floor of the Malacca Straits comprises a great depth of thick mud and only a small portion of the aircraft wreckage was picked up. Once again, everyone congregated in the mess bar, drank heavily and then got on with life, my log book recording that I flew two trips, one by day and one by night on the day following John's accident.

Late May 1970 saw the first detachment to the Far East of the newest RAF fighter, the McDonnell Douglas Phantom FGR.2 when 54 Squadron flew out to Tengah from their base at RAF Coningsby. The first two pairs flew the entire way non-stop in just over fourteen hours, flying unaccompanied at high speed in between rendezvous for a refuel by the ever-helpful Victor tankers, and could do so because this versatile aircraft could carry three external fuel tanks, upping the total fuel load to 22,500lbs, well in excess of the Lightning. It could also fly supersonically with these tanks, whereas ours were simply for ferry only and were limited to 475kts. 54 was there to take part in Exercise Bersatu Padu, designed to reassure the Far East nations that Britain could still defend them if necessary. This was the largest exercise we saw in Singapore and involved not only the Phantoms and Victors, but six Vulcans from 44 Squadron as well as a detachment of 58 Squadron Canberras from the UK. It was also the last time that 14 Squadron RNZAF deployed their Canberras from Ohakea in North Island, New Zealand, as they were to disband soon afterward. There was also a sizeable naval presence for this exercise as well, including the Australian carrier *HMAS Melbourne* with its A-4 Skyhawks and we enjoyed a lot of trade over the month's flying. Early in the exercise, however, I very nearly came to grief when I flew a sortie defending the naval forces well up the east coast of Malaysia. The plan was that a tanker would be stationed overland and available for us to take on fuel whenever required, so when I was advised of a fast low-flying target approaching from the north I chased it down and claimed a kill on the Skyhawk before climbing up, and once high enough I contacted the GCI at Bukit Gombak for vectors to the tanker. Then came the shock 'Sorry, the tanker's been delayed and is not yet airborne from Tengah.' I had pressed on too long on the final intercept and now could not make Singapore with my remaining fuel. The RMAF base at Kuantan, 150 miles north of Singapore on the east Malaysian coast, was feasible but it had only 6,000ft of runway, short for the Lightning, and had no suitable ground facilities. I could not reach Butterworth either so I would have to divert to the international airport at Kuala Lumpur, which would be embarrassing for all concerned, not least because they had no facilities for handling jet fighters. I continued south toward Singapore and asked how long the tanker would be, to be told that he was just getting airborne. This gave me a ray of hope and I pressed on south, convincing myself that the tanker would be there very soon. It was not to be, however, and 'just getting airborne' meant that he was taxiing out! When I eventually learned that the Victor was now airborne I no longer had the fuel to reach Kuala Lumpur – in fact, I no longer had the fuel to reach any airfield in Malaysia. My anxiety was obviously apparent to the Victor who simply asked which hose I would like and encouraged me to fly an intercept on him and he would level out from his climb when I was twenty miles away. I was 'clear astern any hose and clear for contact wet to full'. When I raced up to the Victor and settled astern the centre hose I had just over 400lbs of fuel in total in my tanks, just less than that necessary to fly a circuit and in my haste then fluffed my approach and missed the basket. I knew that realistically I only had one more attempt so I took a little longer and this time the probe went smoothly into the drogue and fuel flowed. When I was full the tanker cleared me to break but instead of passing me the amount of fuel transferred as usual, the call was 'We'll give you the amount transferred in the bar!' I was very grateful indeed to be able to buy them beers later that day as I had taken on appreciably more than the Lightning's tanks would hold!

Although June provided a lot of good flying and fun times, the end of July was to be another bad time. The aircraft was well known for its display take-off, termed a rotation take-off, where the aircraft was kept low after lift-off until the end of the runway when it was pulled sharply into a steep climb. Whilst the early, light, marks could perform a very snappy and impressive rotation, the heavy F.6 could usually only achieve about 3g with the climb attitude checked at about 50°. On the morning of 27 July Frank Whitehouse, an exuberant and popular squadron member, carried out a rotation take-off but what no one had realised was that leaving 'Flight Refuel' selected until after take-off, the procedure we had adopted after Paul Adams' fire in April, had resulted in the aircraft centre of gravity (CG) moving much further aft than usual, and not even the manufacturers at Warton had noted that the CG movement placed it so far aft that it was now at or beyond the aircraft's cleared handling limit. Fate had also had a hand on this day, as Frank had been delayed after starting and the extra fuel burned prior to take-off had exacerbated the problem. The effect on the aircraft handling was that the stick forces were much lighter than usual and so his rotation was startling: as I watched from outside the mess the Lightning appeared to snap to the vertical with its tailpipes only feet from the ground. If I had a camera to hand and the quick reflexes to have taken the photo the result would have certainly rivalled the famous one of George Aird ejecting from an early Lightning and being observed by a tractor driver. Frank's aircraft wallowed upward on 'Rolls-Royce versus gravity' as someone would later put it, fish-tailing as it went, and it was obvious to those of us watching that a crash was inevitable. Frank, however, tried to fly it away for too long and when he eventually ejected he was so late that he had not separated from the ejection seat when he hit the trees and was killed instantly. As if this tragedy wasn't enough, two weeks later Mike Rigg was forced to eject from his aircraft at night when one main undercarriage leg would not lower, though fortunately he was not injured. In the space of four months from 6 April to 12 August 1970 the squadron had lost four aircraft and two pilots, this from a complement of fourteen aircraft and sixteen pilots. It says much that we bounced back and continued to enjoy the time remaining to us in Singapore.

We continued to visit places such as the Tiger Brewery, where many attempted (usually successfully) to drink the 'Boot', a glass boot of over three litres of ice-cold Tiger Beer, to be drunk in one go. We continued to enjoy the nightlife in town, in hotels such as the Singapura, Malaysia and Goodwood and of course, to enjoy ending evenings at Bugis Street. *Carpe Diem!*

Downtown 14 August 1970

Back Row:
Erik Bennett, Chris Strong, Jim Bates, Colin Webster, John Lawes

Centre Row:
Russ Peart, Barney Bullocke, Ian McIvor, Self, 'Johnny' Johnson (BAC), Vernon Small (CSDE), Paul Adams, Dennis Caldwell / Mike Rigg / Pete Carter / Nick Acons / John Rochfort

Front Row:
Nick Buckley, Phil Yates, Roger Munyard, Keven Mace, Chris Peile, Tony Ellender, Tom Minns, Les Elgey

I I

ONE YEAR TO GO

IN THE MIDDLE OF September 1970 I spent a pleasant ten days in Bangkok on leave, at the end of which I joined *HMAS Stuart* for the return trip by sea. *Stuart* was a River Class Australian frigate and was basically similar to the Type 12 ships operated at that time by the Royal Navy. She was in company with a sister ship, *HMAS Parramatta*, and each ship had taken two officers unfamiliar with the sea for familiarisation. Along with me was a RAAF Mirage pilot from Butterworth and we both learned much during the three days sailing back down to *HMS Terror*, the Naval Base in Singapore. One particularly poignant moment was when both ships passed over the spot where *HMS Repulse* and *HMS Prince of Wales* still lie following their sinking by Japanese aircraft in December 1941. The captain ordered the entire ship's company on deck to line the rails and 'piped' a two-minute silence as both ships passed over the war graves.

No sooner was I back from my leave in Thailand than the Boss announced that there would be a detachment of two aircraft to Don Muang Airport outside Bangkok for a display. 'I don't know who else will be going,' was how he announced it, but the eventual decision was that Dennis Caldwell and I would fly the two aircraft up to Bangkok, and the Boss and Roger Pope would fly them back. In addition, a ground support party would travel up by 48 Squadron C-130 Hercules from Changi. The six days were interesting, not least for the arrival at Don Muang Airport where the resident Thai Air Force squadron was now commanded by an officer who had completed staff college in England on the same course as Dennis. He met us as we shut down and insisted that we would now

With Buddhist monks at Bangkok Air Show 1970

'all go for Thai tea', which apparently came out of a whisky bottle, and grasping Dennis' hand he set off. In Thailand it is not unusual for male friends to hold hands and it does not imply anything about their sexuality, but Dennis did not like this at all and as they walked in front of me he was walking as if his left arm no longer belonged to him. My suggestion (as the squadron diarist) that I would just get some photos of our arrival was met with a very firm negative! At the air display the USAF flew in what was then the largest aircraft in the world, the C-5 Galaxy. With its clamshell nose up and twin rear doors open, the cavernous hold was open for all to see – 'longer than the Wright brothers' first flight' as the aircrew were keen to point out – and when the VIP cavalcade came around in a fleet of cars they were simply driven up the ramp and stopped in the centre of the hold, exiting later at the other end!

It was around this time that I met a girl who lived at the British Military Hospital (BMH) in Singapore, working for St John and Red Cross. Her name was Pippa Cratchley and we started going out together, though our relationship was a bit on and off for the remaining time in the Far East. Two days after meeting her I was asked at no notice to go up to Butterworth on a two-week detachment to replace another pilot who was

Top: Tengah Officers' Mess July 1971 Note Wg
Cdr Erik Bennett's Yellow Ferrari 275GTB 4

Left: One week before leaving RAF Tengah 1971

sick and when I came back and rang BMH I got a stony response, as I had promised to call. Not a good start!

All the RAF personnel at Tengah were involved to a greater or lesser degree in the preparations for the fledgling Singapore Armed Forces (SAF) to take over as the RAF left the Far East. I had been the station combat survival and rescue officer for two years by then and in December 1970 we ran an exercise to test the Singaporean preparedness for search and rescue following an aircraft accident. Three intrepid pilots, Wg Cdr Erik Bennett, OC Flying Wing, John Rochfort the station flight safety officer and I were taken out into the Malacca Straits by a British Army tank landing craft from which we climbed into single-man dinghies of the type carried by the Lightning and cast ourselves adrift. At the appointed hour we set off our SARBEs, the personal locator beacons we all carried, and at the Rescue Centre at Changi the supervisor informed the staff that a two-seat Lightning and a SAF Strikemaster had collided and the aircrew had ejected. Some of the SAR organisation was still operated by the RAF and a Shackleton of 205 Squadron rapidly found us and dropped a Lindholme Gear.* We climbed aboard the large dinghy and once we had

---

* The Lindholme Gear was developed at RAF Lindholme by Group Captain Waring during the 1940s to provide a simpler rescue system than the air-dropped lifeboats then in use. The Lindholme Gear dropped to us was three cylinder-shaped containers joined together by lengths of floating rope. The centre container housed a nine-man inflatable dinghy with the other containers housing survival equipment such as emergency rations and clothing. The containers were discarded containers for the tail-units of 500lb and 250lb bombs.

Singapore Harbour 1971

pulled in the ration packs we settled down and awaited rescue. However, we were surprised when fifty yards from us a black 'sail' rose from the sea, followed by the rest of *HMS Orpheus*, a Royal Navy submarine. On the conning tower an officer appeared and bellowed 'Good Morning! Can we be of assistance?' Although we rather fancied the idea of going aboard and leaving the empty dinghies like some *Marie Celeste*, to be found some time later, we told him of the trial, thanked him and let him go on his way! We were 'rescued' by launch soon afterward and the exercise was judged a success, so much so that we set out to repeat it in January 1971, but this time at night. This time there were four of us bobbing around as Lt Tim de Souza of the SAF joined us to see for himself the rescue organisation. By now the SAF had taken over the maritime side of search and rescue, and were operating pinnaces which had earlier belonged to the RAF Marine Branch. It was a good thing that Tim de Souza had come along because although we were picked up quite quickly by the launch, a few minutes later while pulling in our single-seat dinghies a calm descended as the engines died. We thought little of it until all the dinghies were safely aboard and deflated, but it then transpired that no one could re-start the engines and once the crew had radioed back to inform base of the problem they were happy to sit below deck and chat while they waited, despite the protestations of Lieutenant de Souza and ourselves. We were now distinctly worried. Eventually the launch batteries died and we were now drifting in the middle of one of the world's busiest shipping lanes unlit and at night. After a large merchant vessel passed us by about a hundred yards without seeing us yelling and flashing torches, we rigged up a couple of emergency battery-powered 'McMurdo' lights on the mast, and as the coastline of Sumatra drew ever closer we started to prepare to abandon the launch for our dinghies again. After what I remember to be about five to six hours adrift, we were very pleased indeed to be found by a professional crew from the Naval Branch of the SAF and taken in tow back to Singapore. There was a lot still to be learned!

By April 1971 and with only six months to go before the squadron disbandment, our postings began to come through and along with three others from 74 I found that I would be going to become a student at the RAF Central Flying School (CFS) at Little Rissington in Gloucestershire to become a flying instructor. It was not my first choice: indeed, I had been given to expect a posting back to the Lightning OCU at Coltishall helping to run IRE courses and I had no great wish to be a QFI. I argued but to no avail, my

About to depart Tengah – 4 Sep 71

Departure from RAF Gan on 6 Sep 71 – and my last ever Lightning take off

XS897 with Roger Pope between Gan and Akrotiri – 6 Sep 71

posting would stand. And so we began to do things 'for the last time'. Our last Tiger Rag detachment to RAAF Butterworth ended in July during which I managed to get a ride in the two-seat Mirage IIID. On 1 July the half-yearly promotion list commonly known as the 'Feast of the Passover' had brought three promotions: Erik Bennett became a group captain, Peter Carter a wing commander and Robin Hargreaves, another 74 pilot, became a squadron leader. At the beginning of August we also made our final foray up country to spend a long weekend on Pulau Babi Ujong off the east coast of Malaysia. Those times were very special indeed, sleeping on the beach, and now the tourists who go to those islands find 5-star hotels at 5-star prices!

On 25 August 74 Squadron disbanded with a parade and flypast, and from 1 September we started to fly the aircraft out to hand them over to 56 Squadron in Cyprus. First to leave was the Boss, leading a pair to Gan on a four-hour sortie before the following day flying on non-stop to Akrotiri, where 56 Squadron took over the aircraft. He and Paul Adams were followed later the same day by Robin Hargreaves and Russ Peart, while the next day saw Kevin Mace and Mike Rigg depart along the same route. Tengah had received a typically bureaucratic signal from HQ Near East Air Force in Cyprus instructing us that the aircraft were to be devoid of any squadron markings, an order which received the Nelsonian 'blind eye'

Self over Iran en route to RAF Akrotiri – 6 Sep 71

treatment and our groundcrew took great pleasure and pride in ensuring that not only did each pilot fly his named aircraft, but that all aircraft were burnished to a beautiful shine with 74 Squadron markings resplendent.

I was detailed to lead the pair departing Tengah on 4 September and decided that I wanted to say goodbye to Tengah with an extra pass across the airfield on departure. The Victor tanker crews confirmed that there was no shortage of fuel so I asked for this to be approved. My briefing that morning to my wingman, Roger Pope, and to Nigel Holder, who would be the airborne spare as far as the first refuelling bracket over Sumatra, had some important witnesses as my flight commander, Barney Bullocke, was accompanied by none other than Gp Capt Erik Bennett and Tengah's Station Commander, Gp Capt Peter Latham. I remember the words well. After taking off and forming up to the north of the airfield, we would run past Tengah with my aircraft closest to the air traffic control tower, and Roger and Nigel widely spaced in line abreast. We would be at 350kts, as the overwing ferry tanks we were all carrying precluded high speeds. I made no mention of height and there was no response to my request for any questions. We did as I had briefed, but an air traffic controller friend who was on duty that morning later said that the two group captains lost sight of me as I flew so low past the tower that I was below their line of sight. This did not sit well with the station commander and he insisted that I was to be recalled and placed under arrest prior to court martial, but Erik Bennett pointed out to him that as they had both attended the brief and asked no questions, any court martial might rebound! Instead, Erik sent a signal to Gan detailing my punishment, which I read on arrival there. I was to fly on Roger's wing for the last flight I would make in a single-seat Lightning, meaning that I would take my fuel from the left hose instead of the right. I still owe Erik Bennett at least a couple of beers for convincing Peter Latham of that action.

The final leg was northwest from Gan to make landfall over the Iranian coast east of Oman, from where we routed up past Tehran and Lake Van before turning west into Turkey and finally flying southwest past Adana toward Cyprus. I landed at Akrotiri on 6 September 1971 after a final trip of eight hours, thirty-five minutes taking on fuel seven times during the trip and I had fallen short of my target of achieving 1,000 Lightning flying hours, ending up with 925 hours on type. So ended my first (long) tour, spending exactly three and a half years at Royal Air Force Tengah, itself to disappear as an entity less than a fortnight later when the base was handed over to the SAF and renamed Tengah Air Base. Although I didn't then know it, I would re-visit the base nine years later to fly there again.

After arriving back in the UK on a VC10 I now had three weeks' leave before starting the course to become an instructor and I needed a car to get around, after selling my beloved TR3A in Singapore for $600 more than I had paid for it. My tour extension had allowed me to save up some extra cash and so I bought my dream car, a 1963 Aston Martin DB4 Series V Convertible. There were only forty convertibles of this particular model and only twenty were fitted, as was mine, with the more powerful Vantage engine. I paid £1,295 for it and recently I saw the guide price for a similar model put at over £900,000. If only I could have kept it!

12

PATTER, PATTER, PATTER

ESTABLISHED IN 1912, THE Central Flying School of the RAF is the oldest flying training school in the world. When I arrived at Little Rissington in September 1971 258 courses of flying instructors had already passed through and the twenty-seven members of 259 Course included three officers from overseas, one each from Australia, Kenya and Sudan. The course was a notional six months and would teach us to instruct on various fixed-wing types (helicopter instructors were trained at Ternhill in Shropshire). The largest proportion of instructors would fly the RAF's basic jet trainer, the Hunting Jet Provost, while others would learn to instruct on the elementary trainer, the de Havilland Chipmunk, and some on the multi-engined trainer, the Vickers Varsity. Those destined to become advanced flying training instructors on either the Folland Gnat or Hawker Hunter would be selected from within the Jet Provost fraternity after some forty hours of the course. Even though most of us were returning to an aircraft on which we had learned to fly, there was ground school to undergo but at CFS ground school was more than the technical, aircraft knowledge. Aerodynamics, meteorology, navigation, high-speed flight, the list of subjects and the detail into which we went in every one seemed endless. It was late October before I flew my first course trip and after a short conversion to type, an instrument rating and some general handling and navigation, we flew a progress check before settling into the course routine: first a sortie out of the training manual, perhaps effects of controls or stalling. During this the staff instructor would give, or 'patter', the sequence to me while the second trip would be two of us students off together, one acting as the QFI and the other as the student. The third trip reversed the roles of the two students and finally the fourth trip was the giveback, when I pattered the sequence to the staff instructor, so the course went 'give, mutual, mutual, giveback' for each of the lessons flown by real students. After completing eight of the sequences I had flown thirty-three hours on the course and the time had come for those who would become advanced QFIs to be selected. Four places were available and those selected were Mal Grosse, an ex-Hunter pilot from Bahrein in the Gulf, and the three of us from 74 Squadron: Roger Pope, Mike Rigg and myself. But fate once again took a hand when a Gnat from Kemble, where the CFS Gnats were based as Rissington was too short for regular Gnat operations, crashed at Upper Heyford on 13 December 1971 killing both the staff instructor Dave Longden and a student on the course above ours, Dick Storr. The Board of Inquiry found that the fin had separated from the aircraft during a rapid roll and all Gnats were grounded until rectification was completed. As a result, our Gnat flying was delayed until January 1972 and even then, as they returned from repair at Bitteswell the aircraft were given to the Red Arrows for their display work-up and we would cadge rides in the back seat of these practices. Kemble closed at 1600 sharp but Rissington stayed open for an extra hour, so the early part of our Gnat course was often to take off around 1545 in a Red Arrows aircraft and land at Rissie just before 1700. The next morning we would be airborne first thing at 0800 and land at Kemble as they opened at 0900 to give the aircraft back to the team and we would then have to kick our heels until mid-afternoon again.

In the end the Gnat fleet was back to full strength and we went on to complete the course in late May 1972, but not before I had learned a good lesson (which most instructors admit to doing at least once). I was flying a mutual sortie with Roger Pope and it was agreed that we would each fly some aerobatics before heading back to Kemble. After some clearing turns I expected Roger to start his aerobatics but nothing happened and we gently meandered around over Gloucestershire. After what seemed like a good couple of minutes I said something along the lines of 'Come on, Roger, when are you going to start?' only to hear the reply, 'I'm not flying it, you still have control.' In fact, neither of us had been flying the aircraft and we both learned that handing over control in a tandem seat aircraft must be carried out in a definite way so that there is never uncertainty. I never made that mistake again!

13

BACK TO YR FALI

I ARRIVED BACK AT RAF Valley in June 1972 along with another instructor called Ron Pattinson who had just completed a tour as a QFI on the Jet Provost and was now posted to Valley as a Hunter simulator instructor (he had flown Hunters in the Gulf in the late '60s) but Valley was still undergoing runway re-surfacing and the flying training school was operating from Fairford in Gloucestershire so Ron and I had the place to ourselves until the aircraft and aircrew eventually returned in July. Having just been the leader of a Jet Provost formation aerobatic team – the Gemini Pair – at Leeming, Ron was not looking forward to what was intended to be a ground tour but it didn't take him long to get back into the Hunter and he led the Valley display team of four Hunters for the three years from 1973. I joined 2 Squadron of 4 FTS as a brand new B2 QFI. B2, the lowest instructor rating, is 'on probation' and one was expected to ratify one's ability by regrading to B1 – the average category – within six months. All B2s are given students who are of such a standard they probably get through the course despite their instructor and my first student was no exception. Paul Hopkins went on from Valley to fly the Harrier and ended up as Chief Test Pilot on the Eurofighter for British Aerospace at Warton, Lancashire.

At the end of July I managed to get a few days off with the excuse that I was getting married, and on 29 July I married Pippa Cratchley, the girl I had met in Singapore. When she returned to the UK she had gone to live with her parents at their home in Stroud some thirty miles from Little Rissington and this allowed our relationship to progress. Two days before the wedding I parted with the Aston Martin, the proceeds of the sale going into the deposit for a house, and I bought a motorbike to complement Pippa's Fiat 600. I was not, however, permitted time off for a honeymoon and had to be back at work on Tuesday of the following week! There were no married quarters available and so we rented a house a couple of miles away on the road to Trearddur Bay, but this house came with an old lady who needed care and so we didn't stay long, moving into our first house in Valley village, bought for the princely sum of £6,100. The mortgage repayments were £39 a month which I remember as crippling but it was nice to have our own home. Our first child, Stephen, was born in January 1974 but it soon transpired that he had been born with both hips dislocated, known as congenital dislocation of the hip, or CDH, and this required him to go into hospital at the orthopaedic hospital outside Oswestry for long periods. The treatment given to him was started when he was four months old, two months later than should have been the case and included long periods of traction and three operations (one of which proved to be a failure and had to be repeated; even then it was not really successful) and Stephen's problems continue to limit him even now in his forties. We were told to expect that the treatment would take about three years, but Stephen's last operation took place when he was eighteen years old.

It would be fair to say that I didn't find the transition from fighter pilot to instructor an easy one. The patter didn't come easily and the repetitive nature of the sorties, together with the pressure of the course requiring between three and four trips on most days, with the occasional working weekend as well, was quite different from life on a squadron. However, there were occasions which broke up the monotony and one in particular was when we were asked who wanted to go on an exercise in the South of France in November. Volunteers were there many, but the phrase 'if it appears too good to be true, then it probably is' most certainly applied.

An inquiry held in 1971, chaired by Sir Edmund Compton, into allegations of physical brutality by the security forces in Northern Ireland, had found *inter alia* that some actions in regular use in interrogation constituted physical ill-treatment, including posture of the suspect against a wall, hooding, noise, and sleep and diet deprivation. As a result of this report, the use of these methods in the *training* of UK armed forces into their resistance to interrogation methods they could be expected to suffer following capture by an enemy was called into question; eventually their continued use was permitted *only* for those judged to be prone to capture, and RAF aircrew and UK special forces fell into this category. Exercise Quantify, an exercise in escape, evasion and resistance to interrogation, was to be held in France at the end of November 1972 and Valley was asked to provide officers. As I was the Station Combat Survival and Rescue Officer I was a natural selectee and Roy Gamblin, having expressed interest in how he would cope with interrogation, joined me. Bob Eccles and Gavin MacKay made up our team of four and as preparation for the event we, along with other RAF aircrew, went down to Stirling Lines outside Hereford, the home of the SAS, to be briefed and trained. Here we learned how to travel (at night), how to hide (by day), where to go and where to avoid.

One morning we were told the recommended way to cross a river, with the instructor advising us to strip off all clothing before wrapping it up in a cape or groundsheet to make a waterproof package and then floating it across the river before donning the 'dry' clothes and moving on. We (the RAF) considered this to be quite unpleasant and so turned up at the lake used for the demonstration wearing our immersion suits in which we flew during winter when the sea temperature dropped below 10°C. These were dry suits and inside them we would stay dry and relatively warm. The SAS instructor sniffed at us, implying that we were very foolish, but while the Army guys did as they were told we simply walked into the lake. On the other side there was a mobile canteen dispensing hot coffee and as I emerged from the water an extremely cold soldier was clutching a coffee and shivering so badly he was spilling most of it. He watched as I came up the bank and unzipped my suit to display my dry clothing and simply said, 'W-w-where c-c-can I g-g-get one of t-t-those?' We did not, of course, admit that we were never going to wear the suits on the actual exercise, as while they are fine for surviving in water they are no good for walking long distances!

We had been told that the exercise was to be held in the South of France but our notions of the area around Nice were soon corrected as the start was to be in Pau, to the north of the Pyrenees and east of Biarritz, and that we were to be asked to cross the first foothills of the Pyrenees. Being the hardy souls they are, the special forces personnel would parachute in by night but we, on board a C-130 Hercules, were landed at Pau Airfield and set off from there. Although we had been given a 'pass' for the first ten miles or so, we could expect to be evading from then on, and we learned that ranged against us were units of 'Les Paras', the French elite force, the local police and indeed the populace, as there had been announcements on television and in the press about the exercise asking that everyone should be 'en garde' and to report unusual activity 'pour la gloire de la France'.

Pretty soon we came to our first river, which appeared to be in full flood. We had been warned that chokepoints such as bridges were most likely to be guarded but we didn't like the look of the water and instead wormed our way along a ditch until we had a clear view of the bridge. After a good twenty minutes nothing had happened and we agreed to try to cross. Seconds before the first of us moved we saw movement from the opposite ditch and another RAF team of four rose and sprinted across the bridge, attracting no reaction at all, so we followed. At the debrief following the end of the exercise it transpired that all the RAF teams crossed that river by the bridge!

After a night's march through fields and woods we knew that one of the places to avoid was any habitation, as every farm seemed to have a dog and every dog loudly warned its owners of any nearby movement. We made concealed hides for each of us in the woods as dawn approached and spent the entire day successfully hidden from all passers-by, before setting off again for the second night. We knew travelling through a forest was quite perilous, as dry wood snapped as we walked and an ambush could lie around every corner. We therefore split up and walked about twenty yards apart in the hope that if an ambush was sprung we might not all get caught. We also agreed that every so often we would take a five-minute break and on one such break I was sitting with my back to a tree when, without warning, a hand came tightly around my neck and a voice said, 'Speak!' I swore and he said, 'OK, you're English,' and the pressure was relaxed. After establishing that the others were spread ahead in the same manner, the man ordered me to stay a further ten minutes before moving on. I protested and he said, 'I'll tell the others the same thing,' and he was gone. I neither heard him arrive nor leave but it reinforced my admiration for the SAS.

QFIs of 2 Sqn 4FTS Valley – 1973

On aircraft: Roy Barber / Dave Rees / Keith Marshall / Self
On ground: Roger Taite / Roger Pope / Simon Bostock / Rod King / Roy Gamblin
Wally Black / Roger Smith / Steve Gruner

It rained for most of the second night and on the third morning we made a serious error. Despite warnings that buildings were dangerous places in which to hole up, we elected to do so after finding a deserted farm. We spent a few warm and dry hours there, but then we saw a French Army unit of about four approaching the barn. As they threw back the door I ran out of the far end and raced down the muddy track with one of them in pursuit. It became obvious that he was gaining and so I skidded to a halt and swung round to face a young officer. I was semi-crouched, partly to maintain my balance, but he must have thought I was about to attack him and drew his pistol, saying, '*RAF ou SAS?*' My admission made him relax and I walked back to join the others, now all held under the soldiers' weapons. We were marched down to the nearest road, where they radioed for transport and waited for it to arrive. As we did so, we noticed that the soldiers were being very casual, placing their weapons against a wall and lounging around smoking. In undertones we elected to try our luck and on a call we 'jumped' our captors, grabbing all their weapons except the officer's pistol, which he attempted to draw from its holster. As the closest to him, I took the muzzle cap off the gun I was holding, cocked it and held it closely to his face – the look in his eyes told me that it was loaded! Now we had a standoff. We explained that if it had been wartime they would now all be dead and we would be running again, but this was clearly not going to happen and eventually we gave them back their weapons as a truck arrived to take us away. The soldiers on the truck were not as easy-going; our hands were tightly tied behind our backs and we were driven into a nearby village where we were handed to the police station until further transport arrived. This old policeman was most surprised, and this surprise was compounded as he took our identification details. 'Un officier,' he said. 'Deux officiers! Ah, trois, non, quatre officiers!', his voice rising with each identity card. He now found himself holding four English pilots in his cells and was most apologetic. He (and his quite attractive daughter) found us some cheese and bread, and even some wine, so by the time we were taken onward to our interrogation we were quite relaxed!

Interrogation was not fun, however, and was conducted by the Joint Services Interrogation Wing from Ashford in Kent. Initially we were strip searched and left only with our trousers and shirt, and the laces were removed from our boots. This all contrived to make us captives feel demeaned, unable even to walk properly as we shuffled in the loose boots. We were hooded the whole time except when facing an interrogator and most of the time we were kept outside in a cold courtyard, standing motionless in 'stress' positions, one of which was standing an uncomfortable distance from a wall and made to rest on our fingers against the wall, hands and feet splayed. Speakers played 'white' noise similar to a radio off-station and any movement or speech was rewarded with a rifle butt in the kidneys, none too gently. Most of us stood quietly but every now and again one of the captives would shout at his treatment which, of course, simply brought him more of the same. The guards never said a word.

After what seemed to be an age (we all quickly lost all sense of time) we started to face the interrogators, all of whom were wearing what appeared to be Russian Army uniforms. They played the well-known 'bad cop, good cop' routine, where the first interrogator shouted and threatened, not accepting our 'name, rank, number and date of birth' offerings, all that is demanded of a captive by the Geneva Convention. I think one of my interrogations was nothing more than me, still hooded, repeating this information again and again with the interrogator shouting 'Again! Louder!' each time and lighting a match close to my ear to make me do so. Then into the room came another man who berated the first, who he appeared to out-rank, saying that he was being inhumane and cruel. He removed my hood, sent the man out of the room and adopted a friendly tone, inviting me to sit down and proffering cigarettes and tea. When I still did not offer any more information he sounded sad, saying that he couldn't prevent harsh treatment if I didn't cooperate and, sure enough, my next interrogation was 'bad cop' again. Now we 'escapees' had one piece of information we had to try to retain, the coordinates of the final rendezvous of the exercise where, if we reached it, we would be safe. It was this that our interrogators wanted. I don't think any of us gave up that information throughout the forty-eight hours they were permitted to hold us, but at the end of my period I had contracted quite a cough and the staff decided that it was not a good idea to send me back out, so 'for me, the war was over' and I spent a couple of days in the base camp on Pau Airfield before we were all flown home, much the wiser.

Eventually I buckled down to the training routine (or was ground down if I looked at it differently) and I successfully gained my B1 category in April 1973. It would be wrong to imply that life was not fun, for no one flying the Gnat could fail to enjoy the flying and we ranged widely over the UK during the progress of each course. In particular, the later navigation exercises involved landing away, usually at Kinloss or Leuchars in Scotland, with some of the sortie flown at high level, where the jet engine has a reduced fuel burn and therefore enhanced range, before descending to low level in Scotland and flying the second half of the sortie at 250ft above the ground. The return sortie was often interesting as the planned route, starting at low level and culminating in a high-level recovery to Valley, was drawn longer than the Gnat fuel would permit. This required the student to realise, as he carried out his fuel consumption checks during the flight, that the low-level leg could not be completed safely: he had to decide when to pull up and climb to high level if he was to make Valley before his fuel ran out. So many students believed that, as the line on the map went on at low level, so the route must be flown, even though the fuel was showing that they could not make Valley. Many an instructor would arrive back at Valley 'on the gases', having allowed the student to press on just that little bit longer in the hope that he (the student) would make the decision and not have to make it for him, and there was the occasional diversion to airfields other than Valley as fuel had been run too short. However, the staff knew that the fuel consumption of the Gnat at 40,000ft was only 17lbs per minute so we had a little buffer. Many was the time that I arrived back overhead Valley still at 40,000ft or so having just crossed above the airway, and then select idle and airbrake, invert the aircraft and pull down through the vertical, diving very steeply all the way to the break into the circuit to land. One of the other tasks which we found fun was that the small cross-section of the Gnat made it a good aircraft to simulate a missile. In those days the Soviet Tu-16 bomber, known to NATO by the code name of Badger, carried a stand-off missile known as the Kelt and for large-scale NATO naval exercises this combination was simulated by a Vulcan with one or two Gnats in very close formation. The Vulcan would fly a low-level profile over the sea and 'fire' its missiles at the appropriate range. The Gnat would then continue on at very low level before overflying the target ship. Little did I know then that I would be doing this very same type of flying almost forty years later.

I also enjoyed teaching aerobatics and always nudged my student toward entering for the aerobatics trophy at the end of each course. Something must have been working, for on each of the first five courses I saw through Valley my student won that trophy. Occasionally an out of the ordinary task came my way too, like the re-conversion to the Gnat for a Hunter pilot I had known at Tengah who was soon to join Boscombe Down to complete the Empire Test Pilots' Course. I learned a salutary lesson during this time, as he was doing so well that I relaxed until, on a formation descent when the leader signalled for airbrakes my front-seater selected the lever all the way through to undercarriage. In the Gnat, airbrake was achieved by partially lowering the undercarriage, but selection of the undercarriage carried a 250kt restriction, so lowering it at 300kts was an overstress and had to be reported for the aircraft to be checked. Thankfully there was no damage but that was another 'gotcha' to be filed in the capacious 'I learned about flying from that' file.

I was also tasked to convert an ex-Lightning pilot called Stu Pearse, who had been posted in to be the new unit test pilot at Valley and who would have the task of flying all post-rectification and servicing air tests. I was in air traffic control as the duty QFI when Stu took off on his first full air test and as the aircraft passed the tower I heard a bang which I later described as being similar to reheat igniting. The aircraft seemed to stop accelerating away and started to turn right, with the pilot transmitting that he had an engine problem. Very quickly I could see a sink rate developing out over the sea and although he ejected he was outside the seat parameters and was killed, despite the very brave action of a helicopter winchman airborne nearby from the RAF Search and Rescue Training Unit who, seeing Stu in the sea still in his harness, literally jumped out of the helicopter into the water and used his own Mae West to bring them both to the surface.

Instructing on the Gnat was not always easy and night flying was always good for raising the blood pressure. Our relief landing ground was Mona airfield six miles down the A5 where the local area was not built up and so at night it was very dark indeed. Part of the training was to teach how to land the Gnat with no flap following a hydraulic failure when the aircraft had a much higher nose attitude on the final approach to the runway. The view from the back seat was not good at the best of times but at night with little or no light from the airfield surroundings it was often extremely difficult to see the runway once we had rolled out wings level on the final approach and made even harder if in manual (simulating a hydraulic failure) with limited control; every ex-Gnat QFI will remember it well. We seldom got enough practice in these more demanding situations when flying with students, so periodically all QFIs had to spend two weeks flying with the standards squadron instructors whose job it was to ensure we all taught the same, standard, sequences and to give us more practice in the flying of them. After one such spell in February 1974 I was declared ready to upgrade from B1 and flew down to Little Rissington to attempt to re-categorise to A2 with the CFS Examining Wing. This was a day-long grilling on ground subjects and a trip from the Valley syllabus to be taught to the examiner: the exact syllabus number was only given a few hours before flying the sortie. I was delighted – and very relieved – to be told that I had passed the exam and I was now to be classed an above average QFI. I returned to Valley to find that I had also been designated a flight commander on 2 Squadron.

By 1974 we had started to teach some tactical formation in addition to the basic close formation positions. In close formation the leader is the only pilot looking out, as the wingmen concentrate solely on the leader's cockpit and never look away. It is fine for departure from, and recovery to, an airfield and, of course, for display flying, but a close formation is inherently unwieldy and manoeuvres have to be conducted sedately (except where the Red Arrows are concerned!). In a tactical environment the more eyes scouring the sky the better the chance of seeing a threat, and battle formation, as it used to be known, usually started with a pair of aircraft flying with the wingman maintaining a station about 250 yards behind and slightly offset on his leader, roughly 60° swept behind the line abreast. This permits the leader to manoeuvre freely and the wingman to search the sky, particularly below and behind the formation where it is vulnerable. The instructors at Valley came from a great variety of backgrounds, from maritime aircraft such as the Shackleton, from bombers like the Vulcan and Victor and, of course, direct from flying training, creamed off direct from Valley to CFS, so those of us lucky to have completed a fast jet tour on the Hunter or Lightning formulated a plan to teach the basics before progressing to more demanding forms of tactical formation. We could only practise this on Friday afternoons which were, in the main, sacrosanct and reserved for Staff Continuation Training (SCT) but it certainly made the end of the week more palatable than had we practised stalling!

Among its instructor cadre Valley had one Canadian and one American pilot, each on an exchange tour from their own air forces, and in May 1974 we had a visit from some Canadian Air Force pilots based in Germany at Baden Soellingen where they flew the Lockheed F-104 Starfighter. During their visit I was lucky enough to get a ride in their trainer, the Lockheed T-33, an interesting aircraft (aren't they all?) but by then very long in the tooth. Over my time at Valley I instructed on nine courses, but by the time 1975 arrived there was a change afoot in the training of RAF pilots, called the System's Approach to Training. I felt this change to be poorly thought through, as it was based upon the concept that all training could be conducted and assessed in objective terms. Having voiced my opinions I was somewhat surprised to be appointed by Valley's Chief Instructor, Wg Cdr John O'Neill, to be the project officer to bring this into the world of advanced flying training. Off I went to 23 Group HQ at Linton-on-

Ouse in Yorkshire and listened to education specialists who maintained that assessing things objectively on a scale of 1 to 6 was easy. I pointed out that teaching a person to drive a car around a bend as fast as they could go was very different to teaching a Gnat student how to conduct a maximum rate turn. If an expert decided that the maximum speed at which this hypothetical car could take the corner was 80mph then that would equate to level 6. Level 5 could be 70mph and 60mph level 4, the standard to be achieved to pass the course. They nodded, implying 'there, it's easy, isn't it?' But I said, unlike the car, in the air it was important just how the pilot entered the turn (as quickly as possible), the speed at which he gained the ideal speed at the correct 'g' (6g, the maximum permissible) and the level of the aerodynamic buffet that he maintained. All these things went toward a good max rate turn. One of the educational psychologists said that he was still sure that he could teach it objectively so rather unkindly I suggested that he came along in my back seat to experience the event. He did so, although his enthusiasm waned somewhat as the g suit was fitted to him, the Mae West donned and he was strapped into the Gnat back seat. After we took off and climbed away, I gave him five minutes to settle down and then he declared himself ready. Despite warning him to strain against the g suit immediately, he missed everything about the max rate turn from about five seconds into the turn and after twenty minutes of this he declared that perhaps it wasn't quite that easy and '… could we go home now, please?' I eventually produced an objective syllabus for the Gnat course and then requested – and got – a Hunter conversion to do the same for the Hunter, which made my last few months more enjoyable, but I still believe that all instructors assess students, whatever their standard or prior experience, in a subjective way, even though they may apply an 'objective' assessment.

So, in August 1975 I ended my QFI tour on the Gnat and Hunter, although it would not be the last time I experienced either of these training aircraft. I was now to return to the world of air defence but this time it was to be on the Phantom at RAF Coningsby in Lincolnshire.

14

THE MIGHTY PHANTOM

RAF CONINGSBY LIES IN the middle of the Lincolnshire Fens within sight of Boston and its famous church tower the Boston 'Stump', while next door to the airfield is the village of Tattershall whose castle features on the station crest together with the motto 'Loyalty Binds Me'. Opened in 1940 as a bomber station, from February 1941 Coningsby was home to 106 Squadron which for a short time flew the ill-fated Avro Manchester before converting to the famous Lancaster, and the squadron was commanded by Wg Cdr Guy Gibson. In early 1943 Gibson left to form 617 Squadron for the raid on the Ruhr dams in May and following that raid 617 were based here until January 1944, though the squadron retained their officers' mess at the Petwood Hotel at Woodhall Spa. After the war Coningsby operated the Mosquito and later the Washington, the American Boeing B-29, but took the Canberra as its first jet aircraft in 1953, followed two years later by the Vulcan. There is an interesting postscript to the Gibson story for, although he was born in India, his parents separated when he was six and together with his siblings, Alick and Joan, he was brought to Porthleven in Cornwall where I was later to live. Coincidentally it was also to Porthleven that Douglas Bader, who like Gibson had attended St Edward's School in Oxford, brought his wife Thelma on honeymoon. In 1939 Gibson married Evelyn Strike, a family name still very much in evidence in the village to this day. In 1943 when 617 Squadron formed it is possible that Gibson was allowed to choose the squadron coding letters 'AJ' even though they were already allocated to the Station Flight at RAF North Luffenham, but whether because his father had the same initials and was always known as 'AJ' or for his brother and sister, we shall never know. His own aircraft, ED932, was coded AJ-G which are not only his father's full initials but also the initial letters of the three children.

By 1964 Coningsby was starting to prepare for the arrival of the TSR-2, the advanced Tactical Strike and Reconnaissance aircraft cancelled by the Wilson government in April 1965. The subsequent plan for the swing-wing F-111 was also shelved in 1968, a disastrous lack of forward planning by government in general and Roy Jenkins as Minister of Aviation in particular. Jenkins also wanted to cancel Concorde, but the Anglo-French treaty imposed prohibitive financial penalties for doing so, though he did manage to cancel the P.1154, the supersonic V/STOL follow-on to the Harrier and also the HS.681 transport. Eventually the government decided to buy the McDonnell Douglas F-4 Phantom, but even then had to tinker with the order and demand that the aircraft be re-engined with the Rolls-Royce Spey in place of the General Electric J79 powerplant. The pros and cons of this decision have been well exercised elsewhere and I shall spend no more time on it except to say that it caused further delays and problems in introducing the aircraft into service, primarily in the strike and attack role to replace the Canberra. Following the introduction to service of the Jaguar, the Phantom squadrons started to re-role into air defence to replace the Lightning and so it was that in July 1975 I arrived at Coningsby to join 4 (Lightning) Course, a somewhat shortened course for those who had prior air defence experience. There were only five on the course: Gp Capt Davis, due to take command of Leuchars, Wg Cdr Bill Wratten, and Flt Lts Al Wallace (to Leuchars), Pete Hitchcock and myself. Bill Wratten was to command 23 Squadron as it exchanged its Lightnings for the Phantom and was already an experienced Phantom pilot, having been a staff instructor on the Phantom Operational Conversion Unit (228 OCU) on its formation in 1968. Pete Hitchcock and I were also to join 23. The last two-seat air defence aircraft before the Phantom had been the Gloster Javelin and many Javelin navigators had moved across to the F-4, where many were now staff instructors. Although a good bunch, they were older than most of the aircrew I had dealt with before – some said that they dated from when Pontius was a pilot and Mortis was a rigger. There were accusations made that some only flew in the morning and at lunchtime could be found propping up the officers' mess bar (and fruit machine) but they had a wealth of knowledge and experience, some of which must have rubbed off on us students. There were also some ex-Javelin pilots, one of whom was called Arthur Vine, and I later flew with him while I was on the course to become an instrument rating examiner on the Phantom. For reasons long forgotten we were offered some night AAR and this allowed us to complete two course sorties in one trip. However, the weather precluded us returning to base and we were instructed to divert to Kinloss where we landed and put the aircraft to bed for the night before heading for the officers' mess and a well-deserved beer. As we arrived at the mess reception I expected us to take our flying kit, which in those days included the bulky torso harness and our immersion suits, to our rooms but Arthur insisted on heading straight for the bar and on entering asked in a loud voice for the whereabouts of 'Arthur Vine'. An officer told us he was in an adjoining room and who were we and why were we in the bar in full flying kit, to which Arthur replied, 'Just tell him his dad's here, would you?' and we departed to drop off our kit. 'Young' Arthur was a Nimrod pilot, but his dad was a fighter pilot!

Although I had become very familiar with having another person in the aircraft with me a student is very different to a full crew member and all single-seat pilots now had to learn how to work with a navigator. Although the front cockpit of the Phantom had a radar repeater scope I rapidly realised just how valuable another man could be and how much more effective the aircraft was if operated correctly. The Phantom was capable of intercepting aircraft which the Lightning could not even detect on radar and its eight missiles, and sometimes a gun as well, were very advanced after the two outdated missiles carried by its predecessor. Our course lasted just three months before we moved across from the OCU hangar to form 23 Squadron where I and my 'crewed' navigator, Flt Lt Nigel Sudborough, would 'work up' until the following February when the squadron would move to its new base at RAF Wattisham in Suffolk. However, at the formation of 23 Squadron we took on a couple of aircrew from 43 Squadron at Leuchars and so my time with Nigel Sudborough was short-lived and I was crewed up with one of the Leuchars guys, Flt Lt Dave Webb. 'Dweeb' and I got along like a house on fire and thoroughly enjoyed our time together. He was an expert on the black art of fighting a 'jamming' aircraft, one using electronic means to deny the Phantom's radar a normal discrete radar return, so taught me it as well (or a little of it at least!). Together we would work through the combat-ready work-up syllabus, including the whole range of intercepts with targets from 250 to 45,000ft, from targets flying at less than 150kts to high supersonic flight above 1,000mph and qualifying in both day and night AAR on the Victor tankers. However, in December 1975 we got a sharp reminder that having two people in an aircraft did not guarantee safety when a Phantom from 41 Squadron at Coningsby crashed in Cumbria taking two good friends of mine from Singapore days, Brian Jellicoe and 'Chunky' Harrison.

As the new year approached Pippa and I started to contemplate another domestic move, this time from the married quarters at Coningsby down to Wattisham, a station that had operated single-seat Lightnings for a considerable time and consequently had insufficient married quarters to accommodate a large number of aircrew. We bought a house in Onehouse outside Stowmarket, not only for Stephen who was now two, but also for the new baby due in May. In February we all moved down from Lincolnshire to Suffolk and eventually the squadron was declared combat ready: we were now qualified to carry out any AD* task required of us. It also meant that we were qualified to hold QRA** whenever Wattisham was selected to be the southern QRA station. This task was divided between the two remaining Lightning squadrons, 5 and 11 at Binbrook near Grimsby, 29 Squadron's Phantoms at Coningsby and 23 at Wattisham, but scrambles were few and far between for East Anglia so most of the time it was a quiet twenty-four hours in the 'Q' Shed and a good time to catch up on admin. However, one May morning I was called for a different sort of scramble when I took a phone call from home to learn that our second child was on its way. Luckily, I was just coming off QRA and had a twenty-four-hour stand down so I took Pippa into Ipswich hospital where late in the afternoon I had the marvellous experience of being at the birth of our daughter Ellen. There was a dining-in night that evening in the mess at Wattisham but I had cancelled my attendance when I took the morning phone call. Once the birth was over the nurse told me to 'go home and let your wife rest'. I made a swift second phone call to get myself back

---

*   Air Defence

**   Quick Reaction Alert, the maintenance of two aircraft at ten minutes' readiness to scramble

on the dining-in seating plan and ordered a barrel of beer to be put on to celebrate.

Although Wattisham followed the usual air defence routine of one flight of the squadron on 'days' and the other on 'nights', the sensitivities of the Suffolk locals meant that we had to finish night flying by 2300 – very gentlemanly. However, on one night I experienced a heart-stopping moment on a sortie that would never appear in my flying logbook. Wattisham had only a 7,500ft runway, as opposed to the 9,000ft at Coningsby. This meant that when we operated the Phantom with all three external tanks filled we had very little spare runway on take-off and an emergency at a critical moment would be just that – critical. On this particular night I was programmed to take a 'three-bagged' Phantom on a routine intercept sortie with one of the most experienced Phantom navigators, Ian D-J, in my back seat. As usual we discussed the abort speeds should we have a major engine failure or fire during the take-off roll. One of the Phantom shortcomings was that the aircraft brakes were designed for taxiing around a carrier deck and not for stopping the aircraft from high speed, so braking was not a major part of any abort drill and instead the arrestor hook, built into the Phantom for carrier operations, was the main aid to aborting the take-off from high speed. Should the hook fail to engage the cable, a double ejection was almost certainly the next action. We commenced our take-off but at the *'moment critique'*, exactly AT our decision speed of 140kts, the left engine failed catastrophically. To continue the take-off would have meant jettisoning the external tanks in order to fly away safely and so I called 'aborting!' and with both throttles to idle I selected the arrestor hook down and steered the aircraft toward the centre of the barrier, though if we had entered the barrier without any deceleration from the wire I think we might have taken ourselves and the entire barrier down the hill to Bildeston village. Displaying his experience, Ian watched his cockpit mirrors and almost immediately reassured me with the shouted words 'we've got the wire' as he saw the tapes at the runway edge snap out. The deceleration was really abrupt and the aircraft was slowed to a halt in 1,200ft, when the centre dayglo panel of the barrier appeared almost to be touching the aircraft nose. Indeed, we had pulled the cable out to its limits and we were gently pulled rearwards allowing the hook, which I had now selected up, to disengage the wire. As we had

23 Sqn re-form with the Phantom – 1975

not used the brakes we taxied back to the line on the good engine, both fairly well flooded with adrenaline. As we had never left the ground this event was not a flight and could never feature in my flying log book, but it is, perhaps, a good example of the fact that responsibility for the aircraft is not simply when airborne. Civil pilots add ten minutes to actual take-off and landing times to account for this and if service aircrew did the same it would reflect that responsibility.

When military aircrew fly they usually monitor the emergency frequency in order that any aircraft which may have an emergency can be heard and if necessary have assistance rendered. One Friday afternoon at the end of April 1976 I was making my way back toward Wattisham on the final sortie of the day when I heard a 'MAYDAY' call being put out on the distress frequency. Inevitably the adrenaline surge which follows hearing such a call made me pay attention and I heard that there had been a mid-air collision between two Gnats from RAF Valley. I later found out that four friends from Valley days had been killed when they collided in a turn when flying at low level, a reminder that although the number of fatal flying accidents was thankfully decreasing, fast jet flying is very unforgiving of mistakes.

At the beginning of that long hot summer of 1976 our Boss, Bill Wratten, had announced that in August the squadron would be sending two aircraft to the Tactical Flight Meet (TFM) at RAF Leuchars outside St Andrews in

Fife. We then flew a phase of air combat at the end of which he decided that Sqn Ldr Jack Haines and his pilot, our American exchange officer Capt Norman Lowry who was a very popular exchange officer with a great sense of humour, would be one crew and the other would be Dave Webb and me. For just short of ten days we had a great time, flying mostly at low level over Scotland with Harriers, Jaguars, Lightnings, Buccaneers, Canberras and reconnaissance Phantoms to intercept, combat with and (hopefully) shoot down. Some of the engagements were highly demanding and on one occasion we were mixed up with fourteen aircraft all flying at very low level in a bowl in the mountains, trying either to shoot down a target or to avoid being shot down. The whole fighter meet was very enjoyable and successful with no incidents or accidents, and we all learned a lot from the events. Tragically Norman Lowry was to lose his life at the start of his next tour of duty back in the USA during training to become the leader of the USAF aerobatic team, the Thunderbirds, when a failure of his aircraft's control system resulted in a crash in which the whole formation flew into the ground.

The RAF Phantom had no gun fitted internally but could carry the SUU-23 cannon mounted on the centreline pylon. This fearsome weapon fired 20mm rounds at a rate of 6,000 per minute or 100 every second, meaning that there was a round in the air every 10ft. For practice this rate could be reduced to 4,000 rounds per minute and all squadrons used to deploy annually to Luqa in Malta for a gunnery practice camp. In November 1976 we flew out to Malta and were immediately sat down in one of the briefing rooms for the 'Beano' briefs – 'there'll be no high jinks, there'll be none of this and there'll be none of that...' Without doubt one of the reasons for this pre-emptive bollocking was that a Lightning squadron had just left under a cloud for 'marking' the landing of civilian airliners, including a particularly poor (hard) landing by an Air Malta aircraft. As the aircraft taxied past the dispersal, Lightning pilots were lined up with 'score cards' held high, each awarding '*nul points*'. The airline pilots took it in good humour but unfortunately one of the passengers was a close relative of Dom Mintoff, the Maltese Premier at the time, and he complained. We were not to dream of doing such a thing! As is the norm for any squadron detachment's first night, most of us went into Valletta to sample the Maltese Cisk beer and local food before returning happy to bed. Early the next morning I and the two others who shared a room were awoken by the station duty officer who demanded to know which of us had attached a rude note to our door, describing Maltese people in derogatory terms. Whilst we had without doubt consumed a fair amount the night before, the three of us were not stupid enough to attach such a note to our OWN door but no one else would own up. Very quickly the Boss assembled all the aircrew and demanded that the culprit make himself known. The mess staff who had seen the note were very upset and had considered going on strike, so further angering the Maltese government was not a sensible plan. When one of the navigators finally admitted that he was the writer he found himself on the very next flight for home and that was the end of his detachment. From then onward we were all on our very best behaviour.

After this inauspicious start the detachment proceeded well until on 23 November flying was suddenly curtailed and all crews were summoned for a classified briefing. It transpired that Libya was due to receive a delivery of bombers from Russia the next day and these aircraft would be flying across the Mediterranean to the east of Malta. We were to attempt to intercept and photograph each of the seven TU-22s, codenamed 'Blinder', and this we achieved, the first RAF aircraft ever to do so. After landing, all cameras were taken away and only returned once the film had been removed for developing, and we were told that there was to be no discussion whatsoever about the event. When I eventually saw some of our photos in intelligence documents and briefings some years later they still bore high security classification markings.

Although on best behaviour we still enjoyed ourselves when off duty, and Dave Webb and I took a particular fancy to a restaurant on the harbour's edge in Marsaxlokk called The Hunter's Rest which served magnificent snails in garlic. Accompanied by many of the others, we even went there on our last night before flying home, which was probably not a good idea for it meant that we arrived back still smelling strongly of garlic!

So we moved into 1977 and in April I was selected to be one of the crews to go to Valley for missile firing. Having already fired a missile from the Lightning I volunteered to give up the chance of firing another and instead to be the permanent photo chase. This meant that I would be able to watch the firings from close astern which was much more interesting and I got more flying. In fact, on the very first day I flew as photo chase for a Lightning firing a Red Top missile, the same type that I had fired, and then over the next two weeks monitored the firing of our allocation of two AIM-9 Sidewinders and two AIM-7 Sparrows[*]. When we left Valley it was to fly to Wethersfield, as all Wattisham aircraft were now deployed thirty miles down the road for six months while the Wattisham runway was resurfaced. Wethersfield had been an active USAF airfield but was now a bare base retained to receive aircraft flying in from the USA in the event of an increase in tension or worse, the advent of war with the Warsaw Pact. Those of us who had chosen to buy houses north of Wattisham were now faced with a daily commute of thirty-five miles each way, down through Bildeston to Sudbury and on to Wethersfield, but once Dave Webb and I had sold the motorbikes we had used to commute to and from Wattisham and replaced them with cars, it was fairly painless. There was, however, one event which sticks in the memory. Each summer there would be a major air exercise and in 1977 it was called Exercise Highwood. While the flying was planned to use the aircrew in shifts, everyone knew that the culmination of these exercises always simulated a nuclear weapon exchange which necessitated a 'survival scramble', aiming to get every squadron aircraft into the air before the 'missiles' rained down. Somehow the planners got the timing wrong for I was woken at home at about 0300 to hear my flight commander calling 'Survival Scramble, Dave! Survival Scramble!' I tumbled out of bed and into my flying kit at the foot of the stairs, raced to the car and drove across Stowmarket to pick up Dave Webb. Inevitably the traffic lights in the centre of town were showing red but with no traffic at that time of night I eased across and raced on my way. Within a minute I realised I had a 'tail' who was sporting a flashing blue light but I continued to Dave's house. As Dave came out in his own flying kit the policeman arrived and said, 'OK, where's the fire?' to which we responded that nuclear war was imminent! He looked us up and down and then said, 'Well, not even a drunk would wear that sort of clobber – on your way,' and we rattled off. Within fifty minutes we were jumping into a Phantom and ten minutes later we went back over Stowmarket passing 20,000ft at 450kts.

---

[*]   Air Interception Missile – also known as air-to-air missiles

That scramble turned out to be my last sortie on 23 Squadron, for after some leave I was to return to Coningsby and join the instructional staff of 228 OCU. Yet another domestic move was made easier by the fact that we sold our house in Onehouse within twenty-four hours of putting a sign in the front window and bought one in Lodge Road in Tattershall, once again within 500 yards of Tattershall Castle.

Despite having enjoyed 23 Squadron enormously I also enjoyed being back on the OCU, this time on the staff. I flew my first staff work-up trip on 19 July and with the work-up completed, flew with a student on 1 August. Pilots joining the course flew three dual sorties before going solo with a staff navigator in the back (the staff navigators certainly earned their pay on some of those trips) and once the conversion phase was over each individual exercise in the radar phase was normally flown as a pair with the student crew split, student pilot/staff navigator and staff pilot/ student navigator, so much of my flying was still in the front seat. Rear seat flying in the Phantom was certainly not as difficult as it had been in the Gnat although some approaches (flapless at night springs to mind) still got the adrenaline flowing. All carrier aircraft must be able to absorb huge rates of descent at touchdown and the Phantom's main gear legs had

23 Sqn En route to Malta Nov 1976

oleos almost one metre long, so providing you got the aircraft pointing at the correct spot you could simply wait for the impact and the aircraft DID NOT bounce.

Now and then we also got some non-instructional tasks. Indeed, while 228 OCU existed to train crews for the Phantom, its *alter ego* was 64 Squadron, which was declared to NATO as a combat-ready squadron of ten aircraft and for every exercise we operated exactly as that, a fully functional frontline air defence squadron. Moreover, in every exercise and Taceval, 64 Squadron always got the highest of assessments.

In September after an aircraft generation exercise at Coningsby I flew as part of a four-ship formation to attack Leuchars as part of an exercise there. After the 'raid' we climbed back up to height over the Firth of Forth only to be told that Coningsby was now 'out in fog' and we were to divert to Leeming. We landed there and taxied in to park on the pan directly in front of air traffic control. What we didn't know was that Leeming's station commander had his office on the ground floor of the air traffic building looking directly out over the pan, where we were refuelling and preparing the aircraft for the trip home to Coningsby. The Phantom had the facility whereby the braking parachute could be refitted into its housing in the tail in what was known as 'the US Marine Corps repack'. This involved taking the parachute outer bag off before attaching the main shackle to the aircraft and simply stuffing the 'chute in until only the small drogue 'chute was left. This was closed up around its spring, pushed into the recess and the door pulled down and locked. I never knew this method to fail and on this morning, standing on the bonnet of the 'chute recovery Land Rover that had just brought our used tail 'chutes from the end of the runway, I had just completed the repack when I heard, 'Just what do you think you're doing?' and turned round to find myself facing Gp Capt Peter Vangucci, Leeming's station commander and an officer who I knew had been a pilot with 74 Squadron in its early days with the Lightning. I tried to explain that the Phantom was not like the Lightning, where trying to repack the tail 'chute without professional packing in the parachute bay was almost certainly doomed to failure, but he would not hear of it. I was being totally unprofessional and he would be phoning my station commander at Coningsby forthwith. 'What's more,' he said, 'I shall not authorise you to fly that aircraft in such a state.' I thought that to mention that, being a self-authorising OCU staff member, I wasn't about to ask him to authorise the flight was probably not a good ploy and 'PVG' stormed off to make the phone call. Exactly what was said in the exchange between himself and Coningsby's CO, a man with the nickname of 'Doctor Death', I shall never know, but I authorised my own sortie and flew back to Coningsby once the fog had cleared!

Many enjoyable non-instructional tasks presented chances to do something different and there was nothing more different than the following experience. The Empire Test Pilots School based at Boscombe Down has the motto 'Learn to Test, Test to Learn' and as part of each course to produce a fixed-wing test pilot the school would send a small group of three students to evaluate an unfamiliar type of aircraft. This is called a preview and their task is to approach the aircraft as if they are prospective customers: they must find out what is good and what is bad, what is acceptable and what is not. They then return to Boscombe Down and put their assessment together for the tutors. In 1977 the three students who came to Coningsby, all experienced pilots in their own right, were a lieutenant commander in the United States Navy who was very experienced in carrier fighters, although not the Phantom, a Dutch Air Force captain who had flown F-16s and a Harrier pilot of the RAF. They had ten hours of flying allocated to them and as they could not complete any type of conversion in that short time I was to be their pilot for each of the flights, all made in one of our dual-control Phantoms with me as the captain in the rear seat. For the flights they would each carry a kneepad tape recorder on which they would record their findings for the eventual written report. The short timescale meant that much had to be compressed into each sortie and the three arrived with a pre-prepared set of aims and requirements. Together we discussed them, fitted them into sortie profiles and the majority went without a hitch. However, one of the preview aims was to evaluate AAR and so we booked a slot in the North Sea with one of the RAF Victors from Marham. It would have been logical for this sortie to be flown by the US Navy pilot who was very familiar with the probe and drogue method of refuelling used by both the RAF and USN, whereas the Dutchman had only been exposed to the boom system employed by the USAF, and the Harrier pilot had refuelled only rarely, albeit off RAF tankers. However, two years earlier a Buccaneer aircraft had collided with a Victor tanker resulting in the loss of the Victor and four of its crew, and an edict followed that no pilot was to 'tank' from a Victor without having completed the one-day Marham course to ensure that the procedures were known thoroughly and the receiver pilot could be assumed to be safe. There was no time for our American to do this course so as the RAF Harrier pilot was the only option he and I duly took off one morning to conduct a series of exercises for the preview report. We went first to the tanker on his 'towline' off the Yorkshire coast and after using the centre hose for several 'dry' contacts when no fuel was given the Victor transferred our allocation of 6,000lbs, leaving our Phantom close to full fuel to complete the remainder of the sortie. For our next task we put ourselves at 30,000ft and at 0.9 Mach ready to assess how much back pressure on the control column was required to maintain a turn at 4g. To do this the front seat pilot had an instrument akin to a tuning fork and by placing it in front of the control column the pressure of his hand on the stick could be measured. It was agreed that I would fly the aircraft into this turn and once steady, the front-seater would take control to carry out the measurement. However, one of the vagaries of the Phantom now became apparent. The fuel tanks in the fuselage were divided into cells, with No.1 just behind the rear cockpit and the last, No.7 tank, just forward of the fin. On all but two aircraft, the fuel fed from No.7 tank only when the fuel state had reached a critically low level and so in general this cell was isolated by pulling the 'A' and 'F' buttons in the starboard wheelwell. However, the delivery pressure of fuel from a tanker, particularly when using the centre hose capable of transferring fuel at 5,000lbs per minute, was sufficient to overcome the valves and we found that No.7 tank had been filled. This placed the aircraft's centre of gravity well aft and I rapidly became aware of this through the lightness of the stick (No.7 tank fuel was not gauged) and at 4g the aircraft was on a knife-edge, close to pitching up. I told the front-seater of the problem and suggested that we looked at a different speed or g, but he was adamant that this would be an excellent example of a Phantom handling problem (of which there were many waiting to catch the unwary or inexperienced pilot). He assured me that he could cope with this and so I handed control to him and released the stick, although I cupped my hands behind the control column, but *not firmly enough*! Without any warning the stick moved rapidly aft and the aircraft nose pitched quickly up to about 40° before a massive nose slice in both roll and yaw took place through the inverted and back to upright. Although it was the first time (and the last) that I experienced a spin in the Phantom it didn't take much to recognise it and as I grabbed the stick again and planted it firmly in the centre the thought that flitted through my mind was that the 30,000ft entry altitude would give me a fair time to recover before reaching 15,000ft when the rules said to abandon the aircraft if still spinning. I was also aware of falsetto swearing from the front-seater: his kneepad tape recorder had flown into the top of the canopy and beaten itself to death, dispensing batteries as it went. He was nevertheless receptive enough to act on my instruction to cancel the reheats and NOT to employ the last-ditch recovery option of streaming the braking parachute. During conversion to type all OCU students had seen the famous USAF film on spinning the F-4 and sat mesmerised as the commentator intoned the words 'there is no known recovery from the flat spin' over film from both internal and external cameras of a Phantom descending in a flat spin with the brake 'chute (an extra-large anti-spin 'chute fitted for the trial) deployed vertically above the doomed aircraft and having absolutely no effect whatsoever. The crew eventually ejected and the aircraft reduced itself to its component parts in the desert. I had no intention of doing this and since we were not in a flat spin (the nose was pitching up and down with each rotation) I went on with the recovery technique: as soon as I applied in-spin aileron the aircraft rotation slowed and the nose fell to hold a steep dive. We recovered to level flight at around 18,000ft and I set heading for base. On the way back the ETPS student became quite unhappy when I said that I would be telling the engineers and my superiors what had happened. He felt that we could just say nothing and 'keep quiet' but I knew the aircraft should be checked for a possible overstress. Furthermore, although I was cleared to self-authorise my own flights when conducting OCU syllabus sorties, the unusual nature of the ETPS preview required authorisation by OC 228 OCU, a wing commander. When I told him what had occurred he simply confirmed that use of the brake 'chute had not been required and said, 'Well done. On Friday's ground training you, as the most current pilot in Phantom spinning, can tell us all what it was like!' The final piece of humour was that the ETPS student no doubt thought that his falsetto

DANCING THE SKIES

swearing at the spin entry had not been recorded as his own recorder had stopped but he had forgotten that the Phantom had its own cockpit voice recorder which had worked throughout and the other two students used it to produce the final report. At the end of their time at Coningsby they kindly put on some beer in the crewroom and the replay of this voice recorder tape provided considerable fun for all but one ex-Harrier pilot!

It was fairly common for OCU staff instructors who were familiar with flying from the rear seat to hold the additional qualification of IRE* and I had completed the course soon after joining the unit. Each pilot had to carry out his rating test annually and one day I was programmed to fly an IRT with none other than Coningsby's station commander, 'Doctor Death'. We set off with me in the back seat expecting nothing unusual as the group captain had been one of the initial batch of OCU instructors in 1968 and was very experienced on the aircraft. However, part of the rating involved steep turns while supersonic and as we decelerated after completing these the left engine decided that it had had quite enough for today and flamed out. There appeared to be no good reason for this and the drill at the time was that 'no good reason' meant that the engine was not to be relit so we returned to Coningsby on one engine, but instead of positioning the aircraft for a straight-in approach, as was the norm for a single-engine landing, the station commander joined the circuit on the downwind leg. At this point he then insisted that I, as the aircraft captain, should take control for the landing. As we turned off the runway he said, 'I bet that was your first real single-engine circuit and landing in the F-4, wasn't it?' I admitted that it had been so and he replied, 'I've done quite a few, so I thought it would be good for you to do one!'

Many of the pilots coming through the OCU at that time were straight off the Lightning as more air defence Phantom squadrons were forming. It was fun to show these pilots just how much of an advantage they would have once they mastered the Phantom even though many were adamant that they wanted to remain 'single-seat'. It was important to remind them that the fuel capacity of the Phantom in its usual two external tank fit was roughly 18,000lbs and almost double the fuel available to a Lightning pilot at take-off, so as fuel was no longer the most critical item reheat could

---

*   Instrument Rating Examiner

now be used freely. The other big change came when they started to use the radar and I well remember climbing away after take-off toward the North Sea with an ex-Lightning pilot in the front seat. 'Oh look,' I said, 'the radar has locked automatically to a target,' and then cycled through the ranges until we could see a contact at a range of 180 miles, probably an airliner coming out of Amsterdam (the Lightning could not select a range scale greater than sixty nautical miles and would not pick up an airliner at ranges much in excess of thirty). 'Blimey,' said the front-seater, 'we've got time for a cup of tea before doing the intercept!'

One of the extracurricular advantages of being an OCU pilot was that we could apply to join the Battle of Britain Memorial Flight (BBMF) and I did so at the earliest opportunity. To fly the Spitfire and Hurricane had always been a dream and I was over the moon when told that I had been selected to join for the 1978 season. Before flying either of the fighters we practised in the rear seat of the Chipmunk held by BBMF. When flown from the back seat of the Chipmunk the view ahead was not dissimilar to that from the 'baby' Spitfires, the Mark IIa, the V and also the Hurricane, and we were trained to fly the curved approach necessary for maintaining vision when landing in those aircraft. There was also a requirement to fly Boscombe Down's Harvard which was much more representative of the power of the small Merlins. Now came a problem: the Harvard was unserviceable and stubbornly refused to become ready to fly. Time dragged on and by mid-February when I went off to Valley on another missile practice camp to fire a Sparrow missile I still had not achieved this milestone. In the event it proved unnecessary. We landed back from Valley and were met by Horace, the crew coach driver known to all Phantom aircrew of those days, and he informed me that the station commander wanted to see me as soon as I got into the squadron. I couldn't think what I had done to incur the man's displeasure but when I walked in he had my boss, Wg Cdr John Allison, standing with him. 'What do you mean by this, Roome?' was the station commander's opening line and then as I searched my mind for an answer he went on to say, '... getting promoted to squadron leader?' I was to be promoted and posted with only a month's notice to the Examining Wing of Central Flying School as Officer Commanding Advanced Squadron. Once I had gathered my wits my response was 'Oh, s**t, what about BBMF?' and behind the station commander I saw John Allison's eyes light up. He had wanted to join BBMF himself but had been told that being OC 228 OCU was a full-time job. Now that I was posted there was a vacancy which had to be filled quickly, John Allison managed to get 'Doctor Death' to re-think and he flew with the BBMF that summer, the first of many historic aircraft he later flew in his auspicious flying career. The position couldn't have gone to a nicer man who I would have the great privilege of working for in later appointments.

15

THE TRAPPERS

IT WAS USUAL ON the first day of the multi-engine refresher course on the Jetstream at RAF Leeming for the instructor to go around the new students and ask about their flying experience and how long it had been since they last flew. 'I flew two tours on Hercules and have just completed a ground tour at High Wycombe' was a typical answer but I set the cat amongst the pigeons by saying, 'Air defence fighters and I last flew the Phantom last Friday.' My new post required me to be an examiner (called a 'trapper' by all Service pilots) on those aircraft used for advanced flying training. The fast jet element of Gnat and Hunter, together with the new Hawk just entering service, was familiar to me but the Jetstream and Dominie multi-engined training aircraft were completely new, as was the way in which they were operated: it was to be a baptism of fire. Flying these aircraft I would now be expected to preface any words on the intercom with 'captain to crew', or 'captain to nav', 'co' or 'eng' if I wished to be specific. Flying was expected to be as smooth as possible and to pay great attention to the comfort of my crew and passengers. I would have to be an expert on such things as scheduled performance and weight and balance, not simply 'fill it to full, kick the tyres, light the fires and last one off's a cissy!' I would *plan* to fly in controlled airspace instead of avoiding it like the plague and I would fly all sorts of strange procedural patterns and procedures instead of running in for a break into the circuit to land. It was very different. In just three weeks I completed the ground school on the Jetstream and flew twenty-five hours, much of it under the patient supervision of the delightful Fred Hambly, before leaving it (for the moment), qualified first pilot by day and night with an instrument rating.

Next stop was Valley toward the end of May – much more familiar territory although the Hawk was another new type to learn. Some very familiar faces remained at Valley, including 'Wally' Black, who had been my squadron commander during my QFI tour, Sqn Ldr Roy Gamblin, about to become OC Standards Squadron and Flt Lts Derek Fitzsimmons and 'PV' Lloyd, all instructors with me on the Gnat three years earlier. The Hawk was not simply a conversion as I had to qualify as both an instructor and examiner, and at the end of July I flew with Sqn Ldr George McIntosh, my predecessor on Examining Wing, to regain my A2 QFI and gain the additional qualification of 'examiner'. It was then back to Leeming and to join Headquarters Central Flying School. This included arrival interviews with the Commandant CFS, Air Cdre Anthony Fraser, a fascinating and very likeable man who had an amazing grasp of languages (more of which later), with Wg Cdr Mick Ryan who commanded Examining Wing and one with Leeming's station commander, still Gp Capt Peter Vangucci, who started the interview with the rather acerbic comment that I would not be 'packing' any more Phantom brake 'chutes during *this* tour! During my interview with the Commandant, Anthony Fraser asked whether we planned to stay in married quarters at Leeming or buy a house in the local area? We had just sold our house at Coningsby which had been our third house in less than seven years of marriage (plus two stints in married quarters) and we were keen to buy, but he advised caution and said that it was by no means certain that CFS would stay long at Leeming, and even that a return to Gloucestershire and Little Rissington, from where CFS had moved to Yorkshire, was possible. We therefore decided to bide our time in quarters and as a result we stayed in married quarters for a tour that lasted over three and a half years while house prices everywhere rose steadily!

We sold our house at Tattershall quite quickly but I still had a period when I lived during the week in the Leeming officers' mess and travelled up and down the A1 at weekends. One Sunday I arrived back late in the evening and popped into the bar for a quick drink before bed. Horrors, the bar was out of beer! It was the time of the brewery strike and there had been no deliveries over the weekend. On Monday morning I went into work and was bemoaning this problem when Sqn Ldr Jim Willis, one of my examiners, offered to try to solve it. He made a phone call and within a couple of hours a very heavily laden estate car drove in through the main gate before delivering several barrels of Theakston beer to the mess. It transpired that Jim had been based at Leeming on the Meteor some years before and had lived in a house at Masham, southwest of Leeming and the home of the Theakston family brewery. Jim and his wife had often acted as babysitters for the Theakston family and the baby they had 'sat' was none other than Paul Theakston, now fully grown and working in the family business. Paul ensured that the mess remained supplied with beer throughout the strike and naturally, the officers developed a considerable loyalty toward Theakston beer in general and Paul in particular. In 1992 Paul broke away from the family business and started his own brewery, still in Masham, and gave it the name of 'Black Sheep' for obvious reasons. I feel duty bound to drink this ale wherever I can find it! Thank you, Paul.

At the end of August, the monthly summary of flying in my logbook showed the variety that would be the norm for the rest of my tour, with hours flown in the Hawk, Jetstream, Jet Provost and another new and unusual type in the Meteor, for I would also qualify on the Meteor and Vampire flown by the Vintage Pair of CFS at Leeming. Advanced Squadron was a small outfit: I had two fast jet experts in Sqn Ldr Bruce McDonald, a highly experienced instructor and examiner who I had known since Lightning days, and Flt Lt Mike Underdown, who had instructed with me at Valley on the Gnat. On the 'heavy' side were Sqn Ldr Jim Willis and Flt Lt Mike Naylor, both very experienced 'truckies' who would teach me a lot about this very different form of flying. As well as being responsible to the Commandant for the standards of flying and flying instruction at the advanced flying training units, I was also to be responsible for the administration of the CFS Agency Scheme. Up until the end of WWII CFS was directly involved in the maintenance of flying standards on all aircraft operated by the armed services but as aircraft became more complex this was no longer feasible and so for each frontline aircraft a 'CFS Agent' was appointed (several for large forces). I was tasked with maintaining good communication with all these agents and to that end we held an annual gathering at Leeming to which all agents were invited. Throughout the year I made a point of visiting as many agents as possible and equally obviously I tried to fly with them all in their aircraft.

During my spell on CFS Examining Wing many overseas air forces requested visits by a team of RAF examiners to assess their own air force pilots. Each visit lasted twelve days in theatre (it was said that the Inland Revenue limited us to fourteen days total or the host air force would be asked to fund our pay) and within a month of joining I was the fast jet examiner for the 1978 visit to the Royal Jordanian Air Force. We had sufficient examiners to cover the basic training aircraft, the transport aircraft and the helicopters but there was a requirement for two fast jet examiners to fly the Northrop F-5 aircraft at two separate bases. I knew just the man to accompany us. I had first known Roy Gamblin as a Hunter pilot at Chivenor in 1967 and he had been an instructor with me on the Gnat, but he had recently completed a two-year exchange tour with the Royal Norwegian Air Force flying the F-5 and so he was co-opted to come with us to carry out the examining task at the base at Mafraq just outside Amman. His Majesty King Hussein, himself a pilot, was very keen to hear our report and planned to fly with one of our examiners during our visit but a visit to Amman by the then American Secretary of State, Cyrus Vance, to review the Camp David Accords meant that HM was otherwise occupied! I spent my time at Prince Hassan Air Base which is situated in the northeast of Jordan, along what was initially the oil pipeline from Mosul in Iraq to the Mediterranean at Haifa. Airstrips had been laid down by the RAF along the pipeline between 1932 and 1934 and were designated H1 to H5. H1 to H3 were within Iraq, H4 just across the border and H5 was now a fully operational airfield though still retaining the old figures 'H5' in pristine white paint inside a stone circle just off the airbase. This was only five years after the Yom Kippur War and the entire air base remained on a high state of alert. The aircraft, always armed, were dispersed in readiness shelters off the end of the runway with no more than 30° to turn to be aligned with the runway, and the air and groundcrew worked from underground bunkers close to the aircraft. All the above-ground buildings were unused, although they retained such displays of vehicle parking, squadron flags and noticeboards. I flew the F-5F for ten days, an excellent light fighter and advanced trainer, carrying out air combat, gunnery and low-level navigation around Jordan. I got on well with the RJAF pilots and two, called Saoud and Saeed, were ever-present to aid and assist.

Toward the end of my short stay I was treated to a special classic Jordanian dish of lamb (or goat) called *mansaf*, seasoned with nuts and spices and served with rice and an accompanying sauce. It was a speciality of the Bedouin who would take the meat dried from stop to stop and then mix it with reconstituted camel or goat's milk as it cooked. Taken outside rather like a barbecue, we all gathered around large stainless-steel platters of about three feet in diameter and piled high with this special dish which smelled wonderfully of cardamom and nuts. Unfortunately, reconstituted milk of whatever kind has a smell, texture and taste highly reminiscent of vomit and they proceeded to cover this lovely meal in masses of the sauce. We then had to eat with our right hands only by forming the food into a ball before popping it into our mouths. As I am naturally left-handed I had a slight problem but the base commander on my right helped me by feeding me with large amounts, covered liberally in the sauce! He then made a speech about this honoured guest and at the end he reached up to the top of the mound and took hold of a sheep's eye, placed on top of the food. Without further ado this was fed directly into my mouth! I never before realised that something about the size of a table tennis ball could rapidly resemble a football and was now much too large to be swallowed without chewing to break it down. For those still following this nightmare I can confirm that aqueous humour is very bitter. I thought hard about England and managed to get this down but the next day when I spoke to Saoud and Saeed I asked why neither of them had been present. Their reason was simple: 'We can't stand that stuff and went to the village for a burger!' At the end of the visit we gathered in Amman at the air force headquarters and gave our report before being treated to a VIP tour when we were flown from Amman in RJAF helicopters to Petra to visit this fabled city and the day culminated in a flight back up to Amman at low level, including flying at almost 1,000ft *below* sea level up the Dead Sea.

Back in the UK following the Jordan visit it was time for me to get back into the Hunter, to renew my A2 instructional (and examining) category and to become a command instrument rating examiner on type as well. In fact, October 1978 was a fairly typical month's flying of just less than thirty hours, split between the Hawk, Hunter and Jetstream, and including almost two hours on the Canberra to experience the peculiarities of asymmetric flight in that aircraft. Similar in layout to the Meteor, there had been many accidents when simulating an engine failure (and there were to be several more before the type was eventually retired). There was also one Hawk flight which gave me considerable pleasure. I had been contacted by Tony Craig, who had been the Senior Engineering Officer on 74 Squadron in Singapore and who had previously completed a tour as a pilot with 23 Squadron on Lightnings. Tony was leaving the RAF and had applied for a post as a company test pilot with British Aerospace at Hawarden outside Chester where the BAe125 business jet was made. The company required Tony to prove his piloting skills and would accept a report of a test sortie with a CFS examiner. I was only too happy to oblige and after around an hour's briefing I put Tony into the front seat of a Hawk, an aircraft he had not flown before and gave him his head whilst he did an hour's general handling. Tony had always been an exceptional pilot so the write-up was easy and he got the job. He was obviously grateful and in 1988 when I was commanding a Phantom squadron at Leuchars he repaid the favour in spades when he took me low flying around Scotland in the de Havilland Mosquito operated by British Aerospace. During that trip we 'bounced' a four-ship formation of Jaguars who must have found it difficult to believe their eyes when they identified a WWII piston-engined fighter turning in on them (though not overtaking, it has to be said!). November brought another new event, a CFS visit to the Italian Air Force. We took a Dominie (the RAF version of the BAe125) with Air Cdre Fraser and five others, initially to Rome for meetings in the Italian Air Force HQ. With only one VHF radio and one UHF box, the Dominie at that time was not blessed with a comprehensive radio fit. The military generally operates on UHF while the civil world uses VHF and only one box in this frequency range made airways flying harder than it should have been. As we crossed from French to Italian airspace the French air traffic control told us to 'advise when two-way with Rome Control on (a different VHF frequency)'. This meant that we had to leave the France Control frequency and dial up the Rome frequency to establish contact. We then had to leave the Rome frequency to tell France that we were now 'working Rome' and for a period we would be unable to hear any instructions passed by Rome. Then a serious problem arose as the selector knobs on our VHF box started to slip so that although a frequency was displayed we were not necessarily *on* that frequency and what was more we couldn't even guarantee to return to the previously selected frequency! Eventually we heard another aircraft transmitting on VHF but his grasp of English was insufficient to understand our problem that we didn't know what frequency we were actually on. His response to our question was, 'Why do you not know what frequency you are transmitting on? Surely it is displayed to you?' and underlaid with the unspoken 'stupid English!' Luckily Anthony Fraser was occupying the right seat on the flight deck and his linguistic abilities proved invaluable. He spoke to the other aircraft in perfect French and outlined our problem to France Control who managed to get Rome Control to operate that frequency as well. Anthony Fraser now switched seamlessly to Italian and so we continued all the way to landing at Practica di Mare Air Base on the Mediterranean coast near Rome. The radio problem was sorted during our stopover there and the next day we flew on down to Lecce Air Base on the heel of Italy where as part of the liaison visit I flew a familiarisation trip in a Macchi 326.

Then in February 1979 I went on the first of many trips to Berlin. The Russians then controlled East German airspace and were always looking for excuses to close the routes to and from Berlin, the three corridors resembling the spokes of a wheel with Berlin as the hub, so regular usage by the Jetstream and Dominie fleets was essential to maintain British rights to go to and from this beleaguered city. Usually the route followed by the Jetstream was from Finningley to Wildenrath or Gütersloh in West Germany, where we would refuel so that we had sufficient fuel to return to West Germany in the event that a landing at Gatow was not possible. In the Dominie we usually flew to Stavanger in Norway for a refuel and then flew down the northern corridor to Gatow. Over my time with Examining Wing I completed no fewer than twelve 'Gatow runs', usually staying the weekend in the officers' mess there. Just to the west of the airfield perimeter was the East German army training area near Krampnitz and on one occasion I landed at Gatow for the weekend in a Dominie just after another similar type and we were parked alongside each other while we refuelled before putting the two aircraft into the hangar for the weekend. A shout from the airman underneath the wing of the other aircraft stopped the refuelling as he had just found a hole in the wing undersurface where a shot had gone through! Obviously a bored and frustrated soldier on the range had vented his spleen on an English aircraft only a few hundred feet above him and let off his gun. Thankfully the round was not an explosive one and the hole was patched up with 'speedtape' for the return on the Monday.

Another unusual event took place one day as we took off from Gatow for the return to the UK. As we turned toward the west we flew over an East German Army parade in progress and below us we could see troops formed up in a five-pointed star. This was too good to miss and so we dropped down a bit and cameras were pointed to get the photo. This must have irritated the Sergeant Major on the ground and the five-pointed star rapidly broke up!

Travelling around the city in those days was free if we wore uniform and this was a requirement if we wished to go into the eastern (Russian) zone. The British, French and American powers did not recognise the East German authorities and we dealt only with Russian soldiers while in the east. Crossing was usually completed at Checkpoint Charlie and we were always submitted to endless photographs and document checks before being cleared to proceed, though always with our 'tail'. The Russian zone was a grim place and it was always sobering to go to Unter den Linden east of the Brandenburg Gate, there to look over the wall to the western sector. How easily we could go back and how difficult, if not impossible, it was for the East Germans who watched us in our smart blue uniforms. Traffic was a fraction of that in West Berlin though the ubiquitous Trabant cars were everywhere, more kit car than normal saloon. Coming back through to the western half of Berlin always brought a sense of relief and a feeling of near normality. Then suddenly in the middle of West Berlin one would see a platoon of Russian soldiers marching in their odd slow march goose-step as they changed the guard at the Russian War Memorial in Tiergarten. It was a strange city.

The same month we went down to Kemble for the annual standardisation of the RAF Aerobatic Team, the Red Arrows. This was to be their last season flying the Gnat as it had now been phased out at Valley and so at the end of the visit I asked Brian Hoskins who was the Red Arrows Team Leader if I could have a final solo Gnat sortie. Brian kindly agreed and I spent half an hour flying around Gloucestershire in that lovely little aircraft. At the time I wrote 'final solo!' in my logbook against the trip but little did I know then that I would be flying the Gnat again from Kemble almost twenty-five years later.

April brought another new experience when I was part of a five-strong CFS Team to visit New Zealand and Australia. We flew to Hong Kong from

Brize Norton on a regular RAF VC10 trooping flight and spent three days there before going on to Auckland by Air New Zealand. Once again Anthony Fraser's language skills were in evidence when he elected to take us all to a Hong Kong Szechuan restaurant for dinner. When we arrived, the staff were not particularly attentive until Anthony Fraser let off a long and loud bollocking in fluent Szechuan. Suddenly the staff were very keen to give these white men excellent service and we enjoyed a very fine meal while Anthony Fraser explained his background to us. He was brought up in Shanghai and suffered internment by the Japanese forces during the war, so he learned most of the Chinese dialects in the camp and that was why we got a good meal.

In New Zealand we started with a visit to RNZAF Whenuapai and then we went down to the air base at Ohakea from where the RNZAF Canberras of 14 Squadron had flown up to visit us at Tengah in the '60s and I was delighted to meet three officers who had been there on the Canberra in those days. I also again met Stu White who had left the Royal Navy to come out to Tengah in 1970 as a civilian to teach the fledgling Singapore Air Force. He had later left Singapore to join the RNZAF and was now a squadron leader at Ohakea flying the Skyhawk. I had flown Stu in the two-seat Lightning on a trip in June 1971 and he now repaid the favour by putting me in the front seat of one of their Skyhawks for an unforgettable low-flying trip around South Island including Mount Cook and the Westland areas around Queenstown, and Doubtful and Milford Sounds. After Ohakea we visited RNZAF Wigram outside Christchurch to fly the CT-4 Airtrainer and then crossed to Australia and RAAF East Sale outside Melbourne where the RAAF Central Flying School was based. This also gave me the chance to fly again in the Maachi 326 which I had flown in Italy, though this time it was with the RAAF Aerobatic Team. We also visited RAAF Point Cook, RAAF Fairbairn near Canberra and eventually flew back to the UK via Hong Kong.

Once I had qualified on all the types that went with my job there were a large number of check rides to be carried out each year (with the difference that it was me that was being checked) as I had to renew my instructional (and examining) category on the Hawk, Hunter, Jetstream, Dominie, Meteor and Vampire. Of course, I was also required to renew my instrument rating (and Command Instrument Rating Examiners' rating) on all these types. Each aircraft displayed idiosyncrasies and it made for demanding sorties of up to two and three-quarter hours.

Bangladesh Air Force FT-5 – Dhaka

The routine of Examining Wing involved annual 'trapping visits' to each flying training unit, and those to the larger stations like Valley, Brawdy and Finningley were very busy fortnights. There were also regular re-categorisations of instructors who wanted to gain their A2 qualification, denoting that they were assessed to be above the average as an instructor. Most of these were carried out at our home base of Leeming where the candidate would fly in and then carry out a sortie selected from the appropriate syllabus before undergoing a period of ground questioning to establish his knowledge of technical (his particular aircraft) and theoretical subjects including aerodynamics, meteorology, air traffic control procedures and, if appropriate to his role, high speed flight. In the main we had a good rapport with the staff of the standards squadrons at the flying training schools who prepared the candidates before presenting them for re-categorisation; after all, if the candidate was not really ready but had a lucky break and passed the tests it was his flying training school which would then have to work with a sub-standard A2.

Examining Wing was invited to Bangladesh in late 1979 and a five-strong team flew out for the standard twelve-day visit, led this time by Wg Cdr Mike French, the new OC Examining Wing and an ex-Hunter and Harrier pilot. Mike and I operated from Dacca and flew both the two-seat Chinese-built version of the MiG-17 called the FT-5 and also the French-built Fouga Magister which the Bangladesh Air Force used as a trainer. One problem for us to fly the FT-5 was that it had all-Chinese instrumentation and switch labelling which necessitated us drawing a diagram of the switch layout and functions for our kneepads. The FT-5 was the only trainer for the Bangladesh fighter, the MiG-21, which meant that a trainer with the performance of a WWII Meteor led to a fighter with the performance of a Lightning and the lack of a viable two-seat trainer for their high-performance fighter had led the Bangladeshis to land the FT-5 at close to the MiG-21 landing speeds. I found that at these high speeds I had to force the aircraft onto the ground and this resulted in a long landing roll. This was unadvisable as the aircraft brakes were supplied from an air bottle that was not rechargeable in the air so that too much braking risked the brakes running out of air at a *moment critique*. No one could tell us the correct approach speeds for the FT-5 so I flew a sortie to establish them (all displayed in kilometres per hour). I carried out stalls in the approach configuration at about 5,000ft, then 2,000 and finally at 1,000ft above the airfield. The aircraft was very docile at the stall and there were no hazards provided that slam throttle movements were avoided, as there were no protection devices on the engine. When I landed I used the speed that I had found to be the stall plus about 15kph and it was much more comfortable. We used that speed for the remainder of the visit and everything was much smoother. During our time at Dacca we were promised a flight each in a MiG-21 but in the event the aircraft were grounded for lack of ejection seat spares and looking at the state of them it was probably a good thing. On the ground the Bangladeshis were extremely hospitable and tried to make our life as comfortable as they could. Convinced that British palates would not be able to cope with Asian highly spiced dishes they served us an approximation of steak and chips for each meal. Eventually Mike French and I sat at a table in their mess dining room and proceeded to eat an entire dish of green chillies placed on the centre of the table, after which we were permitted to eat the same food as the rest of the officers – and very nice it was too.

At the start of 1980 I carried out the first of several trips to Gibraltar in the Dominie, staging via Nice as Spain did not permit any aircraft operating into or out of Gibraltar to overfly Spanish airspace. Gibraltar trips were always pleasant and we were looked after at Nice Airport by British Airways staff who supplied us with the in-flight rations for the next leg of our flight. As they always gave us the BA Club Class meal tray (less the wine) it was a great improvement on RAF in-flight rations. However, it was on one of these trips that I suffered frustration with a capital 'F' and what follows is an abbreviated version of an article I later wrote for our flight safety magazine in which there used to be a regular feature entitled 'I learned about flying from that' where writers would admit to errors made in the air or recount events that had a possible lesson for others. My article was entitled:

I Learned About Frustration From That

It all started with a car journey, as by 1980 all the major types on which I examined were based away from Leeming, so it was another 'O crack sparrows' rise for the six of us to drive down to Finningley. However, we were off to Gibraltar where the aircraft would be displayed as part of the static display for the Battle of

Britain weekend. Everything at Finningley was the usual polished, smooth-running machine that we were familiar with and we were airborne on time for the first leg to Nice. London Military Radar was helpful, it was a lovely day and all was well with the world. Something had to go wrong and it started even before we had joined controlled airspace at Ibsley, to route via the Ortac airway reporting point and onward. 'France has given you a one hour delay at Ortac,' said London Mil. Now, although everyone routing through France was used to being messed around by their air traffic, this was a bit much and definitely worse than the usual 'I cull yew beck'. A Dominie could not hold for an hour over southern England and still make Nice but to go back to Finningley for more fuel was impossible within the hour. The nearest airfield was Boscombe Down and they kindly agreed to us landing, topping up and re-clearing customs outbound, and we made the revised time. We landed at Nice on time, where the flight plan for the Nice to Gibraltar leg had to be re-written on the French equivalent of the 'international' flight plan form, where everything was exactly the same except that the titling of each box was written in French before English.

I remember nothing special about the Nice-Gibraltar leg other than the usual problems of aiming to fly exactly on the international airspace boundary because Spain prohibited us from flying in Spanish airspace if landing at Gibraltar. Although Spanish air traffic talked to us quite happily and kept telling us to call Algiers, if we did so Algiers would insist that we were in Spanish airspace and we should call Seville! Eventually the Rock appeared and the landing there was uneventful. Being Battle of Britain weekend, the airfield was quite full, with four Buccaneers, four Jaguars, two Nimrods, Canberras, Hunters and us. They were all going to carry out a flypast on the Saturday afternoon, while we would salute them with a green bottle from the beach. On arrival there was the usual rush to get the after flight servicing completed on the aircraft, clear customs, organise the duty free to be picked up on the Monday morning and still get to the bar in the officers' mess in time for Friday Happy Hour. As captain I delegated the first to our trusty flight engineer, the second to the cunning but surprisingly honest-looking navigator and the third to one of the passengers and despite all of this we were late for the last!

I shall draw a veil over the events of the next few hours. Suffice it to say that fed, and very well 'watered', we returned to the mess around midnight for a well-needed sleep, but the station duty officer was waiting for me with a surprise. I learned that there was now a Category 'A' compassionate case, a soldier who needed to get back to the UK by the fastest possible means. When a serviceman or woman serving overseas informs their unit that there is a family problem, usually sickness, the case is referred back to MOD for categorisation, and 'A' is the most urgent. On that weekend in Gibraltar there were no civil aircraft leaving until late the next day, so a Service aircraft could be requested and a Dominie was much cheaper than cranking up a Nimrod. I realised that it was 'Hobson's Choice' and after agreeing to do it, subject to getting at least six hours' sleep, I then collected the 'below the belt' extra: his eighteen-month son was going too, as it was the serviceman's wife who was dying in a London hospital.

I had taken out the maximum of six in my aircraft and three of them agreed to stay in Gibraltar (selfless devotion to duty I thought), leaving me with one navigator and a co-pilot who was actually the CFS Helicopter Examiner, along for the experience. When I peered out of my window just before 0700 I thought the condensation was heavy for Gibraltar, but opening the window only improved the visibility to about ten yards in thick fog. Nevertheless my navigator had been on the ball and put the flight plan in before going to bed, and the weather at both my diversions of Tangier and Alicante was fine. We met up with the Army corporal and son, got the aircraft prepared and were ready to start on time just before 0800. Once more, frustration arose when the tower would not grant us clearance without the permission of the senior supervisor, who had promised to be in air traffic thirty minutes before our take-off but had yet to make an appearance. In the end we started, got the airfield information and taxied out, which in Gibraltar requires the main road that crosses the runway to be closed, stopping all vehicular and foot *traffic. At last the appropriate supervisor was located and we were cleared to go. I had to trust that nothing was jumping the lights and barriers for the road traffic as my take-off was completely 'on the dials', but we broke out into dazzling sunlight at 300ft and set course for Nice. Here they had been advised of our urgency, they were most helpful and we were airborne again in forty minutes, this time heading for Northolt. French air traffic also knew that speed was of the essence and handed us to London Control before we had even passed abeam Paris. In turn, London cleared us to proceed direct to Northolt and turned other traffic out of our way. On the ground at Northolt, transport was waiting to whistle our two passengers off to Great Ormond Street and we learned later that he arrived thirty minutes before his wife died and managed to speak to her, so the flight had been well worth it and it was touching just how everything can come together now and again.*

However, it was about to go all pear-shaped for us as I was asked to go to operations to take a phone call. As I left I told the nav to get the turn-round done and file a return flight plan for one hour's time. 'We'll be back in time for tea and medals,' I thought. The phone call was from the duty staff officer at our Command Headquarters at RAF Brampton, demanding to know on whose authority the flight had been made and also to find out what my ETA at Finningley was, as he had got that station to open up especially on a Saturday to accept us. I had completed my overseas SCT and was to go directly to Finningley. I explained that half my crew and all our baggage, including the keys for the car parked at Finningley and even the co-pilot's wallet were all waiting for us at Gibraltar. Getting no joy at all from this 'jobsworth', I now played my ace card and rang my air commodore commandant. Although he sided with me, the delay in obtaining his permission meant that we could not get back to Gibraltar before they closed and what was more I would run out of my crew duty time somewhere around Nice. I considered staying overnight at Northolt and getting off early on the Sunday but that idea failed immediately as they were not opening on Sunday for me at any price. I had only one other option and that was to go to any RAF Master Diversion Airfield, those that were open 24 hours a day, and luckily Leeming, my own base, was one so off we went and I spent Saturday night at home. On the Sunday morning we set off in fine pitch, with the Leeming air traffic controller passing our clearance from London – 'You are clear to join at Ibsley at minute 45...' etc etc – and off we went. As soon as we talked to London however, the bad news started. 'Be aware that your join time is now delayed one hour.' France had done it again and being a Sunday, Boscombe Down was closed, but Brize Norton was open and they accepted us, fuelled us, cleared customs for us and saw us off again, this funny bunch with the muttering pilot whose fingernails were now bitten to the elbow joint. The journey back was old hat but there was still one more body blow to come. We were informed later that the staff at Brampton had docked us for 2 Gibraltar landaways from our annual entitlement of 3.

I certainly learned about frustration with a capital F from that.

March 1980 was my first visit to Oman to fly with the Sultan of Oman's Air Force (SOAF). Here I flew primarily as a multi-engine examiner from the main SOAF base at Seeb and renewed an old friendship with Bob Kirkham who had been with me at South Cerney and who now introduced me to the Britten Norman Defender, the military version of their Islander twin piston. This was a rugged aircraft as I found out almost immediately for we went to operate from a rough strip not far from Seeb called the Hajjar Bowl. The size of the rocks on which we landed and took off was such that it was inadvisable to stop unless on the small concrete hardstanding for fear that a rock would lodge in front of a wheel and act as a chock. Another important lesson was to raise the flaps as soon as possible after landing to avoid them being hit by stones thrown up by the wheels. Bob later also took me around the various landing sites used by the Defender, including up to the Musendam Peninsula and the strip at Khasab on the point of land which juts out into that vital shipping route, the Straits of Hormuz. While at Khasab I transferred to a Bell 205 helicopter for a familiarisation sortie around this area with its very rugged terrain and we followed the coast around toward Ras al Khaimah. Two days later came my conversion to a similarly rugged light utility transport called the Shorts Skyvan as Kerry Drew took me off to the strip at Saiq, 6,000ft up in the mountains of the Jebel Akhdar (green mountain), where we stopped for 'breakfast' with a British Army major. I had heard from friends who had completed a tour with SOAF of the 'Firq/Saiq' run, and I could now see the geography of the land. Firq was, apparently, a strip just outside Nizwa and pronounced 'Ferk'. At 1,600ft above sea level it lay 'in the valley', while Saiq ('Sake') is 4,400ft above it. In the early days the only way to get supplies up to Saiq was by mule train but following the arrival of aircraft such as the Beaver and later the two types I was now flying it could be supplied by air much more quickly. The loaded aircraft would lift off fully laden and climb up to Saiq before quickly offloading and dropping over the edge of the escarpment back for a reload. Those that did this run four times qualified for 'the four Firq/Saiq tie'! After a restorative breakfast Kerry sent me off solo with the words 'If you have an engine failure on take-off don't worry, as once you cross the runway end you go over the cliff and then you will have plenty of time to gain speed!'

For the last three days of this visit to Oman I went down to Thumrait to fly the Hunter T.66 there in dissimilar air combat with Jaguars and Hunters, a little different to the first part of the visit. The rule book governing the fast jet squadrons of SOAF was a very thin one indeed and such niceties as a minimum height for air combat were dispensed with as 'the ground' became the minimum! At the end of one sortie of combat between four Hunters and four Jaguars we all arrived back at Thumrait together and eight aircraft broke into the circuit from heights of around 10 to 15ft. One of the ground crew later said that they needed to dig slit trenches from the hangar to the aircraft parking area in order to avoid getting knocked down by aircraft joining the circuit!

At the end of the visit we went to the SOAF headquarters at Seeb to present our report and here I again met Erik Bennett who had been my OC Flying Wing at the time of my departure from Tengah in 1971 and who had ensured that my punishment for a low-level flypast was not too onerous. He was now Commander SOAF and an air marshal, so I apologised once again. All he said was, 'You owe me a beer!'

This period was another good example of the variety of flying we did on Examining Wing as my next trip in the UK was to renew my Command Instrument Rating Examiner's ticket on the Jetstream and then fly a Dominie down to Kemble from where we carried out the annual standardisation visit to the Red Arrows who were now flying the Hawk. I returned to Leeming in a Meteor, went to and from Berlin in a Jetstream over two days, did a continuation sortie in a Dominie and then a Valley Hawk QFI upgrade to A2, and for the last two days of the month went down to Lyneham to fly in a Lockheed C-130 to familiarise myself with their *modus operandi*. Fascinating and thoroughly rewarding.

Later that year I went on a nostalgic trip as I was the fast jet examiner on Examining Wing's visit to the Singapore Armed Forces, permitting me once again to fly around Singapore almost exactly nine years after flying my Lightning out to Gan and Cyprus. On this visit I was to fly three different types, with the first two being reasonably familiar, the Hawker Hunter and the Northrop F-5F that I had flown in Jordan. The third was the trainer version of the A-4 Skyhawk in use in Singapore and was a very odd aircraft. Instead of a lengthened canopy as is usual in trainer variants, the second cockpit was 'stuck' on behind the front, with each pilot having his own windscreen and canopy. Flying from the rear cockpit gave the impression of sitting on the aircraft spine, as I had to look around (or through) the front cockpit in order to see forward – not an easy task.

Back in the UK it was another first, this time to 'trap' 8 Squadron at Lossiemouth. This squadron flew the venerable Shackleton Mk.2 in the airborne early warning role and this was a real eye-opener for me right from the beginning, as a Shackleton landed at Leeming to take us up to Scotland. I was accompanied by Flt Lt Fred da Costa who had replaced Mike Naylor as one of the multi-engine examiners and we arrived to find the aircraft sitting on one of the dispersals just off the main taxiway with its four Rolls-Royce Griffons gently rumbling and turning the eight contra-rotating propellers. Entry was by means of a ladder and through a fuselage side door similar to that seen in the famous photograph of Guy Gibson and his crew boarding their Lancaster for the 'Dams Raid', and that was unsurprising, given that the Shackleton was a direct descendant of that famous bomber. I was told to go forward and found Sqn Ldr John Elias occupying the right-hand seat and indicating that the vacant left-hand (captain's) seat was for me. I duly strapped in and found that I could now see a great expanse of wing and nose but no ground within about a hundred yards. This, John explained, was the reason for the three lookouts, 'Nose', 'Beam' and 'Tail', who would warn me of any problems as we taxied. In particular, the nose lookout would inform me if I strayed more than three feet from the taxiway centreline when one mainwheel would be approaching the edge. The next interesting point was that the brakes were pneumatic and applied by pulling the appropriate handle within the control column 'spectacles', with every release signalled by a loud hiss. Overdoing the braking would quickly empty the reservoir and necessitate stopping the aircraft for a while to recharge the accumulator. I should therefore control my direction where possible by use of a judicious application of power to either No.1 (the port outer) or No.4 (starboard outer) engine. I kept reminding myself that thirty-five years before, thousands of young pilots had mastered a similar aircraft (and I wasn't going to war) but it was a very steep learning curve. We eventually reached the runway and once lined up with the tailwheel locked we commenced the take-off. As the tail rose and I saw where we were going for the first time I got a distinct thrill from this noisy vibrating, almost living, aircraft. We set a sedate course for Lossiemouth and I started to learn about the Shackleton from John, who had flown an amazing 30,000 flying hours, mostly on Shackletons. I visited 8 Squadron again the following year and my final Shackleton trip was especially memorable in that it culminated in a landing back at Leeming on the short runway of 4,800ft. When I informed air traffic we would be landing they passed the surface wind speed and the engineer made the calculation before passing it to me: the runway ground roll would be 4,000ft. I therefore worked hard to put the aircraft down on the very end of the runway and this proved my undoing. Instead of reaching the touchdown point and holding the big aircraft off until it settled down on all wheels I tried to fly it on and it responded with a series of bounces from oleo to oleo. Eventually these subsided and from the depths of the rear fuselage came the comment, 'There are two sorts of Shackleton pilot: those who have bounced it and those yet to do so; I suspect you've just changed groups!'

Soon after my return to Leeming I joined another overseas visit, this time to Ghana where I was to fly the Fokker F27 Friendship and the F28 Fellowship. The F27 was a turboprop airliner and troop transport 82ft (25m) in length, with a wingspan of 95ft (29m) and capable of carrying up to fifty-six passengers. As was usual I spent the first evening studying the flight manuals and checklists before starting the check rides and here I was aided by the Ghanaian squadron commander who had been trained to be an instructor in the UK at CFS Little Rissington. His instruction gave me a good grounding on the F27 and proved invaluable when I was flight checking a different Ghanaian pilot a week later and our aircraft suffered a real engine failure. The other pilot failed to take any of the necessary

F-28 of Ghanaian Air Force at Accra

actions such as applying power on the live engine, put on no rudder to counteract the yaw and did not even feather the failed engine propeller, so we flew sideways due to the drag and slowed down very quickly for the same reason. On transport aircraft such as these there is an audible warning should the aircraft approach a stall and if this is ignored and the speed reduces further the control column is physically pulled forward in an effort to avoid the stall. I let things develop until both the stall warner and stick push had operated and it became apparent that the left-hand seat occupant had frozen. Luckily Sqn Ldr 'Jock' Gordon, the CFS Helicopter Examiner, was along in the jump seat for the ride and I threw him the checklist while I recovered the aircraft to level flight. We returned to Accra to land safely on the one engine but that pilot did not get his category renewed. Thankfully the remainder of the visit was uneventful, including flying the Presidential F28, a twin jet of similar size with a very luxurious cabin fit and a crack from top to bottom of the co-pilot's windscreen!

One of the minor annoyances of my tour was that only the Meteor and Vampire were based at Leeming and these were types I seldom flew. For the remainder I had to travel either seventy miles to Finningley for the Dominie and Jetstream or 200 miles to Valley for the Hawk, while the Hunter was even further away at Brawdy in the far southwest of Wales. Carrying out periodic continuation training often took place in blocks to ease these journeys and very often I arranged to arrive at Finningley late in the day. I would then take an aircraft away at the end of the afternoon after the usual last landing and bring it back the next day. Then an approach from a friend on the Jaguar OCU at Lossiemouth opened up another option. The Jaguar QWI* course included a visit to industry and I could ease their transport problems by carrying the staff and students from Lossiemouth to BAe Warton in an hour instead of a long rail journey and an overnight hotel stop. On the appropriate date I would take a Jetstream to Lossiemouth, spend the night there and with the course aboard we would leave the following morning at 0800 sharp, landing at Warton just before 0900 for their visit to British Aerospace (which I would join) and later in the day fly on and drop them off at Northolt to continue their industry visits, before flying back to Finningley and getting my continuation training while being useful at the same time.

One of the most interesting overseas visits during this tour was that to the Sri Lankan Air Force, during which I qualified as first pilot on no fewer than five types: the Cessna 337, the twin-engine de Havilland Dove and its stablemate the four-engine Heron, the re-engined Riley Heron and the venerable Douglas DC-3. I should clarify that in order to qualify as first pilot, CFS rules insisted that one must display the ability to start, taxi and take off, operate safely, land and shut down either solo or operating as captain with a co-pilot if the aircraft demanded more than one crew.

As the end of 1981 approached my replacement was nominated, but before I handed over my post I got in a final 'first' when I went down to Honington in Suffolk and flew in a Tornado GR1 with Rob Sargent, making him the first RAF Tornado CFS Agent. In the middle of January 1982 I handed over at the end of a truly remarkable three and a half years, during which I had flown almost 950 hours on no fewer than thirty-nine types and forty-four different marks of aircraft.

Now came my first ground tour after seventeen years of flying.

---

*   Qualified Weapons Instructor

16

TACEVAL AND
STAFF COLLEGE

IT IS SAID THAT trappers have no friends, most certainly not in their particular world, and if I had got rid of all my friends in the flying training world my next job would ensure that I got rid of any remaining ones on the frontline!

I now apologise and issue an abbreviation warning, but it will be short and not repeated! My new home was to be at the headquarters of RAF Strike Command (STC) at High Wycombe, but this was also the HQ of the UK military aviation commitment to NATO and was therefore not only HQ STC but HQ UKAIR and the Tactical Evaluation Team worked on the NATO side for the Commander-in-Chief, or CINCUKAIR. We were a small team of seven squadron leaders under a wing commander, later to be replaced by a Canadian Armed Forces lieutenant colonel. Each of us had a particular speciality and I was Taceval Air Defence (AD).

Every RAF strike command station in the UK was required to be assessed on their preparedness for war and we planned to visit each station annually. To meet the standards set down by the Supreme Commander in Europe (SACEUR) who was a 4-star US general, all stations had to be able to generate 70% of their assets and personnel within twenty-four hours with no prior warning and this became known as the Part One Taceval or readiness phase. 'Generation' meant to prepare and arm their aircraft with the ready-use weapons needed for war, and to have a minimum of 70% of their personnel physically present on base within the stipulated time. Our Taceval team would be augmented by a select few and we would often arrive in the early hours of a morning at the station main gate. Our specialists would attempt to ensure that no word of warning reached station personnel by sanitising the main guardroom and this allowed the team members to disperse themselves to all the major squadrons and units around the site before the alert sounded and everyone started to generate assets while we monitored actions and noted the results for the report. Aircraft would be towed out and prepared for war, including a full armament load and all the station manpower would report for duty as quickly as possible. This phase was usually terminated once 70% of the requirement had been achieved and we would return to High Wycombe. Occasionally we would arrive on base during the working day and we would have to resort to subterfuge to remain undetected. For example, we arrived at Marham mid-morning one year where I was to monitor the Canberra squadron. For some reason unknown there was a delay in the signal announcing the start of the Taceval and so I found myself walking into 100 Squadron in normal service uniform (but with my Taceval armband secreted in my pocket) and was met by a squadron member who, understandably, asked my reasons for being there. 'Oh, I was passing and thought I would pop in and see Dave Ward,' I said, Dave having been on my early training courses. Dave was called and said that he would be with me in a couple of minutes and I should, meanwhile, have a coffee in the crewroom. As he walked downstairs, Dave was trying to remember what job I was currently doing and he remembered just as he walked into the crewroom. 'Aren't you on the Taceval...?' was partly drowned out by the sound of the station 'hooter' starting up!

The second phase was unsurprisingly called the Part 2 Taceval or battle phase; this was a much longer event lasting three days and was pre-planned to evaluate station personnel under simulated wartime conditions. For the larger UK stations this required us to mount a team of around fifty evaluators and involved all manner of scenarios including air raids, ground incursions and survival to operate in nuclear contamination. Understandably we were not the most popular people around. Despite the knowledge that success or failure in Taceval could have a major impact on the careers of all station executives, the squadron and wing commanders and certainly of the station commander, most treated the event as a necessary evil and even managed to have a good time for at least some of the evaluation. There were some amusing moments, such as an evaluation of the Harrier station at Wittering when the station commander – the very popular Pat King – aimed to impress the team by announcing that he had removed all his rank braid to minimise the chances of being captured by any infiltrators on the station. He then donned his uniform hat with its 'scrambled egg' peak (the only officer on the station to have such a hat) and wondered why the evaluators were reduced to helpless laughter. On another evaluation, this time of Leuchars, the station was running so smoothly that I decided to 'kill' two of the senior officers following an air raid. The station commander was none too pleased when I told him that he was 'dead' and could take no further part in the evaluation and we escorted him back to his married quarter. Twenty-four hours later I took a phone call from his wife. 'Please let Mike back on base, even if it is only to his peacetime office,' she pleaded, 'he's wearing out the hall carpet!' At the debrief, however, when we announced that Leuchars had earned the best possible assessment in all four assessed areas, Mike Graydon was mollified and it did his career no harm, as he later became the Chief of the Air Staff, the head of the Royal Air Force.

On the afternoon of 4 May 1982 we were standing in a hotel room in Edinburgh about to carry out a surprise Part 1 Taceval of Leuchars when the television announced the sombre news that *HMS Sheffield* had been struck by an Exocet missile in the South Atlantic and the Falklands War suddenly became very real. Tacevals were put on hold for the duration and I found myself working underground in the old Bomber Command bunker at High Wycombe from where the Strike Command assets operating in that war were controlled. I joined the Tanker Cell which became very busy indeed as the requirements for tanking grew exponentially. The greatest of these was without doubt the bombing of Stanley Airfield known as the 'Black Buck' missions flown by Vulcans which utilised the entire Victor tanker force (some aircraft more than once). Plenty has been written about these events, but there was much 'biting of fingernails to the elbow joint' over the period. Thankfully the end of the war was not too long in coming and it was later acknowledged that many lessons learned during Tacevals, particularly the *ad hoc* fixes that enterprising personnel had adopted to overcome a problem, had proved very useful in the South Atlantic. In the two and a half years that this tour lasted I still managed to get airborne whenever I could in aircraft ranging from the C-130 Hercules and Victor to the Lightning, Phantom and Harrier, but the tour involved a lot of travelling and we were away from High Wycombe for eight months of every year. Family life suffered as well for we had bought a house between Peterborough and Huntingdon as I had been led to expect a tour in the Ministry of Defence in London after Leeming (which thankfully never happened), so I got to know the route from Ramsey to High Wycombe very well. But in December 1984 I handed back my Taceval armband and UKAIR badge and we moved to married quarters at Bracknell for a year at Staff College.

At the end of WWII, Ramslade House on the edge of Bracknell town was the HQ of the Second Tactical Air Force, but this formation moved to West Germany for the Cold War period and the house and its grounds became the RAF Staff College. I joined 76 Advanced Staff Course which ran from February to December 1984 and together with roughly ninety others from countries as far apart as New Zealand and Norway, Japan and Chile, we learned the RAF approved way of making cogent arguments both on paper and verbally. We travelled extensively around the UK and Europe and we socialised amongst ourselves on a grand scale. I am proud to still call many of those on the course my friends to this day over thirty years later. Some had stellar careers and at least five became the head of their own air force, and we all had a good time. During the course we had had many distinguished speakers talk to us including senior NATO officers, politicians (often boring) and a trade union general secretary (very interesting). There were also periods when we received visits from the other Services' colleges, the Army Staff College at Camberley and the Royal Navy College at Greenwich; the RAF College visited each of these colleges as well, with the visit to Greenwich for the Tri-Service Dinner being particularly memorable as the Bracknell and Camberley officers, all resplendent in full mess kit, boarded a launch at Chelsea Pier in the mid-afternoon and sailed down to Greenwich to be addressed there after dinner in the beautiful Painted Hall by the Secretary of State for Defence, the Rt Hon Michael Heseltine.

After enjoying a great August summer break we knuckled down for the final term and eventually we found where we were all going next to make best use of all the staff knowledge we now possessed. I was delighted to be told that I would be changing my rank braid on promotion to wing commander and would become Wg Cdr Training at HQ 11 Group, responsible for the RAF's fighter force and based at RAF Bentley Priory outside Stanmore in Middlesex. The course ended just before Christmas 1984 and with several of us remaining in the Bracknell married quarters over the festive period our final party was a barbecue on Boxing Day in the garage of an empty quarter. The theme was 'Aussie' and we duly turned up in shorts and thongs (flip flops to the uninitiated) and drank lots of Australian beer around a barbecue. We were in full swing halfway through the afternoon when a car pulled up at the end of the drive and a bemused Australian and his wife got out. They had just arrived in the UK to join the 1985 Course and would be living in this very quarter so they joined the party and soon felt quite at home! So although I was now to have another ground tour it came with promotion and was also back to the fighter world.

17

A VERY SPECIAL PLACE

IN 1775 ON THE site of a medieval Augustinian priory in Harrow Weald, the architect Sir John Soane designed a large mansion house called Bentley Priory for the wealthy businessman James Duberley and in 1788 the house was significantly extended, again by Sir John Soane, for John Hamilton, 1st Marquess of Abercorn. The Priory was the final home of the Dowager Queen Adelaide, queen consort of William IV, before her death there in 1849 and it subsequently served as a hotel and girls' school before the buildings and forty acres of surrounding land were acquired by the Royal Air Force in 1926 for about £25,000. It then became the headquarters of Air Defence of Great Britain, the organisation which in 1936 changed its name to become RAF Fighter Command. In the run-up to WWII the priory underwent many changes. Chief among these was the hurried adaptation of the two largest rooms into the Operations Room and the Filter Room (when the priory later became the officers' mess these would be the Anteroom and the Ladies' Room) and the old school classrooms in the east wing were converted into accommodation. Brown and green paint was sprayed over the outside of the building including the clock face and many of the windows were blacked out.

In 1939, the magnificent conservatory was pulled down and replaced by wooden offices for the operations staff and this set the scene for the wartime era, which in a national context is considered to be the most interesting and significant part of the priory's history. In January 1940 work started on the underground operations block with an average excavation depth of 42ft (13m) and this commenced operations on 9

March. The priory itself suffered very little damage from enemy action during the war: two small bombs destroyed a wooden hut near the married quarters, blast from a flying bomb broke a few windows and the windows in the officers' mess were shattered by the blast of a V2 rocket. Ironically, it was an aircraft of Bomber Command that came closest to destroying the priory when a Wellington bomber of No.311 (Czech) Squadron returning to base attempted to land on the lawns in front of the priory. It crashed outside the sergeants' mess narrowly missing the priory and there was only one survivor. After the war Bentley Priory remained the HQ of Fighter Command until that famous name disappeared in 1968 as the operational commands amalgamated to form Strike Command. However, the Fighter Command Badge remained above the main entrance, displaying a portcullis from the crest of the City of London surmounted by a sword to signify the Command's role as the defence of the capital and the motto 'Offence Defence'. The priory now became HQ 11 (Fighter) Group, the officers' mess remained in the priory building and much of the mess silver still proudly bore the Fighter Command Badge. However, in 1974 the Department of the Environment ordered a thorough investigation into the priory building and their findings were extremely disturbing, for the spread of dry rot in the timbers meant that the only safe parts of the mess were the kitchens and dining room, and these would only last until March 1975 when they too would have to be closed. The decision that the mess would have to close came at a particularly bad time as some four months earlier the Royal Air Force Association had been given permission to hold a Fighter Command Commemorative Ball at the priory and invitations had already been sent out. Given the serious concern about the integrity of the building's structure it was decided to use marquees for the majority of the function and the lower floors were temporarily strengthened. The ball was a resounding success and one of the guests, Her Majesty Queen Elizabeth The Queen Mother, who had a long association with the mess having visited with King George VI more than once during the war, displayed a particular interest in the priory's future. Had she not done so it is almost certain that the building would have been condemned. It was from that night that the campaign to save the priory really began and it was eventually decided that it should be renovated at a cost of approximately £1 million. Most of the paintings and other valuables were removed for safe storage and work was started. The removal of the valuables was fortuitous as on the evening of 21 June 1979 smoke was seen coming from the priory. The London Fire Brigade quickly arrived to fight the fire and several teams went inside in an attempt to get the fire under control. Unfortunately, the electricity had not been switched off and as the firemen advanced to the seat of the fire they were surrounded by great sparks and had to beat a hasty retreat, before spending the next morning damping down the smouldering remains and looking for the cause. Despite some wagging tongues it was quickly established that the fire was an accident and not arson, though it had devastated most of the main staircase, but luckily jumped over the Adelaide Room and bypassed the rotunda, but destroyed the rooms down the other side, including the Dowding Room, which was a museum to Lord Dowding and maintained as it had been during his tenure as Commander-in-Chief during the Battle of Britain. Initially, this fire was thought to be the final tragedy but after legal ramifications were resolved the insurance covered most of the cost of rebuilding and renovations went ahead at a cost of approximately £3.1 million. Although several of the rooms were built during the 18th century alterations to most of them led to the loss of their original character and only the entrance hall remained virtually intact with its eight Roman Doric columns supporting a shallow vaulted ceiling. The 1979 fire peeled off the whitewash paint cover of the ceiling revealing the intricate painted pattern as designed by Soane, but the finances did not allow this pattern to be restored at the time and the whitewash was re-applied. In 1982 a large underground nuclear hardened bunker was built to the east of the mansion to replace the previous wartime one which had been continually upgraded from 1940 up to the 1980s and this new bunker became the Standby Air Defence Operations Centre.

It was to this historic site that I came in December of 1984 to take over a staff of seven squadron leaders and one flight lieutenant, and was responsible to the AOC* Air Vice Marshal Ken Hayr, for the training units within the fighter world flying the Hunter, Hawk, Lightning, Phantom and the air defence version of the Tornado, and operating from Brawdy, Chivenor, Binbrook and Coningsby. Also within my remit were the 8 Squadron airborne early

---

*   Air Officer Commanding

warning (AEW) Shackletons at Lossiemouth and the UK AEW component
of the NATO force at Waddington which was soon to receive the E-3D Sentry
aircraft. I reported directly to Gp Capt Air, Peter Naz, who welcomed me into
the job and showed me the ropes before immediately departing on two weeks'
leave, so I became the acting group captain for the period. The operations
staff who formed the other half of the air staff were led by old friend Ron
Shimmons and he eased me into the intricacies of life at Bentley Priory where I
soon began to enjoy both the job and the locality very much. I adopted the old
adage of 'sit tight for a couple of months and don't change anything until that
time has passed'. It is very good advice to anyone new in a job and served me
well over the years. My staff and I produced papers and briefs for the AOC,
coordinated courses at the various units and tried to ensure a smooth and
orderly progression of aircrew as they headed toward joining their squadrons.
We conducted inspections, called 'pre-AOC's', of each unit annually and they
were exactly that in that they took place, and the report was written, prior to
the annual AOC's Inspection of each station. In my view it was also essential
to liaise with each unit in the air and I not only renewed my acquaintance
with the Hawk at both Brawdy and Chivenor but also fitted in trips in the
Lightning at Binbrook and in the E-3 Airborne Early Warning aircraft. I even
managed a ten-hour Shackleton QRA scramble from Lossiemouth to well
inside the Arctic Circle. Then in the autumn of 1985 I got the chance to re-
visit Singapore, when that country asked for an air defence expert to help to
monitor a large exercise to be held there. I arrived to find major changes to
the air force layout, for the air defence forces were now operating from Paya
Lebar in the centre of Singapore Island. When I had last visited in 1980 this
had still been the international airport but that had now moved across to
Changi and Tengah had become the attack base. I also had one great surprise
when I found that there was an Australian Air Force wing commander also
there for the same monitoring task and he turned out to be none other than
Reg Meissner who had been a flight lieutenant Mirage pilot at Butterworth at
the same time as I was on 74 Squadron at Tengah. We enjoyed chatting over
old times while we shared a Tiger Beer (or three) and found that we agreed
the strengths and weaknesses of the Singapore air defence setup. We wrote
an honest report and presented it to the headquarters staff at the end of the
exercise, only to find that there was no interest in anything that implied any
form of critical comment: only praise would be accepted. An example of this

was the claim that a Bloodhound missile launcher could be reloaded after a firing within ten minutes, when I had watched the event during my time on UK Tacevals and knew that this claim was impossible to achieve: a first-class team took about twenty minutes for a full reload. It was a shame to see this blinkered view prevailing, one that I had only very rarely seen during my time as an examiner and one which did the troops a great disservice.

Back in the UK most of our pre-AOC's inspections went very well but in the spring of 1986 we went up to Coningsby and carried out the usual checks of the squadrons there, including the Phantom OCU which still carried the secondary title of 64 Squadron. We found a unit which would have trumped all other Phantom squadrons had it been a frontline squadron but we felt that the task of training students for the frontline had become somewhat undervalued and we recommended changes be incorporated. As always, we gave our report to the Coningsby station executives before leaving and it is fair to say that the portion covering the OCU was not well received. Nevertheless, we forwarded the report to the AOC who was now AVM Mike Stear. After deliberation and, I've no doubt, a couple of phone calls between Bentley Priory and Coningsby, I was summoned to the presence. Mike Stear told me that he could see my reasoning but asked what I would recommend should be changed. I gave him my suggestions and his response was, 'Well, you had better hope it works, because you are posted to be the next OC 228 OCU – and I shall be watching!'

I was to take over 228 OCU in November of 1986 and immediately prepare the whole unit to move north to RAF Leuchars in Fife the following Easter, but before this I was to attend a month's short course on the Hawk at RAF Brawdy to get me back up to speed in fast jet flying. I had visited Brawdy to fly the previous month and was therefore still in current practice on the Hawk but who was I to argue and I duly turned up at 79 Squadron at Brawdy for twenty-five fun hours doing formation, air combat and live weaponry. By mid-August I was judged to be ready for the OCU and after three weeks' leave I reported back to Coningsby to join 64 Course.

18

COMMAND

WHEN A NEW OFFICER commanding of a squadron is nominated he gets up to speed on the aircraft at the OCU for the type, but when it is the OCU that the newcomer is to command he has to do his training on the same unit. So it was that in mid-September I arrived at Coningsby to join 64 Course. After completion of the requisite ground school and simulator I started flying the Phantom once more in the last week of September and quickly felt at home. After two weeks I was put back in the rear (instructor's) seat and began the staff work-up to allow me to instruct students once more and gained my clearance to instruct one month later in mid-November. I even instructed some of the 64 Course students I had started the course with. On Friday 30 November 1986 on my fortieth birthday and having just passed a flying milestone of 4,000 hours total flying I took command of 228 OCU/64 Squadron.

It is said that the post of a commander is a lonely one but in my experience that is not so if the commander is well supported. For the vast majority of my time in command this was the case but on the second working day at the OCU I was badly let down. One of the staff pilots was programmed to carry out a flypast leading a pair of Phantoms at the RAF College Cranwell for a graduation, and flypasts had to be authorised by the squadron commander. The individual came to me and I asked him what he planned to do. His reply was that it was to be a repeat of a graduation flypast he and I had done two weeks earlier at Church Fenton when we carried out several circuits and low overshoots down the runway with the graduating course and their parents, friends and relatives standing outside the squadron buildings. I saw nothing wrong with this plan and authorised the sortie before I took off with a student to practise interceptions over the North Sea. However, after an hour or so the fighter controller conducting the intercepts advised me that a message had been received from Coningsby recalling me to base. It was only *my* call sign that had to return, not the other aircraft and my heart missed a beat for I was convinced that such a recall could only mean that something major had occurred. I feared a crash of one of my aircraft and returned at the fastest speed permissible. When I landed I found that there had been no crash but that the 'flypast over Cranwell airfield' had in fact been a flypast over the College itself and what was more it was in the middle of the graduation parade. Instead of one pass which is the norm for such a flypast this foolish and dangerously headstrong pilot had led the other aircraft round for a second pass over the assembled crowd and bottomed out at a mere 62ft above the ground, low enough to cause hats to be blown off the cadets' heads and very nearly colliding with the wing of the College building. What made him do this has never been established – he certainly could never explain himself to me and what annoyed me most was his barefaced lie when I had asked him his intentions. In previous years when there had been similar situations following an accident or near accident the affected squadron commander was summarily fired and packed his bags, so mine could be one of the shortest command tours ever. Regardless of the fact that the pilot had deliberately told me one thing and then done another, the finger of blame was pointed at me for lack of supervision. I was told that my position as OC was in jeopardy after only forty-eight hours but eventually I was awarded a reproof which is a formal expression of displeasure by the AOC and one that set me back considerably when compared to my peers. I shall always remain bitter that the trust I placed in those four aircrew was abused but years later when I read my F1369* for the period I found that I had received a good and fair report from Gp Capt Chris Coville who was my station commander. The second reporting officer was the AOC and unsurprisingly he had reduced no less than eight of the scores, marking me down in many areas. I was then gratified to find that his superior, the air marshal who was the Deputy Commander-in-

---

*   Form 1369 – the Officer's Confidential Report which was raised annually on all RAF officers

Chief of STC at the time and who wrote the final portion of the report, made the comment, 'I suspect that Wg Cdr Roome has paid a high price for turning up to take over 228 OCU on time,' and duly returned all the scores back to their original marks. I remain very grateful to Air Marshal 'Benny' Jackson for this restoration.

After such an inauspicious start to my tour I was, as they say, 'behind the 8 ball' and had to work very hard to recover. Immediately after Christmas the entire OCU, assisted by air-to-air refuelling from the Tanker Force, detached to Akrotiri in Cyprus for the whole month of January. There we managed to fly training sorties that would in all likelihood have been prevented by the UK winter weather and we returned to the UK comfortably ahead of our task. This buffer meant that the preparation for the move to Leuchars did not cause courses to fall behind and thankfully the move of the unit to Leuchars in April 1987 went without a hitch. It also permitted me to rid the outfit of the dead wood that had dogged it and I was pleased to welcome fresh blood from elsewhere in the Phantom Force. 228 was the largest Phantom unit in the RAF with twenty-two aircraft; nineteen of

'Charlie Oscar' – My aircraft as OC 228 OCU/64(R) Sqn

Arrival at RAF Leuchars 22 Apr 87 – 18 of our 22 aircraft

them arrived all together at Leuchars safely on 22 April and we were up and running almost immediately, a tribute to the forward planning by my squadron leaders and the conscientious approach by all personnel, whether aircrew or groundcrew. From that moment on I always felt that I had the full support of all OCU personnel and we knitted well together. The other squadrons at Leuchars were 43 and 111 (always known as 'Treble One') flying the Phantom FG.1 and as the aircraft were very similar we soon began to cross fly each other's aircraft for reasons of serviceability, particularly as the FG.1s which had been Royal Navy aircraft had not been well maintained and were showing serious signs of neglect, with corrosion being a particular problem. As 64 Squadron the OCU maintained its operational task and so we took our turn at holding QRA and also sent crews down on detachment to the Falkland Islands. Although the number of live scrambles to intercept Russian aircraft approaching the UK had decreased since *perestroika*, Leuchars' position as the most northerly of the air defence stations meant it was still the primary choice for any QRA activity and the Russian aircrew soon got used to seeing fully-armed Phantoms with 64 Squadron markings alongside them.

Mid-September always used to be Battle of Britain Day to commemorate 15 September 1940, the day on which RAF Fighter Command aircraft had faced a series of major air attacks on the UK by the Luftwaffe and beaten them off, and Leuchars was one of the stations which always held an 'At Home' Day with air and ground displays. As part of the 1987 display I led a diamond nine flypast and then a 64 Squadron display of five aircraft but the month also brought a less pleasant side to my position when I was called upon to act as the President of a Board of Inquiry into the loss of a 74 Squadron Phantom from Wattisham with the deaths of both crew. The aircraft had crashed in mid-Wales, yet with the very professional assistance of a member of the Aircraft Accident and Investigation Branch who had never seen a Phantom before that date, we were quickly able to decide upon the cause of the tragedy. We found that the crew had been looking out at their leader and had not noticed the rising ground until just before impact. The full downward deflection of the aileron, visible in the earth of the hillside, proved that the pilot had been conscious and that the aircraft had also been operating normally. He had seen the ground too late and put in full aileron deflection in a futile attempt to miss the hill.

The year passed quickly and in November the OCU deployed to Akrotiri once more to take advantage of the Mediterranean weather and also to take advantage of the social and working cohesion that always occurs on squadron detachments. Halfway through the month one aircraft needed to return to Leuchars for servicing and I took advantage of the Phantom's considerable range when carrying three ferry tanks. I flew from Akrotiri to Sigonella in Sicily and then after a refuel to Leuchars, returning on the Monday in a different aircraft by the same route. Then on the last day of November I flew the final sortie of the day in air combat against one of the four Chivenor Hawks which had come out to Cyprus to support our task. As we landed (with most of the aircrew having already made tracks for the bar) station operations called to say that a Russian maritime patrol aircraft (with the NATO codename of May) was approaching Cyprus and could we mount a rapid QRA scramble? I agreed and was then approached by Wg Cdr Norrie Bell, the commander of the TWU detachment who had been my adversary on the combat sortie just completed: could he come along in his Hawk as my No.2, as he had never seen a 'live' Russian aircraft? This was approved and off we went to find the May. When we came alongside it rapidly became obvious that while Phantoms were old hat the Russians had never seen a live Hawk and all their cameras were trained on Norrie Bell and Dave Ramsden!

Alongside the airfield at Akrotiri was The Princess Mary's Hospital, the large Service hospital always referred to by its initials TPMH and the Akrotiri officers' mess was home to many of the nursing officers. Inevitably there was considerable socialising between them and my aircrew and I came into the bar one evening to find that some banter about big bold fighter pilots fainting if exposed to blood in an operating theatre had resulted in a challenge from the nursing fraternity. When they asked who would be put forward from the aircrew some student had said, and I quote, 'No problem. The Boss will go!' I couldn't extricate myself from this challenge and turned up at TPMH on the appointed day to spend a morning in theatre. After watching three operations I was keen to see more, as it was fascinating to watch professionals at work, so by choice over the next few years I managed to get into various hospital theatres in Cyprus and the UK to watch major and complex operations including hip replacements, serious abdominal surgery and more, and thoroughly enjoyed doing so.

When the Phantom became the primary UK air defence fighter it had been judged unnecessary for its pilots to continue to train in air-to-ground gunnery but after the Falklands War this was reviewed and in early 1988 I first carried out some air-to-ground strafe using the Phantom's phenomenal SUU-23 cannon. Unlike when firing the Aden gun from the Hunter and Hawk, if a target was hit from a gun firing several thousand rounds per minute there was never any doubt and it was impressive to see the impact of rounds on the target at Tain Range northeast of Inverness.

Most of February was again spent at Akrotiri and then in March came a really special 'one-off'. It had been decided to replace the four Phantoms based at Mount Pleasant in the Falklands, returning the other four to the UK for servicing. As there had been a little sabre rattling from Buenos Aires it was decided to show how quickly the Falklands fighter force could be supported. Four aircraft were deployed from Leuchars to Mount Pleasant in the Falklands and were on QRA, fully armed, only eighteen hours after leaving Leuchars, stopping for less than an hour at Ascension airfield in mid-Atlantic to change crews. Two OCU crews led by myself deployed to Ascension a day or two earlier and the sortie south from Ascension was carried out in total silence with no radio or radar emissions from any aircraft for the entire trip; we even took off from Ascension on receipt of a green Aldis light from air traffic. After arriving at Mount Pleasant we stayed on for a week before bringing the other four aircraft home to the UK for servicing, and flew some great sorties as there were, at that time, almost no rules to restrict flying operations. For the entire detachment I flew with 'Ned' Kelly who was one of the most capable navigators I have ever had the pleasure to fly with and when I started this book he reminded me of one of the trips we carried out from Mount Pleasant. Flying five aircraft, the three-and-a-quarter-hour sortie was spent attacking the radar sites at Mount Alice, Byron and Kent, the destroyer *HMS Nottingham* and *RFA Black Rover* on station around the islands, and Mare Harbour and Mount Pleasant airfield to exercise the defences, and between us we drained the Tristar tanker of fuel in two and a half hours and I alone took on 29,000lbs of fuel. We knew that most of the sortie would be spent at ultra-low level and so the radar altimeter would be of considerable importance. This instrument had a warning light that came on in both cockpits if the aircraft was flown below whatever height had been set on the 'bug' and when flying in the UK the usual setting was 220ft, 30ft below the UK minimum cleared height. I asked Ned what height he wanted the bug set and got the reply, 'Whatever you set, Boss, I'm happy with.' Two or three minutes after take-off we agreed that 50ft might be more appropriate but only another few minutes passed before the bug was set for the remainder of the trip at 20ft because, as Ned said, 'If it's any higher the light is always on!' After an enjoyable week the time came to start the return trip and departure was set for very early in the morning when it would still be dark. When he came over to say goodbye to me on the preceding evening the Mount Pleasant station commander, a good friend of mine and a great fighter pilot, said 'Make sure the whole station knows you're going – wake them all up!' We did and the night beat-up of the airfield was talked about for a considerable time afterwards. The Tristar tanker from 216 Squadron at Brize Norton took us back to Ascension Island in just under eight hours, but the Ascension to Leuchars leg was closer to nine hours, which is quite a long time to be strapped into an ejection seat.

The OCU was also tasked to provide the solo Phantom aerobatics display crew for the 1988 season and I had two volunteer pilots so I flew with them both before deciding which to select. Before I could do so, one of the two was himself selected to go to the USA on an exchange tour to fly the F-15 and so Flt Lt Chris Lackman started to prepare a display sequence together with his navigator, Flt Lt Jack Thompson. Toward the end of April it was time for them to be given display authority, but their display still needed work and the clearance to display was delayed for a month before it was finally granted. Now it is well known that hindsight is always 20/20 and the events of 23 September 1988 have been explored in great depth, but Chris Lackman and Jack Thompson had planned an impressive display for the Phantom and for much of the 1988 summer season things went well. Flown with no external tanks the aircraft had plenty of excess power and would gain speed quickly, sometimes when it was least needed and on a practice for their display at Abingdon on 23 September they made a fatal mistake. Having pulled up into a loop, Chris needed to hold the aircraft inverted for a while in order to track back across the airfield, but he omitted two things. In order to hold the Phantom level when inverted the nose had to be held extremely high above the horizon and Chris did not achieve this so a descent started almost immediately. He also left the reheat selected and if it is not cancelled the speed will increase rapidly. By the time they reached the point to pull back down to level flight the aircraft had descended below the safe gate height of 5,200ft which they should have checked before committing downward and also the speed had increased to around 270kts which was much too fast. Why they did not make that critical gate check before committing downward we shall never know but they pulled through from about 4,800ft: both died immediately in the impact. It so happened that on that day Leuchars' station commander was away and so it was me who answered the phone to the controller at the Distress and Diversion Centre at West Drayton. He simply said, 'Are you the station commander Leuchars?' and when I replied that this was so he said, 'Your Phantom has crashed at Abingdon. There are no survivors. The BBC have film and it will be shown on the six o'clock news.'

It was now just after 1700 so the paramount need was to tell two families the dreadful news before they saw it on television within the hour and thanks to my executive officer, Andy Kirk, and both our wives we managed to do this in time. The whole OCU that day had already been in sombre mood as we had all attended the funeral of the wife of one of our officers who had died from a brain tumour, although the preparation for a ladies' guest night that evening had continued at the wish of the family. The officers' mess staff now proved what a great bunch they were. When I told them what had happened they took the food planned for that night, re-made it into bite-sized buffet pieces and then, along with a couple of barrels of beer they delivered it to my married quarter where the wake took place. Almost all the OCU aircrew, their wives and girlfriends and many other officers from the other Leuchars squadrons joined us that night, and it finished around 0700 the following morning. It was a night of raw emotion but it displayed the spirit of family that I have seen so often following tragic accidents and there is no doubt in my mind that such gatherings are an instrumental and vital part of the eventual healing process.

Over the years I had occasionally visited my old school, Reigate Grammar School, and the RAF Section of the school's combined cadet force which had played such an instrumental role in preparing me to join the RAF. Eventually I became the 'Official RAF Old Boy' for the school and in October of 1988 I flew a Phantom down to Farnborough where the CCF were visiting for the day. Along with me in my back seat I took

Flt Lt Alison Booth who was a fighter controller at RAF Buchan outside Aberdeen and also an 'Old Reigatian' who had attended the school, though long after me I should add. It was good to see the girls in the CCF realise that there were many interesting things for a girl to do in the RAF of the time, though now of course all trades are open to them.

As November came around again we headed southeast once more to Akrotiri but this time we had something new to do. Along with the usual student sorties we did several trips of air-to-air combat against the air defence Tornado F3 to help them to plan their best way to fight aircraft such as the Phantom. The ability of the Tornado to sweep its wings meant notionally that with the wings swept forward it could fight a low wing loading aircraft such as the Hawk but with them swept back it could match a Phantom which had a much higher wing loading. That was the theory but in practice the Phantom had much greater excess thrust and being able to fight in the vertical plane allowed us to dictate the combat. If we ever felt threatened we could simply pull the nose up and climb way above our opponent and then choose the moment to re-enter the fray. It didn't take long for the Tornado crews to learn that they had to maintain their speed if they were to have any chance against us and this allowed them to develop their tactics for their aircraft.

During that month I took the chance to visit an old friend and one Friday afternoon I caught the ferry from Limassol to Haifa in Israel, where Col Asaf Agmon of the Israeli Air Force met me on the quayside. Asaf and I had been on the same syndicate whilst completing the RAF Staff College at Bracknell in 1984 and over the weekend he took me all round Israel, staying for two nights with his wife, Raya, and the family in Tel Aviv. It was a most enjoyable and fascinating weekend as Asaf's military pass allowed us to visit areas denied to tourists, from the Golan Heights, captured from Syria in the 1967 war, to the Knesset, the Parliament building. We also visited several religious sites, including the Dome of the Rock, the Islamic shrine built on the site of a Roman temple which itself is on the site of the Second Jewish Temple. Its significance to Muslims is that most believe that the Prophet Muhammad ascended to Heaven from the Rock at the centre of the structure, while for the Jewish religion the Rock is referred to as the Foundation Stone where God gathered the dust to create Adam and as the site where Abraham attempted to sacrifice his son. A little-known fact is that a few hours after the Israeli flag was hoisted over the Dome during the 1967 Six-Day War, Gen Moshe Dayan ordered it to be lowered and the Muslim religious trust, the *waqf*, were given the authority to manage the Temple Mount, in order to 'keep the peace'. The beautiful golden dome is covered with gold leaf, most recently refurbished in 1993 after a donation of US$8.2 million from His Majesty King Hussein which funded the 80kg of gold required. A place of huge significance, complemented by the nearby Al-Aqsa Mosque, the Western Wall and the Church of the Holy Sepulchre. I found the whole area truly awe-inspiring. Then on the Sunday afternoon, having visited Nazareth, Bethlehem, Galilee and Caesarea, Asaf deposited me back at Haifa for my overnight sailing to Cyprus for the Monday morning and return to the 20th century.

Then it was into 1989 and another tragedy. On 9 January I was flying in a pair of aircraft carrying out staff continuation training and practising interceptions under the control of RAF Buchan but after a short while the other pilot made an RT call which shocked me: 'Boss, I have a problem, I can't see.' By the time I had got alongside his aircraft Dave Nelson was not responding at all and eventually the aircraft crashed into the North Sea seventy miles east of Leuchars. Thankfully his navigator, Gordon Moulds, ejected in time and was picked up by helicopter. So, in a period of less than four months we had lost three aircrew and one wife, a difficult time for everyone.

It is commonplace for RAF squadrons to be twinned with units from the other services and we had the good fortune to be twinned with *HMS Liverpool* which was a Type 42 destroyer based in Rosyth just to the west of the Forth Bridges. We had formed a strong bond as soon as we arrived at Leuchars and I had had the pleasure of flying the captain, David Snelson, on several trips, including the long return from Cyprus back to the UK. On that trip we flew from Akrotiri across the Mediterranean toward Sicily where we met up with a tanker to top us up before continuing on unescorted up through Europe and back to Leuchars. Working in the back seat, David operated our radar to find and intercept the tanker, so I awarded him an air force navigator's brevet! As *HMS Liverpool* was an air defence ship we on the OCU did quite a lot of work with them and in February 1989 the ship was working up in preparation for a deployment to a war theatre. David asked me if we could do some interceptions and some attacks and we were very happy to oblige. At the end of one sortie I was surprised to be asked if we could do a supersonic run very low and close past the ship. This is usually forbidden as the shockwave can cause injury and damage so I insisted that the captain himself came on the RT to confirm the request. 'Yes,' said David, 'the entire ship is closed down for nuclear war and we can cope with explosions close by. Your run will simulate one!' I positioned my aircraft and ran past level with the bridge at 750kts or about 860mph before pulling up and asking if that was what they had needed. A different voice answered: 'Yes, that was fine, but we're just getting bits of the bridge door out of the captain's forehead!' It transpired that the internal wooden door from the bridge to the bridge wing had not been firmly secured and although the metal external door had done its job the shockwave had flung the internal door open into the captain's face. The next time I saw David Snelson he was sporting his war wound!

By March 1989 my successor was on the OCU undergoing his conversion before taking over command from me. Graham Clarke and I had graduated together from South Cerney in 1965 and were also on the same courses through Valley, Chivenor and Coltishall. There was also another wing commander going through the course who was due to take command of 74 Squadron at Wattisham but he was eventually suspended from training when it was found that his eyesight had deteriorated so much that he could no longer fly aircraft. Graham Clarke was switched to command 74 and this awarded me a short period of grace, but it didn't take long for another very experienced Phantom pilot to be found in John Walmsley, and he soon started a course. But before I came to the end of my tour I had one final new event, which was a detachment to the instrumented air combat range at Decimomannu in Sardinia. Here we carried a pod on one of the missile stations which transmitted back to the ground station all the parameters of flight and of missile firings. It was now no longer possible to lose the fight but win the debrief by out-talking the opponents, as everyone could replay the sortie and see just how good, or bad, your flying was. The flying overall was excellent, with opponents including Hawks from the TWU at Brawdy, USAF F-15s and Tornados from both the RAF and the Luftwaffe, and culminated in a twelve-ship fight with all those types. I did, however, earn one record and that was the greatest speed in reverse! At one point in a combat my aircraft registered 35kts going backwards, having run out of thrust going vertically up. My nav was telling me to go left but I said, 'Steve, for the moment we're going where the aircraft wants to go, but I'll let you know when I'm in control again.' After a while it swapped ends and we continued the fight!

The following month I went back to Coltishall for the first time in several years, but not for a pleasant reason as it was to attend the funeral of Flt Lt 'PV' Lloyd, who I had known for seventeen years from when we both instructed on the Gnat at Valley and who had been flying Jaguars for some time. For reasons unknown, he let down through cloud and hit the cliffs at St Abbs Head in northern England. It was another great loss. The last few months of my tour were characterised by a series of reasonably short dual checks with the RAF's entire Phantom Force after an aircraft of 56 Squadron from Wattisham had been lost when one of the squadron executives had been carrying out an arrival check on a new pilot and decided to demonstrate an unusual oddity of the aircraft. If the Phantom was put into a very hard turn and then the switch to dump wing fuel was operated, the airflow breaking away behind the wing took the dumping fuel up above the wing and could even be made to track back up the upper surface for some way. This was well known to all OCU staff QFIs and was demonstrated as part of the conversion to type. However, the rear-seat supervising pilot had never been on the OCU staff and so was neither experienced in the exercise nor capable of carrying it out safely. The aircraft flicked and spun before crashing into the North Sea after the crew ejected safely. The Board of Inquiry recommended that all Phantom pilots fly with a CFS Agent to have the correct procedure demonstrated and practised. Three of us from Leuchars went around both the UK and Germany and flew with every pilot to ensure that the accident would never be repeated.

On 10 August 1989 I led a five-ship formation around Scotland, at the end of which we overflew Leuchars and I symbolically pulled out of the formation to leave John in the lead position. My command tour had finally ended and I was to return to the desk from whence I had come, at HQ 11 Group at RAF Bentley Priory.

19

RETURN TO BENTLEY

HAVING SPENT ALMOST EIGHTEEN months as Wing Commander Training at 11 Group before taking the OCU, Bentley Priory was very familiar and it didn't take long to settle in. As well as the day job I took over the post of President of the Mess Committee (PMC), responsible for the day-to-day running of the officers' mess and the same post as I had held at Leuchars for a time. The PMC at Bentley Priory was much higher profile as the mess was the usual location for the regular formal dinners hosted by the Air Force Board – those most senior and important personages in light blue – to entertain VIPs including royalty and politicians from many countries, and I was regularly on parade to welcome some very well-known faces to the mess. It was an especially fascinating time as the renovation of the priory took place during my tenure of office and this gave me both a detailed knowledge of the building and its history and also allowed me to see it as its glory was displayed once more. Once the redecoration had been completed many of the special dinners commenced with a tour of the mess and always included the Dowding Room, maintained as it had been when Air Marshal Dowding used it as his office during the Battle of Britain. Another particularly noteworthy part of the restoration was the entrance hall with its eight Roman Doric columns. The 1979 fire had peeled off the whitewash paint cover of the ceiling but at that time the finances did not allow this pattern to be restored and so the whitewash had been reapplied. Now it came off and after the paintwork had been carefully repaired the intricate painted pattern designed by Soane was there for everyone to admire.

My job had changed slightly as the air defence version of the Tornado was now entering service in ever increasing numbers, so I wangled a conversion to type at Coningsby and also managed to keep my hand in on the Phantom at Wattisham, and the Hawk at Brawdy and Chivenor, but in early 1990 AVM Bill Wratten as AOC gave me a special task. He had been charged by the Air Force Board with planning a special very large flypast over Buckingham Palace on 15 September – Battle of Britain Day – to commemorate the fiftieth anniversary of the air battle and he delegated the detailed planning to me. He and I attended several meetings with the Chief of the Air Staff and other Air Force Board members to rough out a plan. Once that had taken shape I could get down to my detailed work. This flypast was to be the largest seen over London since the Coronation and detailing it could fill a book. In fact, the operation order that I wrote for the event *did* fill a book which was specially printed and sold many copies. The flypast was to start at twelve noon precisely and in the next six minutes 168 aircraft would overfly Her Majesty and the assembled Royal

View from Buckingham Palace on 15 Sep 90 just before Noon

Family gathered on the balcony of Buckingham Palace. In the forecourt below was a large parade and important spectators including the Battle of Britain Fighter Association, that august group of aircrew who had actually taken part in the battle, while outside the railings there were many thousands of members of the public down The Mall and indeed all over London and elsewhere on the flypast route, which comprised four main 'holds', racetracks around which the elements flew as they joined up to form larger formations. There had been a sharp intake of breath when I briefed the C-in-C of Strike Command and his deputy that one formation of no fewer than sixty-four fighters would join behind another formation of the same number over the Norfolk coast with a separation of only forty-five seconds and all without a single word being spoken on the RT. It is little-known that the entire flypast took place without any radio transmissions so that every single aircraft could monitor the one radio frequency without it becoming cluttered. All the major formations would pass over Southwold in Suffolk, the point at which a line seventy miles long extending from Buckingham Palace along The Mall reaches the coast. From there they would fly direct to the Palace. After overflying London the formations would separate as they started their return to their bases, this separation being necessary because the speeds of the elements varied between 150 and 300kts so the later formations were closing on the slower aircraft.

So that I could say honestly that there were no conflictions at any point, and to satisfy one of the requirements placed upon me, I drew out the flight path of every individual aircraft from brakes off on take-off to approaching their airfields on the return to land. However, although the flypast aircraft were deconflicted we had to ensure that no other aircraft could get in the way of such an unwieldy mass of aircraft and so I had many meetings with the Civil Aviation Authority and the National Air Traffic Service which resulted in the setting up of corridors of airspace each side of the flypast aircraft extending from ground level to 3,000ft into which no civilian aircraft would be permitted to fly for the duration. Eventually the Secretary of State signed what is known as a Statutory Instrument to make the closure of the airspace legal and also requiring the closure of Heathrow Airport for twenty minutes. I produced a video film of the route from Southwold to The Mall for use at the briefing and to do this I needed an optically flat glass bubble to film forward, with the result that I lay in the bomb aimer's position of the Avro Lancaster of the Battle of Britain Flight as it flew along the route, giving me a perfect perch from which to film. It was obviously impossible to practise a flypast such as this over London but I found that a line from Southwold to overhead Wittering near Peterborough was of almost the same length and so the element leaders carried out a couple of practices over Wittering before the event. Bill Wratten would fly the one remaining RAF Spitfire that had taken part in the battle as the lead aircraft for the entire flypast and the whole of BBMF detached to Wattisham prior to the day itself. It was also agreed that I could be inside the Palace in a room alongside the main balcony in order to give a report of the weather on the morning and to video the flypast.

On the night before the great day the officers' mess at Bentley Priory hosted its annual Battle of Britain Fighter Association reception for those who actually took part in the battle, but on this special occasion a formal dinner followed to which I as the PMC was honoured to be present, along with a couple of guests not usually seen at these events: some ex-Luftwaffe pilots who had also flown in the battle. In one of the speeches they were welcomed with the words 'We couldn't have done it without you!' and when I finally left the bar at just before 0100 there were still several doing what fighter pilots do best: talking the fight expressively using both hands. There was also one lovely comment from a Hurricane squadron commander called Tom Gleave who had been badly burned on his face as he bailed out of his burning aircraft during the battle and later received pioneering treatment from Sir Archibald McIndoe in hospital at East Grinstead. Gleave was therefore a member of the Guinea Pig Club, formed mainly – but not exclusively – of pilots who had suffered bad burns and subsequently received ground-breaking treatment from McIndoe. They decided to form a club to maintain their morale and this club continued after the war. Each year, they mounted a 'lost weekend' reunion for former Guinea Pigs who had finished their course of surgery. And, of course, they drank. Indeed, at their 1949 reunion dinner 225 former Guinea Pigs put away no fewer than 3,000 bottles of beer, 125 bottles of whisky and seventy-two bottles of sherry. During their revelry, they sang their own theme song to the hymn tune 'Aurelia', usually 'The Church's One Foundation':

> We are McIndoe's Army,
> We are his guinea pigs,
> With dermatomes and pedicles,
> Glass eyes, false teeth and wigs.
> And when we get our discharge,
> We'll shout with all our might,
> *Per Ardua ad Astra*,
> We'd rather drink than fight!

When Gleave arrived at Bentley Priory that day he looked at the others of his generation and mocked, 'What a bunch of wrinklies!' before touching his own face which remained shiny and somewhat pink from the skin grafts and saying, 'You see, bum skin doesn't wrinkle!'

Thankfully the day itself dawned without a cloud in the sky and we knew that weather was not a problem. I arrived at the Palace to be met by Her Majesty's Equerry, Wg Cdr David Walker, and he showed me around several of the rooms, including a tapestry replicating the Battle of Britain window in Westminster Abbey which contained forty-eight panels each with about 48,000 stitches and contributed to by eleven artists and forty-eight embroiderers. This tapestry was presented to The Queen that day and seven years later Her Majesty Queen Elizabeth The Queen Mother handed it to the Spitfire and Hurricane Memorial Building at Manston Airfield in Kent for safekeeping. David and I also walked through the room directly behind the centre balcony where I noticed that the view down The Mall from that balcony is almost completely obscured by the Victoria Memorial in front of the Palace: thankfully the aircraft would be easily visible above the memorial! That day was also the fifth birthday of Prince Harry who early in the day was wearing a present in the form of a personal Red Arrows flying suit. He was obviously getting a bit bored and the Princess of Wales asked me if I could amuse him with my huge professional video camera similar to those carried by the press, so the Prince and I went into the room next door where I would be for the actual flypast and we spent half an hour or so looking at the crowds through the zoom lens or filming Prince Harry and then allowing him to watch the replay. Then as midday drew near I made a final phone call to Wattisham to confirm the perfect weather to the AOC and took up my station to await noon. It all went off perfectly and was immensely impressive.

For the record, the flypast consisted of seven formations. The first comprised the BBMF fighters, five Spitfires and two Hurricanes, led by Bill Wratten in the Spitfire IIa P7350 which had taken part in the actual battle. There was then a gap of one minute before the 'heavies' arrived, the twenty-one aircraft being a mix of VC10s, C-130 Hercules, Nimrods and Canberras, escorted by Tornados, Buccaneers and BAe125s. Forty seconds later the fast jets arrived in two formations totalling 128 aircraft – Harriers, Hawks, Jaguars, Phantoms and Tornados. Just under a minute after the final Jaguar passed over the Palace the nine Hawks of the RAF Aerobatic Team, the Red Arrows, trailed red, white and blue smoke up The Mall and as the smoke cleared the crowd burst into spontaneous applause as the growl of four Merlin engines brought the Lancaster into view. As this sound died away it was replaced by that of two more Merlins, but travelling much faster this time and flying low up The Mall came Bill Wratten in the Spitfire, escorted in line abreast by Gp Capt Martin Widdowson, Coningsby's station commander, in a Hurricane. As they approached the Palace they broke apart and upward in a salute to Her Majesty and those on the Palace balcony. It was now 1206 and in the preceding six minutes 168 aircraft had provided a faultless display of precision flying by aircraft from thirty-two RAF squadrons and one RN squadron, and with aircrew from ten different services and seven nations, including the Luftwaffe!

As well as these aircraft there were twenty-two airborne spares which made a grand total of 190 aircraft flying on the day. From my vantage point next to the balcony I filmed the entire flypast and then, in accordance with my briefing from Bill Wratten, I did nothing until he was back on the ground at Coningsby and we spoke on the phone. I think I simply said, 'Perfect!' after which I heard Bill Wratten say to the other BBMF aircrew, 'OK, you can open that champagne now!'

In the long corridor that runs behind the front face of the Palace I again met Princess Diana with both her sons, and as Prince Harry wanted to view the flypast again through the camera I knelt down to hold the camera while he sat on a chair and watched the aircraft through the eyepiece. Suddenly I was tapped on the shoulder by the Princess who said quietly, 'On your feet...' and I looked down the corridor to see The Queen, The Duke of Edinburgh and various other members of the Royal Family, and accompanied by the Chief of the Air Staff, coming along towards us. I rose and stood back as the group came to us but Prince Harry stepped forward, full of excitement and said to The Queen, 'I've seen it again!' and Her Majesty stopped to talk to him. She then looked toward Princess Diana who indicated me and said, 'This is the officer who planned it all,' and presented me to Her Majesty who was very complimentary and The Duke also commented on a 'faultless performance'. It was indeed a day I shall never forget and in the 1991 Queen's Birthday Honours List I was appointed an officer of the Order of the British Empire (OBE) in recognition of that planning. It was a great honour and the eventual day out at the Palace with the family to receive the medal from Her Majesty herself was very memorable.

After such a special event, the remainder of that ground tour could easily have paled into insignificance but much went on in the air and on the ground. Things had not been good at home for a while and the nine months of flypast planning had taken its toll on family life. Eventually Pippa

Day of OBE Investiture – 1991

announced that she wanted to leave, so we bought a house at Tangmere outside Chichester for her while I remained at Bushey Heath and soon got caught up in the events of Operation GRANBY or 'Gulf War One' as it became known. Although the UK air defence participation in it was negligible I spent the period of tension on shifts back down underground at High Wycombe until thankfully I was able to return to normal duties.

The Bentley Priory mess held many memorable functions, especially following the Gulf War in which AVM Wratten had been the Air Commander British Forces in the Middle East from November 1990 until the end of that war, and as PMC I remember welcoming such personalities as US Secretary of State Alexander Haig, General 'Stormin' Norman Schwarzkopf and General Sir Peter de la Billière who, despite being due for retirement in 1990, had been appointed C-in-C of British Forces in the Gulf War – in effect General Schwarzkopf's deputy. Sir Peter had considerable experience of the Middle East, much of it with the SAS, having won a Military Cross (MC) for actions in the Jebel Akhdar in Oman in 1959 and followed this up with the award of a Distinguished Service Order (DSO) in 1976 for his part in battles in Musendam and Dhofar in the same country. His past experience of fighting in the area, knowledge of the people and possession of some fluency in Arabic overrode concerns about his age and in this role he was largely responsible for persuading Schwarzkopf (who was initially sceptical) to allow the SAS and other special forces to play significant roles in that conflict. He was a fascinating man to talk to over dinner in the mess on the night we dined out Bill Wratten as he handed over as AOC to none other than AVM John Allison, who I had worked for at Coningsby back in 1977.

I had also managed to stay reasonably current on the Phantom, the Tornado F.3 and the Hawk, so when the new AOC indicated that he wished to travel around his patch regularly by air, the Hawk was an obvious choice and to my pleasant surprise he asked that I be his personal pilot. This did *not* mean that I would fly him around, more the reverse, but it was agreed that 100 Squadron at Wyton outside Huntingdon would provide the aircraft and usually I would drive up to Wyton and fly a Hawk down to Hatfield, the nearest suitable airfield to Bentley Priory. There I would prepare the aircraft and then jump into the back seat as John Allison flew to whichever airfield he planned to visit. Sometimes I would wait and return with him to Hatfield, but more often than not I would fly the aircraft directly back to

Wyton solo and drive back to Bentley Priory. The same routine also applied if the SASO*, Air Cdre Mike Donaldson, to be followed later by Air Cdre Cliff Spink, needed to visit an 11 Group station.

The Royal Observer Corps also had their headquarters at Bentley Priory and in July 1991 they held a final garden party in the grounds before being disbanded, and as the PMC I was honoured to welcome Her Majesty and Prince Philip to the mess. Escorting the royal couple through the restored mess we stopped for Her Majesty to sign the visitors' book which had been placed on a small table with a chair alongside. The table had only room for the book and a pen and as usual Her Majesty was carrying her handbag. She had nowhere to place this whilst signing and looked to give the bag to the nearest person which was me. Immediately Prince Philip turned to the accompanying photographer and said, 'Quickly! Take a photo of this RAF officer stealing Her Majesty's handbag,' but thankfully the photographer was concentrating only on HM and no photo of me carrying a handbag exists!

Toward the end of 1992 the RAF was retiring the Phantom from service and John Allison elected to fly the final RAF Phantom sortie out of Wattisham to land at Duxford in Cambridgeshire where the aircraft would henceforth be displayed in the Imperial War Museum. On that day I flew a Hawk out of Wattisham with a Service photographer in the rear seat so that John Allison could formate on my aircraft and we could produce a record of the event. Later we also got a photo of the final landing of that aircraft being halted by an arrester cable fitted specially on Duxford's short runway. When I landed back at Wattisham to drop off the photographer I carried out the last RAF fixed-wing landing in Wattisham's fifty-three-year history as a Royal Air Force airfield before it was handed over to the Army and twenty minutes later I carried out the final RAF fixed-wing take-off from that station as well! By the end of the three years in that post I had managed to fly a total of 108 hours in six different types, which was not bad for a ground tour.

In 1993 I switched roles within the Group HQ and became Wing Commander Air Operations instead of Training and while that meant the end of my Tornado flying it was not the case where the Hawk was concerned, as I had now got quite a name for myself as a flypast planner

---

*   Senior Air Staff Officer

after planning a couple to celebrate the Queen's official birthday on the day of Trooping the Colour. In April the RAF celebrated the seventy-fifth anniversary of its formation and another large flypast was planned: I was nominated to be the project officer. This time Her Majesty was going to review a large static display at RAF Marham in Norfolk before watching a flypast of 148 aircraft. Although the planning went well and the practice was successful the day itself was ruined when the heavens opened and not a single aircraft flew. The television crews wanted proof that the rain was indeed very heavy and wanted me in full uniform to do a piece to camera explaining the reasons for cancellation. By the end of the fourth TV interview I was quite literally soaked to the skin and my best uniform was never quite the same again. However, the weather was on our side for the next one and what a big one it was. To commemorate the fiftieth anniversary of the invasion of Normandy no fewer than fourteen heads of state came to the UK and sailed across to Normandy on the Royal Yacht *HMY Britannia*. Prior to leaving Portsmouth there was a drumhead service at the war memorial on Southsea's waterfront followed by a flypast of aircraft from all the countries that had taken part in the air war over Normandy in June 1944. Aircraft from Australia, Belgium, Canada, the Czech Republic, Denmark, France, Greece, the Netherlands, Norway, Slovakia, the United States (both US Navy and USAF) and of course the UK were to take part. I not only planned the flypast but carried out the weather checks prior to the event in a Hawk of 100 Squadron which I kept for a week near Portsmouth at the naval airfield of Lee-on-the-Solent. Moreover, the Czech participation of four MiG-29 aircraft were required to be intercepted and escorted as they first entered European airspace as their knowledge of English and of western air traffic procedures was limited, so I took a pair of Hawks out to Wildenrath in Germany from where we intercepted the MiGs and escorted them into Wildenrath for a night. The following morning the weather was, quite simply, atrocious, with a cloudbase of around 300ft and cloud tops above 40,000ft. Only one of the Czechs had a working knowledge of English and so we drew the plan out on a board. The power and take-off speeds of the MiGs made any sort of mixed formation take-off impractical, so I got airborne first and carried out a circuit at 200ft, below the cloudbase, before coming back past the Wildenrath runway threshold. Just before reaching abeam the threshold I called 'Go!', at which time the first two MiG-29s commenced their take-off, joined in formation on me as they lifted off, and the three of us then went straight into cloud and climbed up, eventually to break clear above the tops at no less than FL440! The second Hawk then did exactly the same, starting his take-off as soon as the first MiG 29s started theirs, and the second pair joined up on that Hawk. It all worked well and the six of us stayed up at that altitude all the way back to the UK before letting down to join the circuit at Yeovilton, from where the large formation would fly for the event. The final aircraft in the formation flypast was a British Airways Concorde because BOAC (BA's forebears) had flown to the beaches within twenty-four hours of the landings to deliver supplies and troops. After it had flown over *Britannia* I and my No.2 Hawk formated on Concorde and we then flew in formation with that beautiful aircraft all the way along the south coast to pass by Plymouth and then back towards London. Not many can lay claim to have flown in formation with Concorde.

There was another flypast over Portsmouth that day which I also organised, when four Spitfires and a P-51 Mustang flew at low level across Portsmouth harbour to simulate the fighter sweeps that had taken place early on the morning fifty years before. Three of the Spitfires were flown by RAF fighter pilots who needed no help to fly in battle formation but

Formating on Concorde between RAF Lyneham and Portsmouth Harbour

the fourth was a civilian Spitfire IX flown by Carolyn Grace. The Grace Spitfire ML407 has the distinction of shooting down the first enemy aircraft on D-Day when Fg Off Johnny Houlton destroyed a Ju88 over the beaches and so without doubt this aircraft was rightly involved in the commemoration. The aircraft had been restored to flying condition by Carolyn's husband Nick but he had then tragically been killed in a road accident and Carolyn took over the reins. She is now well known in that Spitfire and I shall always be grateful to her for later giving me one hour's delightful flying in it.

Overhead HMY Britannia

20

PERSONNEL AND
TRAINING COMMAND

THE D-DAY FLYPAST ENDED my long association with 11 Group for I
changed jobs in early July 1994. Pippa and I also decide to try again after two
years apart and moved together into rented accommodation eight miles west of
Gloucester as I took up the post of Plans 1 at the newly formed HQ Personnel
and Training Command (PTC) at RAF Innsworth outside Gloucester. I was
in this post for less than a year before I moved once again, though only up one
floor within the HQ to become the Command Flight Safety Officer (CFSO).
At least this was back to dealing with aircraft and I quickly made it my job
to visit the various PTC flying stations. As I had my private pilot's licence
with a qualification to fly in cloud I also flew quite a bit in a Piper PA-28
owned by two ex-228 OCU navigators, Nige Marks and Ned Kelly. For a
time, Nige had been based at Chivenor in Devon and Ned at Wattisham in
Suffolk so I had often been asked to deliver the aircraft from one station to
the other, especially if the weather was at all bad because neither of them had
instrument ratings. Now I also started to fly historic civilian jets and qualified
on the de Havilland Vampires and Venoms owned by Don Wood of Source
Aviation at Bournemouth Airport. He had a total of ten of these ex-Swiss
Air Force aircraft with both the single- (FB.6) and two-seat (T.11) versions of
the Vampire, and single-seat FB.50 Venoms, the Swiss version of the RAF's
Venom FB.1. Back in 1966 when I had completed my Jet Provost course at
Syerston and gone to Valley on the Gnat, several of the course had completed
their advanced flying training on the Vampire T.11 at Swinderby and now
finally I got the chance to fly them as well. The Vampire was a 1950s trainer
powered by the Goblin turbojet but with almost none of the engine protection
systems that by the 1990s we had come to accept as the norm. If the throttle

Vampire FB6 of Source Aviation, Bournemouth

Venom FB50 of Source Aviation, Bournemouth

was advanced too quickly there was a very real risk of an engine surge and the view from the cockpit was quite limited by the metal frame around the front screen and down the centre of the canopy. Nevertheless it was fun to fly and we displayed around the Solent at various events. The single-seat Vampire was quite different, for despite the same limitations on engine handling it had a great view from the bubble cockpit and flew beautifully. The Venom was its big brother and was designed as a high-altitude fighter with a very different wing and more powerful Ghost engine developing 4,850lbs of thrust. Although it was a lot heavier on the controls as there was no power assistance, the light airframe and big wing gave it performance not dissimilar to the Hawk: given the choice I always went for the Venom. One of the problems when trying to display these aircraft was the difference between elevator (pitch) and aileron (roll) forces. The control column was pivoted at the cockpit floor for pitch but about nine inches above this point and therefore between the pilot's knees in roll, making the ailerons very heavy, especially when making large control inputs. The oxygen systems were no longer cleared for use, which I always thought to be a pity as it would have been great to have taken a Venom up to 50,000ft and invited a Tornado F.3 to try to intercept and identify us, as they would never have achieved it!

As CFSO I requalified on the Hawk at Valley and this proved useful as early in 1995 I was asked to plan two more flypasts, to commemorate the fiftieth anniversary of VE-Day in May and the same for VJ-Day in August. These flypasts over London allowed me to fly again as the weather check Hawk, free ranging over London at heights down to 500ft, and that summer I also displayed the Vampire and Venom at places such as St Mawgan, Biggin Hill, Cowes and even Chièvres Air Base in Belgium. However, just after the VE-Day commemoration I made a serious error which could have been life-changing. The house we rented west of Gloucester had a large expanse of grass, much of which was on steeply sloping banks. There was an old petrol-driven Flymo mower that came with the house and one day in May I set out to cut the lawns, carefully lowering the mower up and down the steep banks on a rope in the approved safe fashion. Having completed all the lawns there was a small section just outside the front gate of not much more than weeds and so I ran the mower over it. Standing on the wet grass and cut weeds I eased the mower down the very slight bank and when I pulled it back my foot slipped and I put my right foot, clad in only a trainer, under the mower. There

Myself and Pippa – 1994

was a bang and I immediately saw that my foot was now shorter than it had been. As it was an old mower there was no 'dead man's handle' and so the engine continued to turn the blades until I chased it to shut it off. I then had to walk back the twenty yards or so to the back door and get Pippa to drive me to hospital in Gloucester, where they greeted me with the words 'You're the first of this season's "Flymos"!' The swathe of the blade through my foot had broken my little toe and removed the next toe completely. It then took two thirds off the third toe and one third from the second one but left my big toe untouched. The surgeons stitched up the mess that remained and it healed so quickly that I flew a Venom the following Saturday. I am lucky and suffer no balance problems but now if I fall over in a bar I can always claim that is caused by the 'war wound'!

Thankfully the flight safety within the flying training world was good and we had few accidents to investigate, though one particularly unpleasant one involved the fatal crash of a Hawk on take-off at Valley. As the pilot lifted off the runway the aircraft rolled rapidly to the right and crashed inverted after less than five seconds of flight. It transpired that some remedial work carried out the previous evening had involved the disconnection of the aileron control rod beneath the cockpit floor and this had not been reconnected. The powered flying control system on the aircraft meant that control movements still felt the same to the pilot but a visual check of the control surfaces would have shown that the ailerons were not moving in response to control column movement. Tightening up the engineering practices and a simple visual check as the controls were checked after start solved the problem.

In the autumn I first flew a couple more new types when I flew the Tucano at Linton-on-Ouse and two of the RAF's gliders at Syerston, the Vigilant and the Viking. Then in the summer of 1996 I was offered a very different form of flypast when I was asked to produce a plan for one over Heathrow Airport itself to commemorate the fiftieth anniversary of the opening in 1946. This involved a long line of over thirty aircraft, all of which had been very familiar to air travellers from that date, ranging from the Lancastrian, a modified Lancaster bomber operated by BOAC immediately post-war, through the de Havilland Rapide and its stablemate the Dove, to larger piston transports like the Douglas DC-3, DC-4 and DC-6, and followed by the jets such as the Comet and Boeing 707, DC-8 and Boeing 777 to Concorde. Speeds from 120 to 300kts meant using the same form of staggered timing that I had employed in earlier plans. The flypast also gave the aircrew flying the aircraft a chance to enjoy themselves with no passengers, and much exaggerated wing waggling as they flew along the Heathrow runway made their enjoyment obvious!

This turned out to be the final flypast that I planned, as in July I took a phone call from the officer who posted group captains telling me that I was soon to become one myself. This great news was tempered by his next statement: I was to spend six months from September 1996 living at Incirlik Air Base in Turkey as the commander of the British Forces involved in Operation WARDEN, the maintenance of a no-fly zone over northern Iraq to protect the Kurdish population there from Saddam Hussein's Iraqi forces. Six weeks after that call I boarded a Hercules at RAF Lyneham and headed for a completely new experience.

21

COMMANDER BRITISH FORCES NORTHERN IRAQ

INCIRLIK (PRONOUNCED IN-SHER-LICK) IS a Turkish Air Force base outside Adana in southern Turkey and in the 1990s was also the HQ of Operation PROVIDE COMFORT, a four-nation operation by French, Turkish, UK and US forces under the overall command of a one-star USAF brigadier general; the other three commanders were all of colonel/ group captain rank. During my spell there the UK provided attack aircraft in the shape of attack and reconnaissance Tornados supported by VC10 tanker aircraft, all re-supplied by C-130 Hercules. The French contingent was similar to that of the UK, with Jaguars and the KC-135 Boeing tanker, while the US used F-15s or F-16s and similar KC-135s. Vitally important were the USAF E-3 Airborne Warning and Control System (AWACS) aircraft. The Turkish Air Force usually operated alone and spent much of its time attacking the Kurdish forces who were opposing Turkey: these attacks were called Turkish Special Missions (TSMs) and whenever they were mounted the other three components were forced to remain on the ground to preclude any possibility that damage or casualties caused by these TSMs could be attributed to us. This inevitably made for strained relations between the Turkish Air Force and the other three, so much so that France decided to withdraw its contingent at the end of 1996. The six months I spent there were busy at times but very boring and frustrating at others when the Turkish Air Force seemed to delight in preventing the operation from working as planned. In particular, the Turkish Customs delighted in confiscating items of freight brought in by UK, American or French transport aircraft to support air operations and this caused considerable ill-feeling. There was a little light relief, however, after the

Turkish Air Force complained that they could not operate their Boeing tanker aircraft and blamed the Americans for not sending the necessary items from the USA. It eventually transpired that the items had arrived several weeks previously but had been impounded by Turkish Customs! Domestically we wanted for little as the base was 'little America' and included clothes shops, electronics stores and a large well-stocked food supermarket and liquor store, with everything flown in from the USA and priced in US dollars, as is standard for American bases all over the world.

As 'CBF' I had sole use of a smart white Range Rover that had been appropriated in Iraq at the end of the Gulf War and sent home on a Hercules as one of the spoils of war. However, when the aircraft landed at Incirlik some higher priority freight meant that the Range Rover was offloaded. The UK commander of the time decided that it made an excellent personal transport, affixed an RAF pennant to the bonnet and there it had stayed, handed down from CBF to CBF. The elevated driving position and the white bodywork conferred considerable stature and it was *much* more impressive than the saloons driven by the other nations' commanders!

I only flew once during my stay, but what a trip it was: almost two hours in a USAF F-15E. This aircraft was certainly the most effective multi-role combat aircraft of its time and opened my eyes to what the RAF could have been flying if decisions taken to decide the way forward had gone differently after the Falklands War. When an air defence presence of RAF Phantoms on the newly built base at RAF Mount Pleasant on East Falkland was agreed, the UK was going to be one squadron short of our agreed declaration of assets to NATO and so we were in the market for another air defence squadron. A delegation was sent out to the USA where they were offered options on two different aircraft types already sitting in storage. The choice was between ex-USAF single-seat F-15s and ex-US Navy two-seat F-4J and F-4S Phantoms. The USN was then operating the F-4S but this option was too expensive, while both the other types were offered for roughly the same price per airframe and the Phantom F-4J was eventually chosen, with the reason for doing so often quoted to be 'commonality'. These old F-4Js were languishing in the 'bone-yard' at Davis Monthan Air Base and it was very difficult to see exactly what commonality there was, as the F-4J was powered by different engines, the

General Electric J79. Also, the aircraft had no internal starter and had to use an external unit the size of a Ford Transit to start it, which would cause major problems if one of these aircraft operating in the UK had to divert to an airfield which did not hold such equipment. The wheels and tyres were different, the radar was different, the aircraft could not carry the primary UK missile the Skyflash (though they were later modified to do so), the flying clothing and safety equipment was all American and UK crews had to be issued with new flying clothing and helmets. The list is almost endless although it must be said it was still a more effective air defence aircraft than the FGR.2. Although I enjoyed flying the F-4J there are few fighter pilots who would not have preferred the F-15 and for the same price it might have opened the door to a further F-15 air superiority purchase for the RAF. Who knows, the Tornado F.3 may never have been born and there are many who would not have shed tears had that been the eventual outcome.

My trip in the F-15E showed me just what advantages that aircraft had over any other air defence aircraft I had flown. As part of a three-ship formation we flew at low level from Incirlik to the air-to-ground range at Konya where we carried out some bombing and air-to-ground gunnery, then climbed to medium level and conducted several practice interceptions before some close formation manoeuvring and then a return to Incirlik where I flew several circuits from the rear seat. This was made very easy by the ability to display the view through the front-seater's head-up display on one of the four large screens in the rear cockpit and after one hour and fifty minutes' flying I carried out the final landing. Even then we had sufficient fuel to divert should it be necessary and we hadn't even taken off with full fuel, carrying 4,000lbs less than the full fuel load. I climbed down and reached for my cheque book!

I was very happy to see my own 'freedom bird' in the shape of an RAF C-130 arrive to take me to Cyprus and onward to home at the end of March 1997. I had made some good friends during my six months but the frustrations, particularly those caused by the intransigence of the Turkish Air Force in general and the Turkish General Staff at Ankara in particular, had marred what could have been a very pleasant interlude.

22

PLANS AND BUDGETS

MY RETURN TO INNSWORTH found me working for an air vice marshal who would have much preferred to be running a civilian company rather than the RAF Training Group. He had replaced all the commonly used RAF job titles with mock-civilian equivalents so that my job was now titled Head of Business Planning and Finance instead of Group Captain Plans and Budgets. Everywhere I went outside that particular floor at Innsworth people would ask me what the job title meant and 'What do you do?' was a very common question. Things were not helped as his office (titled 'Chief Executive') had a sign on the front of his desk reading 'It's hard to soar with eagles when working with turkeys'. He was actually in charge of the RAF's flying and ground training systems and I was responsible to him for ensuring that the annual budget of about £630 million was spent and accounted for correctly in order that we remained afloat at the end of the year. This was not always easy as the purse strings were forever being tightened until things squeaked, to paraphrase Denis Healey. We also faced the ridiculous budgetary constraint that whatever amount remained unspent at the end of one financial year would be removed from the following year's budget. The single most easily controllable spend was aviation fuel and each year as the end of March approached I would be found on the phone to the flying stations asking them to spend money by filling all available fuel tanks, aircraft, fuel bowsers and underground bulk storage to ensure that we never underspent. Eventually I managed to get MOD to agree that we could carry over a very small proportion of the budget without fearing that it would be culled from the following year's allocation.

Another challenge was that the 'into productive service' target for new aircrew numbers moved up and down with alarming rapidity. This generally affected only the fast jet fraternity and over my time it climbed from an annual requirement of 15 to 60, yet two years later it was back down to 20. The main bottleneck was always Valley but not for any failure on that station's part – it was the most rigorous of the flying training courses – but the syllabus was always being examined through a microscope in an effort to find ways of improving the pass rate. Someone with the '200-mile fine-tuning screwdriver' suggested more than once the simple solution of lowering the graduation standard, but danger lay that way and rightly the OCUs rejected any notion that a lower input standard was acceptable to them. My department, comprising about fourteen civil servants and three serving officers, did its best and constantly amended the costings and plans as the targets moved. It was not a satisfying time.

In a Source Vampire FB6 leading a commemoration of 54 Sqn Vampires crossing the Atlantic in 1948 – formation with 54 Sqn Jaguars

Thankfully I was only in the post just over eighteen months and throughout both summers I continued my display flying on the Venom and Vampire. I displayed the single-seat Vampire FB.6 in a pairs display with a T.11 Vampire at the Waddington Air Display, and particularly enjoyed a trip in the Vampire FB.6 to Odiham from where similar Vampires of 54 Squadron had commenced the first crossing of the Atlantic by a jet aircraft fifty years before, in 1948. Several ex-54 Squadron Vampire pilots had come to Odiham for the day and it was good to allow them to re-familiarise themselves with the aircraft. This trip also resulted in some nice photos of me leading a pair of 54 Squadron Jaguars, before flying a second trip in the lead of a three-ship Vampire display for the ex-Vampire pilots on the ground. Some more nice photos were taken when I did an air-to-air photography sortie with a Virgin

Formation with Virgin Atlantic B747

Atlantic Boeing 747, captained by a pilot who also flew with us at Source Aviation. The small Vampire leading a much larger 747 looked distinctly odd! There was also one event that summer which was for me a first and thankfully also a last. In the Vampire the lever to select the undercarriage is reached by the pilot dropping his left hand down the sidewall of the cockpit to where two almost identical handles present themselves, both moving in the same way, up and down. One selects the gear and other the flap, although there is a switch designed to prevent inadvertent raising of the gear on the ground by a 'weight on wheels' switch on the left undercarriage leg. However, there is also a caution in the Vampire pilot's notes which warns that if there is a strong crosswind from the left on landing there may not be enough weight on the port wheel to close this switch until the aircraft is moving slowly. On this day I was occupying the right seat while a very experienced pilot flew a practice display and on landing we were still doing 80kts or so when there was suddenly a crunch and the nose dropped, followed by a general sinking feeling and a very loud swearword from the left-seater as he had intended to select the flap up but operated the wrong handle. This error had obviously been quite common in the early days as the Venom had a different type of gear handle which required a separate selection before raising the gear, thereby making a similar mistake impossible. I felt sorry for the pilot in my left seat as he was mortified and made the decision to stop flying forthwith. Nothing any of us could say would make him change his mind and he left that day, never to return. It was, I am glad to say, the only time I ever had an undercarriage collapse.

Then in August 1998 came an event which would decide my future path when I checked out once more in that delightful aircraft, the Hunter. A company called Delta Jets had been set up at Kemble outside Cirencester to maintain and operate Hunters and Martin Stoner, their chief pilot, asked me if I would like to join. I didn't take long to decide, as the flying available at Bournemouth had reduced as the older aircraft suffered the inevitable shortage of spares, particularly on the Venom for which starter cartridges were becoming harder and harder to source. The Rolls-Royce 100 Series Avon used on the Hunter T.7 had cartridge starting and this engine had also been used on the Canberra, where the face of the engine was easily accessible and the cartridges were fitted behind the 'bullet' on the front of the engine. Hunter pilots had to get used to reaching deep into the fuselage from beneath and to have a multi-jointed arm in order to replace cartridges but thankfully this would no longer be a problem as Alan Fisher, the Delta Jets Chief Engineer, had developed and fitted an electric starter conversion to our Hunter T.7A WV318 and later to others. We had two Hunters at the time I started to fly there but I could see that there was potential for growth. By the following summer I had ceased flying at Bournemouth. Much as I had enjoyed the 1950s jets they were very heavy work to display and the drive back and forth could be very slow, also more and more of my spare time was being devoted to Kemble. Delta Jets worked out of the hangars which used to be the home of the Red Arrows and 4 Squadron CFS where I had completed the Gnat phase of my CFS course in 1972, so it was great to be back on the same flight line. I now had my display authorisation for the Hunter and worked up an aerobatic display for the all-black T.7A that was Delta's flagship.

Like all display pilots, I found that as I gained experience in this challenging field I could introduce more advanced manoeuvres and so began to incorporate more of the vertical into my sequence. Low-level aerobatics are thrilling for both the pilot and the spectator, but only if flown safely and sensibly. For aircraft on the civil register – and this included the ex-military aircraft I often flew – the regulator is the Civil Aviation Authority, the CAA, and they laid down a basic set of rules including the minimum heights for a display. Jets such as the Vampire, Venom, Hunter and Gnat had a minimum permitted height above the ground of 100ft but for any vertical manoeuvre the base height became 500ft. The most basic of these is the loop, but even here there are pitfalls for the unwary. First it is essential to enter at a speed that will carry the aircraft through the inverted point at the top with sufficient flying speed to retain control so that the exit from the loop – the second half – will equally be controlled. However, the aircraft should still be easily visible to the crowd throughout and therefore the diameter of the loop must not be excessive but recovery to level flight must be within the parameters set by the regulating agency. What is vital for any manoeuvre through the inverted is to know your 'gate' height and speed. If you know that a minimum height of 4,500ft and a speed of 160kts is safe for you to continue to pull down through the vertical, then *only* continue if you satisfy those gate parameters. Remember too, that excess speed can be just as dangerous as insufficient height. Almost without exception crashes at displays, resulting in some very well-publicised and horrifying film clips, are the result of the pilot continuing a manoeuvre having failed to check his gate, so all pilots must know their 'escape' manoeuvre, whether that is simply to roll the wings level and re-position or to modify the pull out to avoid the vertical. There must be a 'gate' for all manoeuvres, even for the speed at entry, and those for the displays of the early jets such as the loop, cuban eight and horizontal eight are equally straightforward. However, the barrel roll is an apparently benign manoeuvre that has caught many out, some fatally so. The main difficulty is that there is no obvious gate as the aircraft describes its 'egg' in the sky. The pilot has to maintain both pitch and roll throughout, but to different degrees as the speed decreases on the way up and then increases again in the descent. The easiest way to show the variation is to say that on the pull up there is more pitch than roll, and then this is reversed after the apogee. One good description I've heard is to ensure that 90% of the roll is completed by 75% of the whole barrel roll. This allows the pilot to 'let it out' as he comes back down to his base height. Another important point is to be able to maintain good external references throughout wherever possible. If displaying at a seaside venue, make the initial entry to the barrel roll toward the crowd. By doing so, on the way down the other side, the crowd line will be easily visible to the pilot and not simply the sea which, if the horizon is indistinct, can make judgement very difficult.

Delta Jets' Hunter WV318 had originally been built as a single-seat F.4, but like many others was later modified by replacing the nose section with the two-seat layout. It was further modified to have the OR946

Kemble Hunter WV318

instrumentation seen in the Lightning from the F.3 onward and also in the Gnat and Buccaneer. Indeed, 318 had been for a time on 74 Squadron's strength. However, from 1970 it had been in the Buccaneer world until that fleet's demise when Delta Jets bought it. It carried the squadron markings of 111 Squadron when they had formed the RAF Aerobatic Team, the famous 'Black Arrows' and it was a great aircraft to fly. More on the Kemble aircraft will follow in due course, but my post at Innsworth, concerned as it was with spreadsheets, financial stringencies and constant battles with civil servants from Whitehall, was dispiriting to say the least when dealing with those who seemed to have the single aim of preventing us from training aircrew to an acceptable standard to enter the RAF's frontline. I managed to 'find the escape tunnel' in less than two years and the weekends that I spent display flying certainly helped to maintain my sanity!

23

SWANSONG

In January 1999 I changed posts at Innsworth once more and to a much more attractive position as Group Captain Flying Training (thankfully we had a new AOC and our posts were once again titled in the usual RAF fashion) with responsibility for the day-to-day running of all RAF flying training. Another excuse to go flying, as if I needed one! This was a busy post with quite a wide-ranging remit overseeing the training activities of everything other than cadet flying and the university air squadrons who were looked after by HQ Air Cadets at Newton and HQ UAS at Cranwell respectively. Elementary flying training was going commercial and became the Joint Elementary Flying Training Squadron or JEFTS at Barkston Heath just south of Cranwell, with instructors drawn from all three Services, but the remainder of the training system was still light blue. Basic flying training was carried out on the Tucano, fast jet advanced training on the Hawk, multi-engined pilot training on the Jetstream and rear crew training still on the Dominie, while the helicopter world continued at Shawbury with the Gazelle and Wessex, although these types were soon also to change as commercial contracts were introduced. Finally, I also had a wing commander from the air operations branch on my staff with responsibility for the Central Air Traffic School at Shawbury in Shropshire. It was a busy job and I spent a considerable time visiting the various units before feeling that I had a good handle on what was going on and could speak with some authority on matters of flying training. I also knew that this would be my final tour of duty in the Royal Air Force, for fifty-five was the retirement age and I would hit that in November 2001. I went out and about as often as I could and flew whenever the opportunity presented itself, as was the case on a visit to the home of the Red Arrows at Scampton where I flew in the rear seat of Red 6, the synchro leader, on a display for the retiring chief of the air staff. Red 6 that year was Sqn Ldr Andy Cubin and after we had landed he took me aside and told me that he was planning to leave the Service at the end of that year: was there any chance that he could start to fly at Kemble? He did just that and in due course became a pivotal person in the Delta Jets organisation and a good friend.

One of the interesting parts of the appointment was to look ahead and envisage what sort of flying training the RAF might need by the middle of the twenty-first century, particularly for the fast jet training aircraft. The progression at the start of the century was Bulldog to Tucano to Hawk, but what would replace these aircraft? There were some very interesting designs appearing and a couple of us went out to Switzerland at the invitation of the Pilatus Company to look at their ideas. The PC-7 and PC-9 were used by several air forces and there had been many in the RAF who would have preferred to see the PC-9 bought rather than the Tucano, purchased after pressure from Margaret Thatcher for assistance given to the UK by Brazil during the Falklands War. Pilatus gave us a very good presentation about their new aircraft, the PC-21, and we both flew the company proof of concept demonstrator with their company test pilot, Bill Tyndall, who I had known years before on the Lightning. I was very impressed not only with the aircraft, a modified PC-9, but with the plan for the whole training package including simulation, both ground and in the air. We returned and wrote up our report for the AOC-in-C who was also impressed. As we now had devolved budgets where the AOC-in-C had (notional) complete control over how he spent the funds allocated to his Command, it raised the interesting and very attractive possibility that he could purchase a new aircraft which would be cheaper to run and very much more effective than the current fleet. In due course, and this time accompanying the C-in-C, we went back out to Pilatus at Stans on the southern shore of Lake Lucerne and they laid on a very compelling presentation, during which they suggested that if we purchased the PC-21 it could take the place of the Bulldog, the Tucano and also cover half of the Hawk advanced training syllabus. The question of what would happen to the Tucano was raised and Pilatus offered to buy them. The C-in-C asked what the company would do with the Tucano, to which the chairman replied, 'We would probably raise the level of Lake Lucerne with them!' He also said, 'If the RAF buys the PC-21 as the launch customer we will discount the price because we shall not have to advertise the aircraft anywhere else around the world once the RAF has selected them.' Unfortunately, when we returned to the UK the dead hand of MOD could not accept such a radical proposal and killed it. So much for devolved budgets granting the flexibility to spend money to best effect. As I write this, the PC-21 is already in service with Singapore (the launch customer), Qatar and the Royal Saudi Air Force, with orders from Australia, Jordan and France underway. In addition, the Swiss Air Force uses them for advanced training and they replaced the Hawk in that air force. A chance to improve the quality of RAF fast jet pilot training at a stroke, and at the same time save money, was lost.

As the time went on within Personnel and Training Command I felt that I could be doing better outside the RAF and this was not a pleasant realisation, but the truth was that I was not doing much more than marking time and much of what passed across my desk seemed to be reinventing the wheel. Any incentive toward adventurous and exciting plans had gone and all we did was work on savings. It was how to do the same with less: less money, fewer people, particularly fewer uniformed people as we became more and more civilianised. Then the balance was suddenly tipped when I was offered the chance to become the managing director of Delta Jets. This I accepted and on 6 April 2001 *The London Gazette* announced my retirement. I had served for thirty-six years and flown just over 5,000 hours, primarily on short duration sorties. I had started my career at South Cerney in Gloucestershire and ended it twenty-five miles away at Innsworth. My first pay packet as an officer cadet had been £7 per week (£364 per annum), handed to me at pay parades, and my final annual salary had been £68,000. I had had a great time, indeed, my answer to those who asked whether I enjoyed the RAF was 'Her Majesty gave me some superb toys to play with and even paid me to enjoy them!' Of course I had enjoyed it.

But I hadn't finished with flying, not by a long shot.

24

DELTA JETS

WHEN I STARTED FLYING at Kemble at the end of 1998 we had only two Hunters, the T.7A WV318, a T.7 WV372 and one piston, a Yak-52 owned by Ronan Harvey who owned Kemble airfield. WV372 was owned by a syndicate who had purchased it and brought it to Kemble to be maintained and operated by us with our instructors teaching the syndicate members to fly it. It was painted in the authentic colour scheme it had worn in its earlier days when

Delta Jets Hunter T7 WV318

flying with 2 Squadron RAF. Delta Jets also maintained an ex-Swiss Air Force single-seat Hunter F.58 for its owner, Jonathon Whaley, and this was painted in a startling colour scheme and called 'Miss Demeanour', and the one and only remaining airworthy single-seat Meteor F.8 WZ467. This, unfortunately, was sold to Australia soon after I arrived so although I had qualified on the trainer version, the T.7, while at CFS, I never managed to fly the single-seater. At the back of the hangar were three more T.7s, aircraft that had sat outside for years and required a great degree of restoration, so for the time being they gathered dust. There were several other companies operating around the airfield, not all to do with aviation, but Kemble was unique as a privately-owned civil airfield in the south of England, having excellent maintenance facilities, 6,000ft of good quality tarmac runway with arrestor barriers at each end, full taxiways which permitted aircraft to taxi to and from the runway in use without occupying the runway itself and uncluttered airspace nearby. One of the members of the WV372 syndicate was Ian Pringle who was already qualified on helicopters and who displayed considerable ability in the Hunter. I started to take him through a conversion to type and he progressed quickly to solo in August 1999. He continued to progress and eventually obtained a full display authorisation on the Hunter before he returned to live in South Africa. Later he bought his own Hunter and also a Buccaneer S.2, which had been used as a trials aircraft and which Ronan Harvey had brought to Kemble. The Civil Aviation Authority (CAA) would never permit us to fly this aircraft in the UK as they judged it too complex and we eventually sold it to Ian Pringle. After preparation I flew my one and only Buccaneer trip, in the back cockpit with CAA test pilot Ian Hartley before it flew out to join the Thunder City stable outside Cape Town. Ronan Harvey also went solo in the Hunter that year but other distractions meant that he never consolidated his Hunter flying. However, most of the other syndicate members flew their aircraft solo at one time or another.

For the two years that I flew at Kemble while I was still serving I displayed the Hunter at various air shows and also toyed with an offer to become the chief operating officer at Gloucestershire Airport, though this did not progress. There were some interesting air show moments such as the Biggin Hill Air Show in June 1999, when I took the Hunter and flew in formation with the Red Arrows and a Gnat painted in Red Arrows colours to publicise the air show. As well as displays we had a couple of requests to

Hunter 15-ship formation over Kemble 22 July 2001

do flypasts at the funerals of ex-Hunter pilots including Frank Hoare and Dick Wharmby, and we were honoured to do this for those we had known. Then in late 1999 Martin Stoner departed to go down to RNAS Culdrose, there to join an organisation called FRADU, more of which later. I found that Delta Jets was hanging on by its very fingertips and money was very tight, so much so that the attractive salary Ronan had promised me never materialised. Indeed, I drew no pay for the first year in the job but slowly we clawed our way out of the mire and began to make money. As other companies and individuals showed interest in coming to Kemble I could see things were progressing along the right lines.

In 2000 I became a display authorisation evaluator, or DAE, when the CAA signed me up to award display authorisations (DAs) to pilots, clearing them to perform their routines at air shows. Not all were aerobatic displays and I was once asked to award a DA to the pilot of a DC-3, the wartime Dakota. As I had qualified on this aircraft while at CFS I flew the aircraft with him to satisfy myself that he was safe to display this vintage aircraft. At Kemble we also welcomed another two ex-RAF and ex-Red Arrows pilots. Andy Wyatt had been flying with me at Bournemouth on the Vampire and Venom, and had been

237

working with me at Innsworth before joining British Airways, while Gordon Hannam, who I had known since instructing with him at Valley on the Gnat, had been flying with Cathay Pacific Airways for some time. He later bought his own Hunter, XL600, registered G-VETA (from that time always known as 'Gordon's Very Expensive Toy Aeroplane') and it joined the Delta stable.

One very delightful event had occurred in April 2000 when I watched a practice display by nine Tiger Moths at Kemble. I went over to look at them after landing and was particularly taken with one which was pristine in the pre-war RAF training yellow. The owner was Commander Phil Shaw Royal Navy, who I had met before at air displays when he had been displaying various other aircraft. Phil walked over and asked me how many hours I had flown in Tiger Moths, to which I responded that I had yet to fly in one. 'Right,' said Phil, 'go and get a helmet.' He then put me in the rear seat, climbed into the front cockpit and we took off for forty-five minutes of general handling, including some stalls, before coming back to Kemble to fly several circuits on the grass strip as this aircraft had no tailwheel, only a tail skid and so used only the grass. Eventually he told me to land and after stopping, said, 'The view from your cockpit is much better without my head in the way, so go and have some time to yourself.' Without further ado, he climbed out and waved me away. I flew around the Gloucestershire countryside that early April evening as the sun slowly set in the west, flying an aircraft with no radio and

Gnat XR538 Close-up

wearing a simple helmet and goggles; it could easily have been the 1930s and the sublime feeling it produced will stay with me forever.

The summer season of 2000 had been quite busy with air shows and one in particular merits comment, at Baldonnel outside Dublin. The display itself went smoothly but the next morning it took an age to get clearance to return to Kemble as there had been a complete failure of the London Air Traffic Control Centre computer during the night and now everyone was bidding for airspace. Permission to fly back at 500ft was refused as I would be crossing from Irish to British airspace but after a long wait I was eventually given a clearance to climb to FL390 (39,000ft), probably to get me above most of the airliners. It was useless to argue as there was never more than a second's gap between radio transmissions. When I was handed over from Dublin to London the controller immediately said, 'It would help if you could descend out of the upper airspace,' which was exactly what I wanted to do. I said I would be happy to do so and the controller asked me to descend as fast as possible and 'What altitude would you like to descend to?' I said that I would go to 500ft above the ground and after inverting the aircraft and pulling down to a descent angle of some 50° I very soon said that I was passing through 25,000ft and changing to visual flight rules. Some airliner was obviously paying attention for the next transmission was an audible sigh, followed by 'I wish I could do that now!'

During the summer of 2000 I also displayed the Hunter at Guernsey and flew one very memorable display at Valley on 22 September for the disbandment parade of 74 Squadron, which had been operating the Hawk but was finally to cease as an active squadron. Delta Jets continued to expand and on 14 February 2001 I flew a 'new' Hunter, a T.8, WV322 from Cranwell to Kemble. 322 had been one of the aircraft used by trainee engineers at Cranwell since the demise of the Buccaneer Force and although it had not been maintained in flying condition it didn't take much to be cleared for one flight; this was the first time that aircraft had left the ground in ten years and I landed at Kemble to report no snags at all. Two days later I repeated the Cranwell to Kemble trip, this time in T.8 XF995 on its first flight in seven years. Ex-military aircraft on the civil register operate on a CAA-issued permit to fly rather than the more common certificate of airworthiness, as the military types had never been operated by a civil company. These two Hunters would be fully cleared to fly again once a minor service had been carried out and the necessary CAA clearances obtained. Indeed, I carried out the permit to fly air test on WV322 on 13 March, only one month after bringing it into Kemble. We also took on charge an aircraft I was really looking forward to flying, our first Folland Gnat. This aircraft was registered as G-RORI and was in a yellow and black colour scheme but once it was at Kemble I found that it had originally been XR538 and had been coded as Valley's fleet number 01. It was the very aircraft that I had flown to upgrade my instructor qualification in 1973 and after a check ride I was flying the Gnat again from the old Red Arrows flight line, twenty-two years after I had written 'final solo' against a Gnat trip after 'trapping' the Red Arrows. My check ride had been conducted by another old friend, 'Boz' Robinson, another ex-74 Squadron pilot who had the unusual distinction of having flown at Valley as a squadron commander, as the chief instructor and eventually as the station commander. The following year we got the Gnat repainted by Linton-on-Ouse in its 'correct' colours as XR538 (Valley 01) once more and I had the pleasure of arriving at Linton to fly it back to Kemble to find it parked alongside the Hawks of the Red Arrows, making a very pretty picture indeed.

The Yak-52 was a great workhorse and I flew it quite a lot, including trips for each of my children, Stephen and Ellen. Later, I also flew Stephen in the Hunter, a trip he much enjoyed. Sometimes we used the Yak to fly people who had wanted to fly the Hunter but who could not be flown on an ejection seat because of fitness or age. One fascinating gentleman was the man I mentioned early in this book who had witnessed Douglas Bader's flying accident in 1931 and who recounted the detail of the event to us in the Kemble crewroom. He had been cycling back to school after having lunch at home and his route took him past Woodley Airfield outside Reading where he had watched a biplane fighter take off and then start to do aerobatics over the field at very low level. He noticed it start to carry out a slow roll but then touch a wingtip and cartwheel over as it crashed. When he got home that evening his father told him that the aircraft had been one of the RAF Aerobatic Team from 23 Squadron at Kenley. It was Douglas Bader. This fine old man wanted to fly the Hunter but I had to say that at the age of eighty it was probably not a good idea to strap him into a Martin Baker ejection seat and I offered to fly him in the Yak instead, an offer he accepted with alacrity.

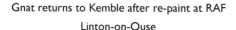
Gnat returns to Kemble after re-paint at RAF
Linton-on-Ouse

In May 2001 we held an Open Day at Kemble and were pleasantly surprised by the interest shown by the general public who streamed in to see what we did. We also held a reunion for Gnat pilots to commemorate the fortieth anniversary of that aircraft's first flight. These were in preparation for the full Kemble Air Show on 22 July at which we would commemorate the fiftieth anniversary of the first flight of the Hawker Hunter, but before that I was asked to ferry one of three Hunters from the UK to South Africa to join the Thunder City stable at Cape Town. Ian Pringle now lived there and he had bought one of the Hunters, so in mid-June I led Andy Cubin and 'Boz' Robinson out of Exeter Airport. Andy and I were each in two-seaters, while 'Boz' was in a single-seater. Although the initial leg from Exeter to Genoa was uneventful things went downhill from there. Andy had a snag getting airborne from Genoa but we eventually headed down Italy intending to land at Heraklion in Crete. Despite our paper clearance for the flight, Greece Air Traffic had other ideas and would not accept three 'military' aircraft in formation into Greek airspace. Our protestations that these were ex-military aircraft fell on deaf ears and we eventually had to divert to Brindisi on the heel of Italy. Many telephone calls later things were smoothed out and the next day saw us land at Heraklion, intending to stay for one night, but another problem arose immediately as although the airfield information for Heraklion showed stocks of gaseous oxygen none was to be found. Andy's passenger must have been breathing hard because the oxygen in that aircraft was getting very low and we knew that by the next morning it would be exhausted. It was necessary to carry out much of the next leg across the Mediterranean to Luxor in Egypt at almost 40,000ft so we pressed on that afternoon and crossed the Egyptian coast as Andy's oxygen gauge reached zero. We could now descend, watching that amazing change from the brown of the African desert to the brilliant

Gnat XR538

Gnat and Hunter

green vegetation on each side of the Nile. After a very pleasant evening and overnight stay at the Old Winter Palace Hotel on the banks of the Nile we prepared to fly on to Nairobi, Johannesburg and eventually to Cape Town but it was not to be and the problems built up one after the other. Luxor is very hot in June and the temperature at the airport that morning was over 40°C, sufficient to make the buckles on our ejection seat straps too hot to hold even with flying gloves on. Next, the cartridge start system on Andy's aircraft was very temperamental and Andy failed to start. Twice I unstrapped, climbed out and went under his aircraft to change the cartridges and rub each with some emery paper in an attempt to achieve a successful start. Eventually there was the delightful sound of the cartridge firing as I climbed back up the wing and into my (very hot) seat to strap in for the fourth time. We taxied out and after a considerable delay were cleared to take off with me leading Andy on a pairs take-off and 'Boz' following twenty seconds later. On a take-off the formating aircraft will inevitably need to use some brake to keep straight until the rudder becomes effective at around 60kts, but after only a few seconds of take-off roll Andy called me saying that he had no brakes whatsoever and was aborting the take-off by bringing the power back to idle and then closing down the engine (better to abort from around 30kts than to need to land at 130 with no brakes). The last thing we wanted was to be spread around

243

Africa so I did the same and managed to drop behind Andy, who by now had no directional control whatsoever and slowly drifted off the side of the runway into the sand. 'Boz' and I taxied back to the parking area and waited for Andy's aircraft to be towed back. It transpired that a couple of days' engineering work would be required before his aircraft would be ready to go and now we learned that the Egyptian rules applied to us were along the lines of 'you arrived as a three-ship formation and you must leave as a three-ship formation. The other two aircraft must stay here until all are serviceable to fly.' This rather open-ended situation didn't work for either Andy who, as an airline pilot, had to be at work in three days, or for me, planned to display at the Waddington Air Display a week later, so we left 'Boz' in the very smart hotel and returned to the UK by hitching a lift on a Britannia Airways aircraft. It was not the great trip we had hoped it would be, though eventually all three aircraft made Cape Town safely.

The Kemble Air Show of 2001 was, however, a great success and along with many displays including the Red Arrows and the BBMF we flew the largest ever formation of civilian-owned Hunters, fifteen in all. It was originally planned to be a diamond sixteen and Boscombe Down had agreed to send a Hunter as the sixteenth. When it landed the pilot announced that it was to be as a static display only as the Boscombe hierarchy would not let their squadron leader fly in a formation with civilians 'as they could not guarantee that the other pilots would have the necessary expertise!' The said squadron leader had fewer Hunter hours than any of the other fifteen pilots!

Throughout every pilot's flying career there will be the occasional unserviceability on his aircraft, some more eye-catching than others, and my engine seizure at Chivenor in 1967 certainly ranked as a big one. However, another very different emergency occurred in August 2001 and I later wrote up the event as an article for a magazine. It was entitled:

THRUST CAN BE TOO MUCH OF A GOOD THING

The weather on 16 August 2001 was ideal for teaching aerobatics and circuits, with puffy cumulus, good visibility and a nice breeze of 15kts straight down Kemble's Runway 27. I was teaching a

Flying my son Steve in the Hunter 23 May 2001

relatively new member on one of the syndicates operating Hunters from Kemble. This individual, who had come with about 300 hours of light piston time, had now flown five trips and this would be another tick on the way to his first solo. We got airborne and worked our way just to the north of Cheltenham and southeast of Malvern before we got into the swing of things with a couple of maximum rate turns and an accelerated stall, also called a stall in manoeuvre. As we had only started with the 3,200lbs of internal fuel we rapidly progressed to some aerobatics and his first loop was reasonable, if a little crooked and lacking a little in the initial pull up.

'Look, you need to get it to the buffet nibble as you enter,' said I, going on to talk of how to maintain wings level during the pull up. 'Let me show you once more. I have control,' and I smoothly took the power back up to the front stop as I pulled into the loop. Now, at the top of most loops with the speed down to around 160kts at the apex, power can be reduced to idle if necessary, depending on what is planned to follow that manoeuvre. As we went through the inverted

I pulled back the throttle and was somewhat surprised when nothing changed: the RPM stayed up at 8,000 with the throttle at idle! The loop rapidly turned into a roll off the top and we started to examine the problem. It was very simple. Regardless of the position of the throttle the engine was delivering virtually full power. I didn't want to play with this too much without the security of a runway underneath me for fear that if I managed to reduce power the reduction might be to idle and the engine might decide to sulk at THAT end of the range, and that would be a whole different ball game!

Back we went to Kemble where I knew there was 15kts down the runway and at 6,000ft long it was suitable even for a forced landing, should it be pressed on me. A PAN call to London Centre woke them up and ensured a smooth passage although the many gliders up from places like Nympsfield and Aston Down might have wondered about this blur doing 500kts or so and every now and again carrying out a couple of 7g turns to get the speed down to manageable figures!

Once in the overhead at Kemble I tried all sorts of things to regain throttle control but to no avail. I was aware of a similar incident which had happened to a Boscombe Down two-seat Hunter a few years earlier: they had arrived at the threshold of a 10,500ft runway going like a train and finished up ejecting as the aircraft was still going so fast that it would have overrun the far end of the runway. I was then on the flying training staff of RAF Personnel and Training Command and wrote a very critical letter having read the Boscombe Down whitewash of the pilot, who had signally failed to control what I perceived to be a minor problem, especially when he had eighty kilometres visibility, one eighth cloud cover at 25,000ft (honest) and 10kts down the aforesaid huge runway. Instead of admitting that the incident could have been handled better there was all sorts of guff about aileron upfloat when going into manual making control difficult and so forth. He had almost certainly misread his RPM gauge as well which was easy to do as it was a two-pointer gauge and it was all too easy to read it as a clock face. When it read 5:30 'clock time' the engine was actually at 6,500 RPM and while the pilot might think that he had only 5,500 RPM, he actually had enough thrust almost to maintain level flight. An important difference as anyone familiar with the Hunter will know. The loss of the aircraft following the double ejection was bad in itself, but the fact that the crew were put into a most dangerous position and ejected close to the seat limits was never addressed.

Anyway, my poor 'student' spent much of this time desperately trying to stay conscious, fighting the regular applications of 6 or 7g, but once I got the speed down to 250kts and could lower the gear, followed by further pulling until I could select full flap, I found that I could control the aircraft reasonably well, turning hard whenever the speed started to run away. I elected to fly the aircraft to a position on finals where, on my call, the student in the left-hand seat could stopcock the engine on the HP fuel cock and I could glide the aircraft in. The engine was closed down at about 300ft and about one mile out, just rolling out of a very tight finals turn and the last bit was very straightforward. The threshold was crossed at about 150kts and the aircraft didn't even make the halfway point of the runway before drifting to a halt. We were towed in and beers were produced! For the technical, the connection from throttle to engine had separated at the engine after a nut had come loose and under the influence of gravity the operating rod had dropped, thereby increasing the RPM. Had I held the aircraft inverted the RPM would have presumably decayed to idle, but that would have been a most interesting finals turn! After the nut had been replaced the aircraft was back serviceable within a couple of days. I got a rather nice write-up in the paper and later the CAA awarded me their silver medal for airmanship.

We now had two Gnats on the strength at Kemble and so prior to the 2002 Kemble Air Day we decided that Andy Cubin and I would work up a synchronised pairs display using both aircraft, with me formating on him. Before leaving the RAF Andy had been Red 6, the Red Arrows synchro lead and so was the natural choice to lead, but I had to work very hard indeed to become a wingman in low-level close-formation aerobatics. June was quite a busy month with the Kemble Air Day and its associated displays, and I took our smart 'Valley' Gnat to Fairford for that year's International Air Tattoo and to Farnborough as another static display before rounding off the summer with displays at Lyneham, Lowestoft and Sleap in Shropshire. Then in late August I got a surprise phone call to ask if I was available to fly a Hunter out to Vancouver from Sweden. I most certainly *was* available and forty-eight hours later I was at the Swedish Air Force base at Sateras north of Gothenburg. In company with another Hunter F.58, the Swiss-built version of the Hunter F.6, we took off from Sateras on 4 September to fly a short fifty-five-minute leg to Bergen in Norway as a proving flight to check fuel feed. All was well and so we flew across to Keflavik in Iceland taking two hours, fifteen minutes, or 2:15, where we learned that storms were forecast within a couple of hours so without delay we refuelled and pressed on across Greenland before landing at Sonderstrom after a further 2:05. This airfield was originally known as Bluie West-8 and is on the west coast of Greenland, sixty miles north of the Arctic Circle and ninety from the northeast end of Kangerlussuaq Fjord, formerly known by its Danish name of Søndre Strømfjord. America used it as aircraft were ferried to the UK during the war but then returned it to Danish and then Greenland control. It is now more correctly known as Kangerlussuaq Airfield and is unusual in that it has a very large hotel on the airport with over 400 beds, built in case a civilian airliner has to land there for reasons of weather or emergency: there was little danger that it could not accommodate two Hunter pilots for a night! Our first day's ferry flying had taken us from Sweden to the west coast of Greenland, not bad!

The next morning we went to file our flight plans for the leg to Goose Bay in Labrador, but our Hunters lacked the accurate instruments that would permit us to fly in the reduced vertical separation airspace where transcontinental flights operate with only 1,000ft between aircraft. We wanted to climb *through* this layer, which was from FL290 to 410, so that we could cruise with maximum efficiency at FL430 or even higher, but air traffic would not let us and gave us a maximum altitude of FL280 where we would face some very strong headwinds. The increased fuel burn meant we could no longer reach Goose Bay and so we elected to fly down to the southern end of Greenland and land at Narsarsuaq to refuel. This allowed us a very interesting 1:15 flight at low level down the west coast of Greenland, not an area I am ever likely to see from low altitude again. This airfield was originally known as Bluie West-1 and was also used by aircraft en route to Europe from Canada and the USA. A quick refuel there preceded a further flight to Goose Bay which still took over two hours

(2:05), and where we stopped for the second night. The next morning, again limited to FL280, we went on to La Grande Rivière (2:05) on the southeast end of Hudson Bay and then on to Churchill on the southwestern tip of that enormous bay, which is much larger than it appears when shown with all of Canada, but after flying across it for 2:10 and 660 miles we certainly realised its size, the equivalent of flying from London to Vienna. At Churchill we stopped once more for our third night and were met by a very friendly lady who ran a local hotel. She warned us as we drove down from the airport in her large US pickup truck not to consider walking out in town that evening 'cos the bears are in town'. Apparently when the polar bears run short of food they start roaming around the town digging through waste bins and seeking out whatever they can find. She had only just got her truck back after a bear had climbed onto the bonnet, stuck a large paw in through the screen and caused a lot of damage by rummaging around inside. When we arrived at her hotel and walked into reception we were confronted by a stuffed polar bear standing on its hind legs and measuring over sixteen feet high, so we ate 'in' that night!

On the fourth day we flew on to Fort McMurray (1:55) for a final refuel before arriving at Victoria on Vancouver Island (2:00). The total flying time had been 16:50 which could have been cut down considerably if we had been permitted to fly at our optimum altitude, but we had seen some very interesting sights, not least going over the Rocky Mountains. Over the next ten days I started to train more pilots on the Hunter and flew four sorties of low-level attacks on Royal Canadian Navy ships *HMCS Regina* and *HMCS Winnipeg*. On each of the trips we started out in close formation on a Learjet fitted with electronic kit to allow it to transmit signals at the target ship, giving the ship the indication that it was being designated by a missile launcher. At about forty miles from the ships I would launch and fly at ultra low level directly at the target before overflying it, climbing back up to the Learjet and re-positioning on a second target. Most of this flying was carried out about 140 miles from Victoria so sorties were all close on two hours long. It was also a taste of what was soon to become my job, although I didn't realise it then.

Had it been given a fair wind and allowed to flourish, I believe that Delta Jets could have been very successful, for by spring of 2002 we had six Hunters flying and another two in rebuild, along with the two serviceable Gnats. We had a pool of experienced pilots on which to draw, both for instruction on the syndicates and for display flying, including some who were very experienced indeed. About that time I had flown over to Duxford, where the Old Flying Machine Company were operating their mixture of WWII big pistons such as the Spitfire, P-51 Mustang and P-47 Thunderbolt, and also some of the early jets. They had a very nice example of a Hunter T.7 that had been restored beautifully but the company's sponsors had decided to focus on the pistons and so the jets were to be sold off. Along with Alan Ponting, one of Delta's engineers, I examined the Hunter and its documentation before discussing a price for the aircraft with Ray and Mark Hanna. I then flew back to Kemble and at the next Board meeting proposed that we buy this Hunter and syndicate it, as we were already doing very successfully with the others. The proposal was carried despite one vote against, that of Ronan Harvey who owned the airfield. The decision did not sit well with him, but instead of discussion I was surprised to receive notification from him the following day that the rent we paid to him as the airfield owner for the use of the hangars was to rise by 250%, effective from ten days' time. I realised then that the plan to expand Delta Jets and to build up Kemble as the centre of excellence for civilian historic jet operations was never going to work, as conflicting priorities were always going to play havoc with such plans. After considerable thought, I handed in my notice as the managing director of Delta Jets, although I agreed to continue to fly and instruct on the Hunter and Gnat. I was sad that I would not see the potential of Kemble realised, but, as the saying goes, when one door closes...

A company called Ultimate High had been operating from Goodwood Airfield outside Chichester but this grass field suffered in winter when rain would flood some of the airfield and preclude their aircraft, small high-performance tail-wheeled pistons called the Extra 300L, from operating safely. Kemble had both the space and a hard runway, and both Andy Cubin and I were very keen to help the company's operations. The two-seat Extra was designed as a competition aerobatic aircraft with the ability to trail smoke, had a great power to weight ratio and its full span ailerons gave it an extremely fast roll rate of over 420 deg/sec. It was a delight to fly and as the passenger occupied the front seat it was particularly well suited to familiarisation trips. Ultimate High's *modus operandi* was just that and it advertised what was called the 'Top Gun' experience. A pair of Extras would fly in formation with one paying customer in each front seat for us to show what close formation flying entailed, before we split up to fly a tailchase and the chase aircraft would try to achieve a 'guns' firing position. If the 'gunnery' was successful, the lead aircraft would start to trail smoke and the tailchase would end; the whole routine would then set up for a second go with the roles reversed.

By March 2003 Andy and I had also built up a pairs formation display in the Extras and in the midst of practising this and flying the various Top Gun sorties I also flew Pippa, Stephen and Ellen in this great little aircraft. For the Kemble Air Day in 2003 we had a very full display and it was the most successful Air Day held up to that time. We raised a large amount of money for various charities and on a personal note, Andy and I flew two Extras in a synchronised display at Goodwood before carrying out another at Kemble, then switched to Gnats for a synchro display at Kemble. We then closed the Kemble Show as part of a larger, three-aircraft display routine. Further displays followed that summer at Waddington, where Hunter WV318 won the Concours d'Elegance prize and at Brize Norton, and our 'Valley' Gnat was again in the Static Park at the International Air Tattoo at Fairford.

In August I flew a sortie which gave me special pleasure and was to celebrate the seventieth birthday of Don Henderson, my flying instructor from my Syerston basic flying training in 1965; it was arranged between me and his wife Doreen without his knowledge. Don had flown Hunters early in his career but had come to CFS and Syerston from the Beverley

Extra 300 at Kemble

heavy transport. It was a delight to put him into the left-hand (captain's) seat and for the next hour I hardly touched the controls.

But then it all went pear-shaped. Kemble had agreed to host the Private Flying Association's annual meeting that year and late on the first day, Andy and I arrived back from a display elsewhere to land. In accordance with the published procedures we had separated to conduct straight-in approaches to land, but the PFA air traffic controller, who was not a regular Kemble controller, asked if we would like to fly a practice display as there was little other traffic. We held off while everyone else got out of the way and then ran in to practise over our home airfield. However, after about three manoeuvres we received a call from air traffic telling us to cease the display and land. This we did, to be met on shutdown by an apoplectic man who turned out to be the organiser for the PFA Rally. He declared that we had flouted the rules, carried out dangerous manoeuvres over a populated area and he announced that he had called the local police asking them to come to Kemble and arrest us! They had refused and our protestations that we were only doing what had been requested by the air traffic controller on duty and what we were cleared to do by the CAA fell

Self flying Extra 300 of Ultimate High

on deaf ears. Still storming around, he demanded that the controller file a complaint to the CAA but the controller refused to do so saying that, in his opinion, no rules had been broken.

The next morning we found that the organiser had rung the CAA himself and that they had arbitrarily rescinded both Andy's and my display authorisations while they considered further action. This struck us both as another example of the usual practice of the 'Committee Against Aviation' and we were both now guilty until proven innocent. In due course we consulted an aviation lawyer who advised us that we had a sound defence but that we could not guarantee being awarded costs when the case was heard, perhaps leaving us each up to £10,000 out of pocket. Neither of us could risk that outcome and so we simply developed a thick skin and let the barbs and arrows bounce off our backs, but that was the end of my display flying.

As autumn approached I spent time away at Exeter teaching a friend to fly a Hunter he had bought recently but upon my return a really major upheaval occurred. Home life had been going downhill for a while as once again my relationship with Pippa was failing and we were leading virtually separate lives while simply existing under the same roof. One evening in the local pub I met a lady called Sandy who had recently moved into the village following her divorce and before long we found ourselves falling in love. In the end I moved out of our house, bought a flat in Cheltenham and wondered what to do while all the unpleasant things that precede divorce took their course.

As all this was simmering along I took a phone call from Brian Hoskins who was now the Chief Pilot at FRADU, the Fleet Requirements and Air Direction Unit at RNAS Culdrose in Cornwall. There was a vacancy coming up in November and a full-time job was mine if I wanted it. It couldn't have come at a more opportune time and I grabbed it with both hands.

25

FRADU

WHILE IT IS NOT difficult to understand the 'Fleet Requirements' part of FRADU's title, the 'ADU' part is worthy of some explanation. Ever since radar was invented, fighter interceptor aircraft have enjoyed the assistance of ground controllers. In the RAF these operators are known as fighter controllers but in the Royal Navy they are air direction officers: the training of such officers used to be carried out by aircraft of the Air Direction Training Unit until the two organisations were merged to form the Fleet Requirements and Air Direction Unit. It was based at RNAS Yeovilton in Somerset but in late 1995 it moved to RNAS Culdrose outside Helston in Cornwall, now operating fourteen Hawk T.1 aircraft leased from the RAF. This move put the unit much closer to its usual operating areas of the part of the English Channel between Portland and approximately seventy miles southwest of Land's End, or over the sea between Eire and the Devon and Cornwall coast. Culdrose is primarily a RN helicopter base and has the twin distinctions of being both the most southerly military airfield on mainland UK and the newest, having only opened in 1947.

I joined FRADU in November 2003 and after a time in various bed and breakfast establishments I rented a house in the village of Porthleven just a couple of miles west of Culdrose. I commuted each weekend back to my flat in Cheltenham although, as my relationship with Sandy deepened, we realised that we couldn't maintain this weekly separation and I bought a small bungalow in Porthleven, a village which we decided we liked very much. Eventually in 2005 both the Cheltenham flat and Sandy's house were sold and we moved down, but the bungalow was too small and we found a house just outside the

My wedding to Sandy 20 Oct 2007

village which required a very large amount of work on it. Treza House had originally been built in 1872 as a two-storey manor house for Lord Churston but had been struck by lightning in 1965 and completely burnt out. In 1972 it was rebuilt as a bungalow, utilising the walls and gable ends of the ground floor only, but by 2006 it was very tired indeed and needed a massive amount of work to make it into a nice house again. Sandy took on the job of project management for the five months the work took while the builders gutted the house and replaced almost everything except the external walls and roof, with new heating, electricity and plumbing. What had been a three-bedroom, one-bathroom house became a three-bedroom, three-bathroom house and with the kitchen moved across the house to be on the south (sunny) side. Luckily, we could keep the bungalow for the duration and work was completed in November 2006 allowing us to move in just in time for my sixtieth birthday. We married in 2007 and settled down very happily in Treza House.

FRADU had a total of eight full-time pilots, seven of whom covered almost all the fast jet types: Buccaneer, Jaguar, Tornado, Harrier, Lightning, Phantom and Hawk. The eighth pilot was very different as he had started his career as a submariner in the German Navy, the Kriegsmarine. Harry Wilhelm eventually decided that he didn't like always going down as, unlike flying where everything that goes up has to eventually come down, everything that goes down does not always have to come up! He transferred within the Kriegsmarine to fly the Tornado and came to the UK for a tour at the Tri-National Tornado Training Establishment at RAF Cottesmore. There he met and married Helen and left military flying for FRADU. He was quite a character and it was tragic that some years later when he had returned to Germany and was flying in a very similar role to FRADU he was killed as a result of a birdstrike at low level.

The Culdrose job was, for the most part, a dream. Our task of support to the fleet was usually to provide low-level targets for ships undergoing operational work-up training in the Channel exercise areas. This would involve from one to six aircraft operating a series of coordinated ship attacks. We were cleared to fly down to 100ft, although without any form of radio altimeter this could only be assessed visually and few seemed to mind if we passed the ships at, or even below, deck level. On many of the attacks we flew in company with Mystère Falcon aircraft, twin-engined jets of business jet proportions but filled with masses of electronic gadgetry and operated by Flight Refuelling (later Cobham) Aviation from Bournemouth Airport. The profiles were very similar to those I had flown out of Vancouver Island after my Hunter ferry from Sweden in September 2002. Two Hawks would

Attacking *HMS Westminster*

formate on the Falcon and run in toward the target ships from around eighty miles range, with the Falcon emitting radar signatures identical to those of Warsaw Pact aircraft. At the appropriate range from the ship the Hawks would be 'fired', leaving us to fly the missile profile to overhead the ship, sometimes descending to 100ft (or so), or sometimes to simulate an anti-radar missile by climbing to 20,000ft and cruising in, until at about six miles from the target we would invert the aircraft and dive directly at the ship at over 500kts. Probably the most enjoyable were the sorties when we would carry out visual attacks in close proximity to the ships, simulating aircraft making strafe gunnery attacks and giving the ships' company practice in manning their close-in anti-aircraft weaponry while the bridge manoeuvred the ship hard to evade the attacks and to bring weapons to bear. Occasionally we got the opportunity to spend a day aboard a ship to experience the 'other side' and I well remember standing on the bridge of *HMS Manchester*, a Type 42 destroyer displaying its considerable ability to turn quickly. A sign on the bridge alongside the ship's wheel announced 'DRIVE IT LIKE YOU STOLE IT'. Very appropriate, I thought.

We also carried out practice interception training for the 'D' School at Yeovilton, so known because it trained directing officers, known throughout the RN as 'Ds'. For the most part these were very basic intercepts, though occasionally enhanced when we did intercept training for the controllers in the back of the 'Baggers', the Airborne Early Warning Sea King helicopters fitted with an external radar to provide enhanced radar coverage for the fleet and which were brought into service following the demise of both the Gannet and RAF airborne early warning. There were also detachments twice a year to northern Scotland for two weeks to participate in the large-scale joint maritime and air exercises that had been running for very many years. For these we were based at Kinloss, always stayed in a delightful hotel in Forres called The Ramnee and operated with the Mystère Falcons on various attack profiles, mostly in the area of sea between mainland Scotland and the Hebrides known as The Minch. At least one Falcon was usually present on our regular one-week detachments to Gibraltar too, working up RN ships in the Mediterranean. When low flying over the very calm sea often seen in the Med it is very difficult to judge height accurately unless or until some shipping is seen but one morning I saw something very unusual when I

Saying hello to Tain Range

overflew a large inflatable dinghy carrying about forty people. It was not under power and as I approached I saw all the occupants huddle down as if to make themselves invisible. I realised that I had found a boatload of refugees crossing from North Africa to Spain. Reporting this to the Coastguard elicited no response and no ship was willing to alter course toward the dinghy as if the refugees got aboard a ship the owners would become responsible for their welfare and for being put ashore. Eventually they were left, presumably to await darkness and the final twenty miles or so to the Spanish coast.

At FRADU we often flew passengers, usually RN personnel from one of the helicopter squadrons based there, but also civilians who the RN felt would benefit from a fast jet trip, or to return a favour. As the Hawk is a two-seat aircraft, the rear seat was available on most sorties and eventually, after much persuasion with the Culdrose hierarchy, we were permitted to give our wives one trip. In their inimitable fashion the RN made it as difficult as possible by insisting that each was a singleton trip of no longer than twenty minutes, thereby forcing us to run a dedicated programme instead of allowing the trips to be planned within a normal daily schedule. It did mean, though, that I was able to fly Sandy around west Cornwall and she could get an all too brief idea of what I did at work. She loved the experience and would gladly have gone again but that was not to be. I flew one other family member but in a most unusual

Us – 2009

manner. My mother had passed away on St David's Day 2008 and after her cremation in Exeter my sisters and I agreed that we wanted to sprinkle her ashes back in her home area of Porthmadog. We considered how to do this and then I had an idea and we all agreed that I would take Mum flying. I placed her ashes in a couple of large envelopes and taped them in place inside the speedbrake on the underside of a Hawk which needed to be ferried from Culdrose to Yeovilton. After take-off I flew via North Wales and, with several relatives watching from Porthmadog harbour, I flew down the Glaslyn Estuary at 250ft and 360kts. As I passed over the embankment that runs from Porthmadog I selected the speedbrake open, the envelopes shredded in the slipstream and Mum returned to her home.

Life continued along these very pleasant lines until 2011 when, with my sixty-fifth birthday approaching, I was informed that on that birthday my retirement from single-seat, fast jet, ejection seat equipped aircraft was mandatory. At the beginning of November I began to wonder what would be my final flight, but it was decided for me by an accident occurring to

Last day in my flying kit!

one of the Red Arrows at RAF Scampton who, while carrying out his after start checks, inadvertently fired his ejection seat and was killed despite the seat having a published zero/zero capability. I landed after a very enjoyable sortie on the afternoon of Tuesday 8 November during which I had flown low-level visual and simulated missile attacks on ships in the exercise areas south of Plymouth, to be told that all Hawks were grounded following the Scampton accident. The grounding continued past 30 November and so my flying career came to an abrupt end, sadly just fourteen hours short of achieving 3,000 hours on the Hawk and just short of 8,000 hours' total flying. It was anticlimactic but it couldn't be fought.

I had spent a total of forty-six years and three months 'dancing the skies'. Did I enjoy it?

I had a 'ball'.

ANNEX

LIST OF AIRCRAFT ON WHICH I QUALIFIED AS FIRST PILOT

Piston
Brittan-Norman Defender
Cessna 182
Cessna 337
De Havilland Chipmunk T.10
De Havilland Dove
De Havilland Heron and Riley Heron
De Havilland Tiger Moth
Douglas DC-3
Extra 300
Yak-52

Turboprop
Fokker F-27 Friendship
Handley Page Jetstream T.1
Hawker Siddeley 748
Shorts Skyvan

Jet
BAe Hawk T.1
De Havilland Dominie T.1 (HS125)
De Havilland Vampire T.11 and FB.6è
De Havilland Venom FB.1
Douglas A-4 Skyhawk TA-4K and TA-4S
English Electric (BAC) Lightning F.1A, T.4, T.5 and F.6
Fokker F-28 Fellowship
Folland Gnat T.1
Fouga Magister
Gloster Meteor T.7
Hawker Hunter F.6, T.7 and T.7A, T.8, FGA.9, FR.10, GA.11, F.58, T.66 and T.75
Hunting (BAC) Jet Provost T.3, T.4 and T.5
McDonnell Douglas Phantom FG.1, FGR.2 and F-4J(UK)
MiG-17
Northrop F-5
Panavia Tornado F.3

SECOND PILOT QUALIFIED
Avro Shackleton AEW.2
Dassault Mystère Falcon
De Havilland Mosquito T.3
English Electric Canberra T.4
Vickers Varsity T.1